)rew
or, 1827-1862

Frank Drew
Actor

= Maurice Barrymore
(Herbert Blythe)
1847-1905

Louise Drew = Charles Mendum
Actress
(d. 1894)

Actor

Georgiana Drew Mendum
Actress
(Mrs. R. L. Stokes)

n
rymore =
382-1942

(1) Katherine
Corri Harris
Actress (div.)
(2) Blanche Oelrichs
Author (div.)
(3) Dorothy Costello
Film actress (div.)
(4) Elaine Barrie
(Jacobs)
Actress (div.)

a
ore
s
wife)

Ethel Barrymore
(Mrs. R. G. Colt (div.)

Colt

John Drew Colt
Actor
(m. Marjorie Dow Bancroft)
Actress

Samuel Pomeroy Colt
Actor

Fiction

By Cameron Shipp

WITH A FEATHER ON MY NOSE
(With Billie Burke)

We Barrymores

WE BARRYMORES

by

Lionel Barrymore

AS TOLD TO CAMERON SHIPP

APPLETON-CENTURY-CROFTS, INC.
New York

The quotations from the following books are used by permission of the publishers: *The Best Plays of 1920-1921* by Burns Mantle. Copyright, 1921 by Dodd, Mead & Company, Inc., *The Du Mauriers* by Daphne du Maurier. Published 1937 by Doubleday-Doran & Co., Inc. *To A Lonely Boy* by Arthur Hopkins. Published 1937 by Doubleday-Doran & Co., Inc.; permission has been granted by the Estate of Mr. Hopkins for quotations from the letter which appears on pages 212–13.

The quoted material on pages 184–86 is from an article by Heyward Broun. It appeared in the *New Republic,* February 2, 1938, and is reprinted by permission. The review of *The Mummy and the Humming Bird* appeared in the New York *Tribune* of September 5, 1902. It is reprinted by permission of the New York *Herald-Tribune.*

Excerpts from the drama columns of *The New York Times* are used by permission; excerpts from the dramatic criticisms of John Corbin are used by permission of Mr. Corbin and *The New York Times;* excerpts from the writings of Alexander Woollcott are used by permission of *The New York Times.*

The excerpt from an interview by Ashton Stevens on pages 230–31 which appeared in the Los Angeles *Examiner* of February 5, 1905 is reprinted by permission of Mr. Stevens and the Hearst Newspapers.

PRINTED IN THE UNITED STATES OF AMERICA

Contents

Illustrations

1. We Barrymores!

In the watches of the night when old thoughts come to roost, some of them slapping their thighs and roaring, others hiding their faces, two particularly baffling notions often appear to beleaguer me. The first, common to most men, involves vast regrets and dilemmas about what I might have been or should have been. This leads always to the conclusion that I have managed to get along all these years through a series of undeserved promotions and by fraud. As an actor, I resemble an amateur fireman who got thrown in with the professionals early, failed to find his métier anywhere else, and had to keep running to various theatrical conflagrations because he couldn't get out of the way.

In addition, I was born with the conviction, to which I still hold, that anything resembling work is a nauseating spectacle. My ridiculous and on occasion serious efforts to discover what I was fitted to do in life have produced a number of bad paintings and etchings, and a large collection of songs, most of which I thefted from real composers, which may some day be played in houses of careless reputation for a cringing posterity; and I have been an actor. My second regret stems from this.

Since I did, in spite of my wails and protests, keep getting promoted in the theater like a pebble pushed toward the top of the heap when its chief talent was for gathering lichen, I think it is not too unreasonable to mourn that I was never able to shove someone aside and carry a spear for my sister Ethel.

This, come to think of it, is odd. My family first appeared on the stage in 1752. In the approximately two hundred years past, the Barrymore-Drew clan has been accused of more nepotism than any other sibling performers, with the possible exception of tight-wire acts and bareback riders. My grandmother, Mrs. John Drew, Sr., my father, Maurice Barrymore, my mother, Georgiana Drew Barrymore, my uncles, John Drew and Sidney Drew, my cousins and my aunts, all played together. I made my first successful Broadway appearance under the startled eye of Uncle John and my first professional bow anywhere under the disappointed frowns of my grandmother and my Uncle Googan—Sidney Drew. I have acted with my brother Jack, with my father-in-law McKee Rankin, and with my wife. With both wives. But I never weaseled my way in front of an audience with the actress I consider the most gifted and distinguished on any stage, anywhere.

With the exception of the motion picture *Rasputin and the Empress,* which we made in 1932, the three of us never took passage together aboard any dramatic vehicle. There was one engagement which found us working in the same theater at the same time. Ethel, Jack and I were together at the Criterion Theater, New York, under Charles Frohman when Ethel played in Barrie's *Alice-Sit-by-the-Fire,* with Jack in support as the diffident lover, Stephen Rollo. We opened on Christmas night, 1905. In the curtain raiser, Jack played the Clown and I played the Old 'Un in another Barrie whimsy, *Pantaloon.* And so I was off stage and my face scrubbed for supper before Ethel read her opening lines.

My main recollection of this engagement is that the weather was uncommon cold and wet and that C. F. annoyed us by demanding that we clean up our dressing rooms on Saturday nights to make way for some Russian performers who used the theater on Sundays. Presumably, my sister was both tidy and polite, as she always is, but the gestures Jack and I made toward being hospitable to the Russians consisted of little more than twisting our soiled shirts into balls and throwing them into corners. It was quite a long time later that we became aware of who the Russians were—Alla Nazimova and Anna Pavlowa.

By the time *Rasputin* came along, Jack and I had both acquired considerable experience in motion pictures, which we found to our taste, especially the money.

Ethel had appeared in pictures but she did not admire her own films or anybody else's. Her films had been, if not cheap, at least not thoughtful. Ethel has always taken her cue from Sir Henry Irving, who regarded his art seriously and respectfully. In any company, Sir Henry took care to appear *as an actor,* and proud of it; his personal distinction raised the profession both artistically and socially. My brother, with almost diffident insolence, met every professional requirement and set new standards of his own, but neither he nor I ever struck a worthy lick to raise the business socially.

Ethel at that time scorned the cinema as a Metropolitan diva might scorn hog calling. It was her opinion, which she stated crisply on many occasions, that her brothers were in cahoots with sidewalk venders and honky-tonk operators. This was her position, so far as we knew, when the proposal was made that all of us work in ***Rasputin and the Empress.***

It seemed, of course, like an excellent notion, one that might be productive of gaiety and perhaps even some good acting; and certainly the front office reasoned that a hullabaloo of Barrymores would be good box office. But there was Ethel's attitude toward pictures to cope with, and there was also speculation about whether she would take a chance on working with her brothers.

Jack and I observed family protocol by refusing to coax Ethel; none of us, Drews or Barrymores, has ever attempted to influence other members of the tribe. We are indeed a tribe, but we respect each other's prerogatives to make his own life and his own mistakes.

But like many a problem which seems insuperable at the time, this one was solved in the simplest way. The late Irving Thalberg, Metro-Goldwyn-Mayer's great production chief, merely picked up the telephone, got Ethel in New York, asked her to act in the picture, and she said yes. Jack and I were both amazed and tickled pink and went about praising Thalberg's powers of persuasion. Privately, we thought that it might not be unreasonable to assume that the lady had been to some extent influenced by $100,000.

At any event, I said "Great!" when I heard the news, and added: "But tell me, what poor unlucky and benighted individual is to direct this opus in which all three of us are to act together?"

My remark was quoted by Edwin Schallert in *The Los Angeles Times* and the pattern was set. Everyone from then on expected that the terrible Barrymores would attempt new forms of fratricide and sororicide when at last we got in front of the cameras. And my brother did the cause of peace no good with his own first remark on the subject.

When Ethel arrived at Pasadena one fine afternoon late in May, I was toiling in some forgotten epic masterpiece and could not go to meet her. Jack was there, along with a number of reporters who were interested in getting some strategic details on what loomed as a fine, funny battle between Barrymores.

One of the welcomers, and I think it was a gentleman from *The New York Times,* inquired of Ethel if she thought she would be nervous appearing in the talkies with two such experienced and accomplished scene stealers as her brothers. Jack interrupted him.

"You need not worry about Mrs. Colt," he said. "Our sister Ethel will be standing right before the camera—in front of us."

There were, I reluctantly admit, more important things going on in a nervous world at this time, from Hitler's activities in Germany to the Japanese invasion of Shanghai, but along the back fences and in the bistros of Hollywood a good conversation piece that summer was the speculation on how much hell would boil when Ethel, Jack, and Lionel began to devour the scenery and each other in *Rasputin and the Empress.* There was a lot of hyperbole about this enterprise, most of it inspired by various tympanists and hornpipers in Hollywood's remarkable press section: it was widely and hopefully predicted that pitting the three Barrymores against each other would result in some interesting carnage.

But now that the clan was gathered and was on salary, the good men at Metro-Goldwyn-Mayer thrust us before the cameras as soon as they could. They had employed Charles MacArthur to write the script, and Mr. MacArthur was turning out big scenes and quaint sayings in a rapid froth of production, but he had not completed his labors when we started to act. This is not as nonsensical as it may appear to those who do not work in the unique medium of the screen: it was somewhat as if, say, Jo Davidson had started on a two-ton statue with only half a ton of clay at hand. As we needed our lines, Charlie supplied them.

Now I have always loved Mr. MacArthur. He is, as you know, that engaging, pixielike ex-Chicago newspaperman of the tough school who wrote *Front Page* with Ben Hecht and married Helen Hayes, not to mention other exciting accomplishments; but as our picture progressed I began to dread his smiling appearance every day behind three to four pink pages of revisions and additions for me to memorize. I began to regard that smiling face with the bitterest hate.

One day, when I felt even worse than usual in the morning, I was about to "give sorrow words" when I realized that the Holy Ghost had lit on my shoulder just in time to whisper that, excepting Eugene Sandow, Charlie MacArthur was one of the strongest and doughtiest men who ever graced this continent. I swallowed my ire immediately, recalled that discretion was the better part of valor, and remembered the dignity of my years.

Our play was about Russians, to be sure, but in 1932 our point of view there was quite different from what it justifiably is now. At any rate, these were *White* Russians, Imperial Russians, and I think I may safely say without fear of being summonsed before a committee that there were then no people more charming than the proper kind of Russian. And so, of course, we were glad to meet some of them. We had met some on several occasions in 1930, and not entirely in the interests of our Art.

Louis Wolheim, my old friend, was himself of Polish extraction but he was prominent in the local Russian Club where many of the ex-great folk of St. Petersburg and Moscow then gathered to recall the fancy days before the Revolution. Jack and I prevailed upon Wally to invite us to dinner.

To begin with, the drinks were superior to anything we were then accustomed to during this period of Prohibition. We were finally seated at table where each course was delicious and each succeeding course infinitely more delectable than the last. We met Countesses, Dukes, Princes, Ambassadors, and each of these was more charming than the other. All of them, too, had the most terrific capacity for beverages, a capacity which, naturally, my brother and I challenged with all the polish and good will we could muster; until it finally appeared to us that the charming Russians were fading away behind some gossamer and glamorous screen. In short, my brother and I became as wall-eyed as embalmed tarpon and had to be escorted to Jack's Tower Road home by Wally, who, soaked as he was, remained as sober as a candidate for the presidency of the W.C.T.U. I spent the night on a sofa, Jack on the floor, from which he refused to budge, claiming it was safer there.

Thus we were introduced to the white Russians and became more or less habitués of their club. We realized, however, that nothing so devastatingly charming as all this had any place in our script, even if we could get Mac-

Arthur to write it in. I must say, therefore, in all fairness, that although all of us may soon become incandescent as a result of Russian thinking today, my only contact with Russians was extremely pleasant.

As we went along with the picture, Mr. MacArthur leaping ahead on his typewriter, we managed after our fashion to inspire more stories for the press, all of them indicating that the Barrymores were having an outrageous time with each other.

Shortly after the start of *Rasputin*, Ethel and Jack were sitting outside one of M-G-M's huge sound stages. They were resting from their labors like any other weary artisans after a period of toil under hot lights and were not in conversation. A studio press agent with a photographer spied them there, saw a chance for a publicity picture, and approached.

"Show some animation, Mr. Barrymore," the eager publicist instructed my brother. "Tell Miss Barrymore something."

"*Tell* her something!" said Jack. "I should say not. But I will *ask* her something."

Ethel herself tossed a fagot on the alleged Barrymore feud a few days later. She came on one of the vast and glittering palace sets in her imperial gown as Tsarina and Little Mother of all the Russians, surveyed the props, and pointed a commanding finger at a certain chair.

"Who used that chair yesterday?" she said. "Mister John Barrymore? Then take the offensive thing away. Get me something different!"

In the idiom of the Barrymores, Ethel's remarks were pet words for a younger brother, but in print they made warm reading and contributed to the belief that the leading players in *Rasputin* were two Hatfields and a McCoy.

The only instance in which Jack and I disagreed over a scene was during a sequence in which I had a long speech to say to him. He was to stand there and listen. But being an actor and a great one he couldn't quite do that. As I would finish, Jack would lay his hand on my arm, upsetting my timing and attracting attention to himself as the sequence ended. I attempted to brush my astute brother off but he seemed to be equipped like an octopus and reached for me every time. Finally, I asked permission to leave the set, went to a telephone, and got Richard Boleslavsky, the director, on the line.

"Will you kindly instruct Mr. John Barrymore to keep his hands off me lest at the close of this scene I be tempted to lay one on him?" I said.

Boleslavsky made tactful representations to Jack, who grinned amiably and presented me with the scene. But this, like the other stories, was soon in print; and the legend grew.

My brother was on his good behavior in *Rasputin* for several reasons. He had always, of course, made out that he stood in awe of me, but this was nonsense. He was awed by only one person in the world, the same person who awed me: Ethel. We gave her the best support we could and were glad to do it. Also, Jack had had several firm conversations with the executive powers and had given his word that he was on hand to work, not to play.

He was not happy with his role because it cast him again as a cameo in a fancy suit. I think I can say without immodesty that my brother was a handsome man, but he despised pretty-actor parts all his life and preferred the roles he had recently been playing in pictures, characters in which he could exercise his mastery of make-up. I, on the other hand, had never up to this time applied much grease paint to myself in pictures, appearing before the camera barefaced and as was. Now our situations were reversed: as the Mad Monk, I was whiskered like an Angora and browed like an Old Testament prophet. Just as he had been in *Peter Ibbetson,* Jack was annoyed by his trappings and by his own overexploited profile. He protested by wearing disreputable britches around the lot between scenes, and once went so far as to attend the world premiere of *A Bill of Divorcement,* his own picture, in a pair of carpet slippers.

When M-G-M entertained a number of the Olympic athletes, here at that time for the games, a number of excitable ladies twittered that John Barrymore had attended in a bathrobe. The fact was simply that Jack wore a yellow, black and white striped sports coat, veritably a conservative jacket for Hollywood, but which, when he was seated at table, could indeed give the impression of being the upper part of a more intimate garment. The incident added to the general talk. None of us minded.

It could be, of course, that my own sour frame of reference added to the feeling that all was far from well on the Barrymore set. I was in torture. I was fur-coated in such a set of underbrushlike whiskers as to make it a punitive experience as they were applied and removed twice a day. I am not a man who endures in silence. I growled, complained, and said wry and bitter things to a number of persons. I offered to spit and broil anybody wicked enough to yell "Beaver!" at me, and I swore that my muff had become infested with deer-hunting dogs. But these howls were merely to relieve my intense feelings of discomfort, and at the same time to amuse my kinfolk. As Gregori Rasputin, the notorious Monk in the court of Tsar Nicholas II, it was necessary for me to look horrible and I knew it. I had to establish my horribleness so that, near the end of the picture, everybody would be happy when the Prince Egodieff, played by my brother, murdered me. It was worth dying to get out of that rig.

I am apologetically aware, to be sure, that it is a pity to spoil anybody's good story or to demolish entertaining folklore. Some legends about Barrymores are too rich to dismiss and had better stand without contradiction for the sake of gaiety. But the delusion, the feeble-brained nonsense that Ethel and Jack and I would be so unprofessional, so peacock-proud and petty that we would actually imperil our own picture, is on a level with—to make it ridiculous but no less accurate—the proposition that three trick bicycle riders would kick each other's spokes out fifty feet above the center ring. Professionals above the standing of cocottes are not such antic fools. *Katzenjammeries* and japeries, perhaps yes, for the hell of it during some of those inexplicable pixie moments which seem to beset all performers and/or artists, but never anarchy.

We were happy, as happy as any Barrymores can be under the impress of gainful toil. We did not quarrel at any time. We did not set fire to the stages. We did not throw things. And I think that most of the high tales of spit-in-the-eye between serious professional performers that have been inflicted upon the reading public are apocryphal.

Rasputin and the Empress started July 18, was completed November 21, and opened at the Astor Theater, New York, December 23, which is fast time for an oversized production. Director Richard Boleslavsky had no trouble with us. All told, this was one of the happiest undertakings our family had ever engaged in, acting together for the first and only time and hailing the arrival of a brand new Barrymore. A man-child was born to Jack and Dolores June 4, 1932. We happily attended his baptism at St. Andrew's Church in Pasadena and named him John Blythe Barrymore.

Jack is gone now, though it seems incredible that such a blithe spirit could be very far away. I am afraid I have neither the words nor the objectivity, nor perhaps even the will, to explain him, the seeker, the mocker, the most brilliant Hamlet of his generation, who could become so quickly bored with his own acting, the unquenchable man scorched by his own inner conflagrations, the good companion, and my brother.

In 1949, Ethel celebrated fifty-three years on theater and sound stage and her seventieth birthday as Metro-Goldwyn-Mayer put her party on the wireless to what seemed like cosmic applause—and to me like simple justice. My sister, after all, is the champion. She has licked the only unlickable person—Time himself.

In these watches of the night I am still pondering the odds and chances which have fetched me along so far, and I am still seeking my proper métier. I suspect that I am a serendipitist. At the moment, considering how cavalierly Ethel has treated the old chronologer with the scythe, and considering how handsomely Time has treated me in spite of my sins, I am bemused by a line that Herr Immanuel Kant put at the head of one of his chapters in *A Critique of Pure Reason.* It is in Latin, but a free-handed translation might go like this:

"Time passeth not, but in it passeth the existence of the mutable."

This, I take it, means that Time stands still while we and everything else move and change according to our horsepower or our durability. I see this as a rather hopeful observation: there is plenty of sheer time for everything, if we could only get the hang of how to use it.

Meanwhile, pondering these things and listening to the ball games when I can escape from work, I act in motion pictures, which on the whole have been getting better lately. It does give me a considerable turn, naturally, to realize that my nephew, John Blythe Barrymore, Jack's son, who was born while we were making *Rasputin and the Empress,* is now acting in them too.

It could be that I will get to hoist that spear for Ethel yet.

2. *Family Album*

THE LIONEL BARRYMORE campaign against hard work and acting was inaugurated April 12, 1878, my birth date. I was born in one of the houses of my grandmother, Mrs. John Drew, in Philadelphia, and spent my boyhood in her vast ménage at 140 North Twelfth Street under influences which should have, but did not, inspire me to diligence and ambition.

I saw, I suppose, most of the great players of the day, including Jefferson and various Booths, as a matter of course; and all the members of my family, including my sister Ethel, who clapped a respectful eye on the theater from her cradle, were working performers. In addition to those current examples, there was the matter of Family Background and Tradition. Well, worse luck for me, I have never taken that kind of thing seriously. As Dr. Collier Cobb, the distinguished geologist, liked to tell his students, "We are what we are largely because we are where we are," and it was more environment than heredity that finally made me apply the grease paint. But for the record, the necrologists and genealogists have unearthed dusty playbills and other archaeological specimens which attest that my rev. ancestors first began to act between 1752 and 1829, and we have been at it ever since. The first actors of the tribe were William Haycraft Lane, 1752–

1829, and his wife, Louisa Rouse, 1756–1804. They were English and both performed in and managed theaters.

From their time on, the family tree is garlanded with mimes and managers. One of the Lane girls married John Kinlock and established an acting dynasty in that branch of the family. Louisa Lane, two generations later, became the wife of a redoubtable Irish actor named John Drew, who is not to be confused with the fashion plate and great gentleman-actor of the turn of the century. The first John died in 1862, leaving three children—another John Drew, Georgiana Drew, and Louise Drew. Georgie Drew married Maurice Barrymore Blythe, the son of a British civil servant who had served most of his life in India—and now I have pulled the tree practically up by the taproots. Georgie Drew and Maurice Barrymore were my father and mother. And Louisa Lane Drew, daughter of Thomas Frederick Lane and Eliza Trentner—Mrs. John Drew—was my grandmother. We called her "Mum Mum." It was in her home that the Barrymore children were more or less fetched up. Mrs. Drew died in 1897 after seventy-two years on the stage—a span which almost equals my whole lifetime up to now, although I am confident that I shall match my granddam in chronology if not in art.

Mum Mum was born in Lambeth Parish, England, January 10, 1820. Her father was Thomas Frederick Lane, an actor who achieved a good deal of fame in the provinces but never made his mark in London. Her mother was Eliza Trentner, whom my grandmother recalled as a beauty and as a sweet singer of ballads. Mum Mum used to tell us at bedtime in her old house in Philadelphia how she herself made her debut at the age of twelve months, being taken on stage to enact the part of a crying baby.

"But cry indeed! I would not, sir!" the old lady told us. "I crowed aloud with joy, and from that moment to this, the sight of audiences have filled me with joy, and I expect it will do so, sir, until the last glimpse I get of them."

Mum Mum came to America on June 7, 1827, along with an entire British company which had been engaged to play at the old Park Theater in New York. They arrived under sail, enjoying a passage that took four weeks. The first European vessel to make the trip under steam, by the way, was the *Curaçao,* which crossed the Atlantic that same year. Mum Mum and company played their New York engagement, then went straight to Philadelphia, where our granddam founded her dynasty and her theater.

She acted, according to the records, in all kinds of parts. A lithograph owned by my uncle, the late John Drew, shows her attired and made up for the five separate characters she played in *Twelve Precisely* at the age of nine. She played with her mother in melodramas and musicals, and was the Duke of York to the elder Booth's Richard III. She also appeared with Edwin Forrest in *William Tell,* and received a fine medal from that gentleman for her performance. (Forrest must have been about twenty-two at the time.) She played, too, with Joseph Jefferson—this is not the Joseph Jefferson you know, but that actor's father.

When she was sixteen years old, Mum Mum was married for the first time, to H. Blaine Hunt, then to George Mossup when she was twenty-eight. There seems to be no record of the first, and the second has long since disappeared from the records, leaving no progeny, but there are chroniclers who allege that his memory was fragrant. Gene Fowler, the reporter and poet who has taken so much friendly interest in the behavior of Barrymores, is authority for the information that Mr. Mossop was a bottleman of vast thirst but that in addition to the odor of barleycorn, there was also about him the persistent scent of onions. The marriage lasted only a few months.

In 1850, Mum Mum became the wife of John Drew of County Clare, Ireland, of whom Joseph Jefferson said there had been no equal as an Irish comedian since Tyrone Power. Grandfather Drew died at the age of thirty-four, so none of us ever knew him. Mum Mum always said that he was a brilliant actor. He took his success lightly and passed quickly into the wings, leaving his widow with four children. These were Louise, John, Sidney, and Georgiana. Georgiana was my mother.

My father's real name was Herbert Blythe. He was born in Fort Agra, India, in 1847. His father was a British civil servant and his mother died when he was a small baby. He used to tell Ethel, Jack, and me when we were children that he was fed on goat's milk in deference to India's superstition about sacred cows; this, he declaimed, accounted for the undeniable fact that his own progeny was extremely odd.

Herbert was sent to England for his schooling with the idea that he too would serve the Queen, and was placed under the charge of the Rev. Mr. Henry Wace, who was to become the Very Rev. Dean of Canterbury, a relation by marriage. It is on record that he attended Harrow and that he went to Lincoln College, Oxford, and that he was graduated. For this I respect my father enormously, myself never having managed to be graduated from anything.

On the advice of his kinsman, the Rev. Mr. Wace, Herbert attempted to read for the law, but it appears that he discovered many things to do of an evening much more entertaining than memorizing *in loco hocus pocus.* He would have made a sensational pleader at the bar, I think, particularly if he could have addressed juries on behalf of clients accused of amusing misdemeanors; but the law bored him. He had no heart in the complexities of old ladies' last testaments and the conveyance of real-estate parcels. He thereupon decided upon a way of life that dismayed and embarrassed his friends and relatives. I presume on my own account that he settled upon this as the best means available for dining in good company without working.

At any rate, he approached his new ambition after a fashion which I seem to have inherited. He did nothing at all about it but became an actor through sheer luck.

As I recall my father's story, it was about like this:

"One evening I was strolling along the pier at Brighton when my notice was attracted by the plight of an elderly gentleman who was escorting an exceedingly pretty *jeune fille.* As if the aged buck were not already in enough difficulty, as you will understand some day, he was beset by dock loafers who were making insulting remarks to and about the young lady.

"Noble fellow that I am, I intervened and bade the scamps be about their business. Upon discovering that they were unbiddable, I naturally knocked their heads together, a matter which required little effort on my part in those days, and having done my good turn for the evening was about to depart. But my elderly friend introduced himself as Charles Vandenhoff, the comedian, and invited me to have a repast with him. Of course I accepted, always being in mood for a dinner, and the upshot of that pleasant engagement was that I confessed to Mr. Vandenhoff that I had lightly considered becoming an actor. He encouraged me, commended my stage presence, particularly when it came to knocking heads together, and so I made the decision. You see, my boys, it was not entirely without a touch of gallantry that your father entered upon his noble profession."

Herbert used "Barrymore" on stage because that was his mother's maiden name. The "Maurice" was his own invention. And that is how we have Barrymores today.

That is to say, we have them because my father came to America under that name and met Georgiana Drew. Herbert's apprenticeship as an actor was brief, but since he toured through the British counties in stock, I presume it must have been thorough. At any rate, he came to America in the early 1870's and wound up with Daly's Fifth Avenue Theater in New York. There he joined John Drew, my uncle, in Edwin Booth's *Hamlet,* a production in which neither young fellow seems to have won much kudos.

The meeting of Maurice and Georgiana might, by stretching imagination, be called classic—fresh from *Hamlet,* in which he had played a small, unnoticed part, Maurice sped to Philadelphia, of all unlikely places, there to sire the greatest Hamlet of them all in the person of my brother. But this of course was not apparent at the time, and Mum Mum, meeting a young and undistinguished and impoverished British actor, treated him as coldly as a dowager greeting a puppy.

But I take pride in my father. I have been knocked out in my time by two heavyweight champions of the world (and by anyone else who cared to lay a fist on me), but when Jack and I as small boys learned that our father had been middleweight amateur champion of England in an era when fighters did not wear pillows on their hands, we accepted him as a great man. On top of that, he had once floored the *heavyweight* champion in a gymnasium bout. It occurs to me suddenly that I am preening my ancestry after all, but in this instance I think the gentlemen in the audience, and some of the ladies, will not blame me.

In spite of Mum Mum's cold opposition, Maurice and Georgiana were married in 1876, and they set about immediately to uphold the family tradition of keeping everybody in the act. They worked together in many plays, some of them under Mum Mum's management, and some of them with John Drew. Unfortunately for me, I never saw my mother and father on stage and never went on tour with them as a boy. I was interested in them, what little time I saw them, but not in what they did in the theater.

Georgiana was kind and gay and I am told that her acting was "natural," as opposed to the stiff conventions of the times. Maurice was a wit and a talented performer to whom there were two abiding mysteries in life: he never correctly estimated either his bank account or his capacity to hold liquor. But if he was a wit, it appears that Georgiana could match him. According to a tale which we now have to accept as fact because it has been sanctified in print so often, Maurice was returning home one Sunday morning after a week's good times. He was in high humor as he greeted his wife and children on the steps of their home.

"I perceive, madam, you are going out," he said with a bow. "Pray, may I inquire where?"

Georgie replied: "I am going to church and you can go to hell."

We lived with Mum Mum in the various great houses she maintained in Philadelphia. By the time we children came along, she had become manager of the Arch Street Theater, a remarkable accomplishment for a woman in those days, and she had residences of some style, although all of them were drafty. The one we were in longest was the house at 140 North Twelfth Street, which became known to the small fry as "The Tomb of the Capulets." We dubbed it so because it was directly across the street from the works of a tombstone cutter who displayed in his yard great numbers of marble lambs, clasped hands, pinioned angels, obelisks, and façades for mausoleums—somewhat, I suppose, in the manner of old man Gant on Pack Square in Thomas Wolfe's *Look Homeward, Angel.* In Mum Mum's big house, where the profession came to call to make their manners to Philadelphia's great lady and great theatrical manager, it was the habit of the acting parents, uncles, aunts, cousins, and visitors to mutter "Go away, child, you bother me" when we interrupted their discourses about the theater and its legends. I did not often interrupt. I was considerably more interested in rats, ghosts, slingshots, and in prowling Iroquois certain to be lurking in the shrubbery surrounding the nearby Academy of Fine Arts. I was, in short, professionally occupied with the arduous business of being a small boy. And so I did not learn anything to my advantage.

I was sent to school, for the Barrymore-Drew-Lane clan had, and still has, great awe for book learning. My family attended St. Stephen's Church, so in the beginning I attended the Episcopal Academy; but while I was soaking up a smattering of religion along Anglican lines, my mother went on tour with Madame Modjeska. Under the influence of that compelling personality, Georgie was converted to Catholicism, in which she lived and died sincerely. I, along with my brother and sister, was decorously spirited from the Episcopacy to the Papacy, was baptized in the Faith, and sent first to St. Aloysius Academy, from which everyone usually goes into the priesthood or into the Eastern League.

From there I went to Seton Hall, in South Orange, New Jersey, from the age of ten to fifteen, setting an all-time record, as yet unapproached, for resistance to knowledge.

With Latin and Greek, though, as I recall it, I had little trouble. Anything that had to do with the spouting of words was a nuisance but could be disposed of. But in arithmetic I remained with the small boys from the day I arrived until the day I departed. In desperation, being convinced that the mysteries of simple addition and subtraction were too deep for me, my masters eventually tried me on algebra, but they gave up this experiment after two weeks. I was firmly of the opinion that algebra was an occult science comprehensible only to persons of extraordinary, low, commercial cunning. I detested it and I still do and I wonder if it really means anything.

But Latin I eventually learned a little about, through a process I will herewith recommend to high school teachers. I came across, at an appropriate time in my adolescence, a book about sex. It might have been Krafft-Ebing's *Psychopathia Sexualis,* if indeed that book was published then. At any rate, it was an absorbing book and contained comments on many matters which at that period seemed to shine with glittering interest. But there were shabby jokers in this wretched book: just at the point where things would become absolutely specific, when life's enigmas were finally to be revealed before my bugging eyes, the author would lapse into Latin.

So I learned Latin.

Jack went to Georgetown while I went to Seton Hall, and Ethel was at Notre Dame, in Philadelphia. Or was it called Sacred Heart at that time? It was on Rittenhouse Square, next to the Cathedral, and there she applied herself, learning a great deal about music, incidentally. She could, I am sure, have become a concert pianist if she had preferred music to the theater.

My brother's advent at Seton Hall, after a misadventure at Georgetown, is still one of the legends of this fine and pious school. Young Jack was taken in charge by one of the good fathers, who in an attempt to interest the lad in school activities, showed him the gymnasium. He pointed to a parallel bar and inquired if Jack, who looked frail at the time, could perform on it. Jack could and did.

But as he gyrated various objects fell from his pockets. These included brass knucks, a pack of cigarettes, and a half pint of cheap whisky.

I presume that the excellent fathers took these outward and visible signs as evidence that my brother earnestly required their ministrations. In spite of this, and in spite of his record at Georgetown, they let him stay.

Jack had been dismissed from Georgetown in disgrace. Less academic than I, at the time, he undertook case history as his method of exploring the mysteries, and accompanied some older boys to a House. It came to the ears of the padres that Jack had been to this place and they haled him incontinent and tight-mouthed before a tribunal.

"If you will tell us the names of the other boys, we will let you stay," they informed him.

Jack refused and so he was canned. Before his celebrated departure, however, his father was sent for in an effort to coax him back into grace, and the following interview took place:

Jack: "But Father, I just went along. I didn't do . . . you know."

Maurice (popping his eyes as big as oysters at this unnatural son): "Well, for God's sake, why not?"

Somehow or other, chiefly through worrying my instructors, no doubt, I wangled my way through Seton Hall. I read some Xenophon. I got through the first canto of Virgil, who impressed me as a tedious old moralist; and Ratio and Proportion, through constant association, became old friends, though I never understood them any more than I understand certain other old friends. I left Seton Hall at fifteen, never again to return to the formal halls of learning. I had learned, of course, to read. I mean to read books, and somewhere along the line, perhaps not in school, I learned to listen when my betters speak wisdom. And that encompasses all my knowledge about anything.

At Seton Hall, by the way, I heard the most amazing understatement of all time. There was a football player who was unfortunately required to go to class. One morning, our instructor, forgetting to treat the great with proper consideration, called on this athlete and demanded of him that he give a short talk on the music of Robert Schumann.

Our hero arose, shifted from one foot to the other, looked desperately about, and uttered this classic:

Spencer Berger Collection

Maurice Barrymore

Spencer Berger Collection

Georgie Drew Barrymore

Spencer Berger Collection

Mrs. John Drew
as Mrs. Malaprop

Museum of the City of New York

John Drew

Spencer Berger Collection

Georgie Drew Barrymore, with her three children, Ethel, Lionel and John

"Well, Schumann, this Schumann, well, he was *all right.*" And sat down.

I was in London several times as a small boy, at one time attending the Gilmore School in Warrington Crescent. I loved London, as I still do—and as who does not? But there are no brass plaques in Warrington Crescent marking my scholarship.

Between terms, or during terms, or almost any time during our adolescence, the three children shuttled around, sometimes on tour with Mum Mum, sometimes on the so-called farm at Staten Island, sometimes in New York. On one of my trips to New York I met Mark Twain.

This came about when Maurice Barrymore was playing in *Captain Swift* at the Madison Theater. During one of my holidays I accompanied him to the Hoffman House, one of his favorite places to hold forth. A bushy gentleman entered and ordered a hot apple toddy. Now a hot apple toddy is a civilized and savory drink, forgotten, apparently, by today's sophisticates in café society. It consists of an apple, hot water, cinnamon, and a bottle of applejack from which a gentleman pours as much spirits as seem to suit the occasion. It is an aromatic, wonderful drink, very solacing, they say. Mark Twain had one of these.

My father took me by the hand and introduced me. He knew Mark Twain well, as indeed he knew all the great people of the day. He introduced him correctly, of course, as "Mr. Clemens."

I sat there like a bump while my father and Mark Twain talked. Finally, my father turned to me. "Haven't you got anything to say to Mr. Clemens?" he asked me.

I muttered that no, I hadn't, and continued to be a bump. There are few things, I suppose, that embarrass a parent so acutely as a doltish child, particularly one who acts the part so ably in the presence of Mark Twain, and so my father was chagrined and tried to cover my non-sociability with small talk and thus-and-so.

Finally, my father made an effort to save me.

"This is Mr. Clemens, Lionel," he said. "But I expect you know him better as Mark Twain."

I did indeed. We were old friends and had mutual acquaintances in Tom Sawyer and Huckleberry Finn. So I looked Mark Twain in the eye then and began to blurt words at him.

I began to tell him his own story, the part about Nigger Jim, and I gave it to him verbatim, mostly whole paragraphs at a time, except for some interpolations of my own which seemed to improve the tale. My father moved to fetch me a kick under the table and tried to stop me from this impertinence of reciting Mark Twain's own story back to him, but Mr. Clemens laid a hand on his arm and gave me his whole attention. At the end of my recital there were tears in his eyes. He beckoned a waiter and bought me an apple with spice and hot water, omitting, of course, the brandy. I was highly pleased with myself, unaware that I had pulled a potwalloping enormity.

I saw Mark Twain often after that, but this was the main time.

Maurice used to say things that amused people but puzzled them afterwards. Once, I recall, a man asked him what another man was like.

My father took this under consideration, thought about it, cocked an eye, rubbed his nose, and delivered a solemn opinion. "I'll tell you," he said, "he looks like a man who might play the piano."

He was at all times an amusing person, had read everything in the world, in French and English, and he liked children. He romped and roared with Jack and me, usually at late hours when Mum Mum would get annoyed, and he told us outrageous stories of derring-do, blood and thunder. He recited spates of Shakespeare on occasion, with leers and winks; perhaps, who knows, influencing the tastes of his sons. And he wrote plays.

These included *Bitter Expiation* in 1880, *Honor* in 1881, *Homeward Bound* (with Julian Magnus) in 1882, a comic opera *The Robber of the Rhine*, with music by Charles Puerner, in 1892, and, most importantly, *Najezda*.

Najezda was first produced in San Francisco with Madame Modjeska as the star and George Osborne as the equivalent of Baron Scarpia. Maurice and Modjeska played it in the East in 1884, including New York and Baltimore, and my father took it to London in 1886 and played at the Haymarket with Emily Rigi.

It was finally suggested that the play was so good that the great Sarah Bernhardt herself should do it. It was argued that the French tragedienne was the only one with the scope and power to interpret this play adequately. And so Maurice, in one of his few moments of real ambition, sent the play to Sarah.

She kept *Najezda* for two years and returned it with scant thanks and no comment. Immediately thereafter, *La Tosca* came out—and it was Maurice's play. There was no question about it. It was an open-and-shut case of plagiarism.

Bernhardt was immediately asked about this. She struck a pose. She flicked a hand in lofty dismissal and said: "If a great man gets the germ of an idea from some—some obscure American, what does it matter? These things often happen."

I shall not forget Maurice Barrymore's reply:

"A man is no less a thief who steals from his own hatrack my walking stick, where I have confidently placed it, and builds an umbrella on it."

Later, Puccini wrote the music for the opera *La Tosca,* from a plot based on the play by Sardou—whose inspiration was plainly *Najezda.* Many years later I met the gentleman, at about the time when he was writing *The Girl of the Golden West.* He sat at a table in the dining room of the Knickerbocker Hotel in New York one evening with David Belasco, John Williams, and John Luther Long.

I approached, and as I did I could hear Belasco whisper to Puccini: "Watch out, here it comes!"

But I merely bowed and said: "Might it be that I could shake the hand of the maestro?" And I was allowed to shake the hand of the maestro.

Still, whenever I hear *La Tosca* played I experience venal emotions. I believe that I should get a rake-off for my father's plot.

3. Flashback

THE STORY THAT I cut my teeth on a bullet extracted from my father's back is another of those figments about the Barrymores too happily told for me to deny at this late date. I was one year old at the time, so the yarn is at least possible.

It is true that Maurice was shot, and the authority is John Drew, who was there. The scene of the fray which almost orphaned me was Marshall, Texas, and this is how it came about that Maurice Barrymore, elegant British actor on the Broadway stage, took part in a Western brawl:

He and Frederick Warde had bought the road rights to *Diplomacy*, which had made a fine hit at Wallack's in New York, and brought Uncle Jack into the company to play the juvenile role, Algie Fairfax.

The troupe was stopping at the Station Hotel in Marshall, preparing to leave for Texarkana. The morning after the performance, Maurice, Ben Porter, and Ellen Cummins went across the street to the station café, the only one open, for breakfast. This café was also a bar, and there was a buckaroo in it who was extremely drunk. It turned out that his name was Jim Curry and that he was a railroad employee and a deputy sheriff. He began to use language which Uncle Jack described with Victorian horror as "extraordinarily vile."

Maurice demanded that he stop.

"I can do anything I want to do with you," Curry announced.

"With a gun to back you up," said Maurice.

"I haven't got a gun," said Curry.

Maurice put up his dukes, pretty sure of himself at this point, but Curry did have a gun. He drew fast and shot Maurice in the shoulder. Porter rushed to his aid. Curry then leveled on Porter, who died almost at once, on the station platform.

Uncle Jack did not see all of this, but heard the shots and the uproar. He ran across from the hotel and entered the bar as Porter fell. Why he wasn't shot by Curry also, or why Curry did not shoot my father again, I do not know. At any rate, the sheriff arrived soon, disarmed Curry, and assisted Maurice back to the hotel, where the bullet was cut out.

Curry was tried for the killing of Ben Porter and was acquitted—by a jury on which, the legend goes, there sat eleven murderers. Many years later he died in respectability and the odor of sanctity and played the leading role in a grand funeral produced by the Benevolent and Protective Order of Elks in Portland, Oregon.

What with Maurice's painful accident and other misfortunes of the road, notably the fact that western audiences were determined to stay away from a play called *Diplomacy,* the trip was not a profitable investment. Maurice and Fred Warde returned East disheveled and out of pocket—for which, you may be as certain as sunrise, Mum Mum had no sympathy whatsoever; vis-à-vis this Barrymore at any time she was a cold queen and not amused. Confronting him as the victim of a barroom brawl, she longed to apply the ostracon. I wonder, indeed, how she managed to endure *any* actors save Jefferson and Booth.

But these affairs never inhibited Mr. Barrymore's high-stepping spirits and good humors. If we were poor, we were poor, in a shabby-genteel kind of way. When we had money, when both Georgie and Maurice were gainfully employed on the stage, we children were handsomely turned out, had fine clothes, and considered ourselves rich. Most of the time we considered ourselves poor.

After my mother's death, when I was fifteen, my grandmother and my father were not seeing eye to eye about anything. In particular, they were not in agreement about the bringing up of children. One of the upshots of this dispute was that Mum Mum took Jack to live with her most of the time. But there was one joyful summer which Jack and I spent together on Maurice's farm on Staten Island.

How he acquired a farm on Staten Island, or why, is one of the mysteries, but he had it, and to it he dispatched Jack and me to be chaperoned and fed by a Negro named Edward Briggs, known as "The Black De Reszke" because of his powerful voice, but more often referred to as "The Black Prince." We were accompanied also by thirty-four dogs. Originally there had been four dogs, presented to Maurice by Commodore Peary, but biological processes took effect, there was plenty of food, putting Malthus in reverse, and we were soon all over dogs, to our great comfort.

Maurice was touring on the Coast that summer, acting in plays with the secure knowledge that he had looked after his offspring well, but he received a scolding letter from a respectable friend, who suggested that he was a lax parent to leave his boys in the charge of that terrible Negro Edward Briggs. He said, indeed, that this was a disgrace.

So Maurice wrote to us to inquire if it was a disgrace and how we were getting along.

Edward Briggs dictated the reply, which Jack wrote. Mr. Briggs described the bucolic splendors in which we resided, reported our good health, and ended the missive with this line:

"And as for Edward Briggs, he is a noble fellow and I love him."

Maurice naturally detected the imposture. Also, naturally, he laughed like hell, showed the letter to his friends, and let us stay at the farm with the Black Prince.

This gentleman later became famous in his own right during the celebrated Maybrick murder trial in England. Maybrick was a cotton broker in Liverpool who perished under circumstances which strongly indicated that he had been done away with by Mrs. Maybrick.

It happened that the summer before Mr. Maybrick's demise, he and his wife had spent a holiday at Newport News where our Black Prince had waited on table. Briggs distinctly recalled that on many occasions Mrs. Maybrick pleaded with her husband, "Oh, please don't take any more of those sleeping pills while we're having dinner," indicating solicitude for his welfare and also that Maybrick was in the habit of swallowing potions.

Briggs was sent for, dispatched to Liverpool, and testified in the courts. But our Prince's word was not enough and poor Mrs. Maybrick, whom all Barrymores believe innocent, was sent to jail for twenty years.

At another time, Maurice was so prosperous, being for

a spell one of the highest-paid actors on Broadway, that he maintained four establishments in town. But there were many times when he was broke, he having a sure instinct against the hoarding and compounding of money and a pretty talent for ridding himself of fiscal matters in a hurry. On one occasion, when he was a four-apartment man, he was even hard pressed to find a place to sleep.

Augustus Thomas emerged one raw, sleet-driven night from the Lambs Club on Thirty-sixth Street to be stopped by a wretched boy of about eighteen who asked for money to rent a room. Gus, instead of giving him money, took him to 205 West Twenty-fifth Street, where he had a room next to Maurice's. He gave him Maurice's bed and bade him sleep well.

A few hours later my father crept in, streaming puddles from a storm that had broken over Manhattan, shook Gus awake, and demanded an explanation for the boy in his bed.

Gus: "Your bed is one of my generous philanthropies. What's the matter with your Fourth Street flat?"

Maurice: "I have a philanthropy of my own asleep there."

Gus: "What about Sturdevant House?"

(This was the apartment shared by Maurice and Georgie when they were in town together.)

Maurice: "Ethel is over from Philadelphia and she's in that."

Gus: "Well, you also have a room at Mrs. Higgins'."

(Mrs. Higgins ran a boardinghouse. Maurice ate there frequently, and had a room reserved also so he could spend the night when it pleased him.)

Maurice: "King Hall has taken that one over."

Gus: "Well, I don't know what you're going to do."

Maurice: "I do." He shed his wet clothes and got into bed with Gus.

These notes on my father, whom I admired inordinately, as you have gathered, are his due, of course, but I have set them down for yet another reason. No one has explained Jack Barrymore, and as I have said before, I do not think I could compose the definitive essay which would explain him. He did not resemble Maurice Barrymore. He resembled his mother more in looks. He did not in any way that I recall affect any mannerisms or techniques of Maurice Barrymore's on the stage. This would have been impossible, Jack being too young to observe these things (and not caring anyway) before his father died. But Jack was like Maurice. They seem to have possessed precisely the same talent, the same imbalance, the same oddly slanted curiosity, the same ennui with achievement once achieved, the same integrity—and the same capacity for hurting themselves. On stage they were brilliant and poised. Off stage, they invariably stumbled and barked their shins.

Maurice Barrymore was a Catholic—after his fashion. Once at a dinner party at William Rideing's in San Francisco, shortly before Maurice died, a guest seemed surprised that my father professed any religion at all. But in his way he did profess it, and he replied: "Yes, sir, I most certainly do—but I am afraid that God does not know it!"

The influences of my youth, as we see, are easy enough to put on paper and fun in the telling, but what they mount up to and why they produced me is another matter. We lived in poverty and in riches, like Bohemians sometimes and like amateur ladies and gentlemen at other times. Jack was full of bounce. Ethel was a talented and serious child who knew what she wanted and soon got it. I was a quiet kid who could be left alone for as many hours as our guardians desired if they put a paint box in my hands. And there was Uncle Googan.

Uncle Googan was Sidney Drew. I am proud to claim kin to him, although in her autobiography, published in 1899, Louisa Lane Drew states that she had adopted Sidney. Mrs. Drew, of course, may say what she wishes in the matter, but Uncle Googan certainly *looked* like her. At any rate, this was an engaging fellow who seemed at all times to have a deal more Barrymore than Drew in him. He did not work all the time, being afflicted with the usual occupational hazard of actors, and was frequently told off as baby-sitter for his young niece and nephews. On such occasions, Uncle Googan would march us sedately down Chestnut Street, a model of avuncular correctness, turn sharp right, and repair some blocks away to a pool hall.

"Would you like to see Uncle Googan hit the pretty balls?" he would inquire. We would. And indeed, taking the children to a pool hall is one of the best ways in the world to keep them quiet and also to educate them, a suggestion I pass on to uncles at no extra cost.

Uncle Googan could hit the pretty balls masterfully. Indeed, Uncle Googan was a shark. It was his habit to lie in wait for suckers, engage them in contests after having convinced them that he was a feeble tyro, raise the ante, and relieve them in the last game of as much folding money as possible.

He once performed this routine upon a credulous customer from out of town who later suspected that Uncle Googan was a ringer and had played him for a fool. This unhappy gentleman chanced to be in the pool hall one afternoon as Uncle escorted the children in. Uncle's victim was a powerful man, topping six feet, and Uncle was an extremely small actor. We backed against the wall as the big man started forward, for there was unmistakable murder in his eyes. We had sense enough to get out of the way so Uncle Googan could run.

He didn't run, though. Cocky and bantamlike in his smart clothes, Uncle stood there and grinned, waiting for the blow. As the big man's fist went up, he struck. His hand contained a billiard ball, and I think he came close to cracking that man's skull. At any rate, he fell like a redwood.

"Come children," said Uncle Googan, never looking back.

Uncle had another disconcerting habit. He liked to get himself engaged to pretty women. In this respect his taste did not coincide with Mum Mum's. Uncle Googan admired ladies from the chorus, fell tremblingly in love with them, and swore to make them his wives. Upon these occasions, Mum Mum would give a grand tea or a dinner party, inviting thereto all the distinguished stage and society folk she could command in Philadelphia—and her commands were respected—and present Googan's fiancée. Both the lady and Googan were invariably intimidated, feeling, I suppose, like bugs under lorgnettes. The girls shriveled under Mum Mum's fierce manners, and decided that this awesome and dangerous family was not a good one to marry into.

In those days, between bouts with Latin and algebra, I went on occasional tours with my grandmother, but I was more interested in the bounties of the lunch boxes and the salutes of firemen on locomotives than in the state of the theater or even in the health of the box office.

I didn't want to act. I wanted to paint or draw. The theater was not in my blood. I was related to the theater by marriage only; it was merely a kind of *in-law* of mine which I had to live with. I compromised with it after my fashion by determining to design scenery for it, and this was the first of my many ambitions and escape impulses, all frustrated. But Mum Mum handed me my fate as a matter of course, like juice before breakfast: I would become an actor.

In a sense, I was in the position of the son of a great athlete who is naturally expected to be a great athlete too; but I was not like the junior Sisler, for instance, who distinguished himself in the Phillies' race for the Pennant in 1950, and will probably do it again. When my grandmother Mrs. Drew and my uncle Sidney Drew considered me, they didn't stop to think whether I could play ball or not; they took it for granted and said in effect, "Oh, put him on second base."

They forgot, to be sure, that I couldn't play second base. To unscramble the metaphor, they forgot that the part of Thomas in Sheridan's *The Rivals* with its front scene between Thomas and Fagg would tax the abilities of both Collie Cibber and David Garrick. The scene goes like this:

Thomas the coachman passes Fagg. As he walks he has to indicate to the audience that he is thinking "Egad! that man looks like Fagg." He goes on, whistling. Fagg shows the customers that *he* is thinking: "Am I wrong? Could that be Thomas?" And they turn and recognize each other, converse, and finally get themselves gracefully off stage. As you can see even from this brief synopsis, to do that scene naturally takes all the consummate skill of a Willie Hoppe delicately clicking the balls into the corner pocket. Well, when I attempted it with my seventy-five-dollar-a-week partner, poor devil, it was as one critic said of Joe Jefferson's production of *The Rivals:* "Sheridan was thirty miles away."

The horrible afternoon of my debut finally arrived and I was a wretched and frightened boy. I am reminded now, these years later, of a story they tell on Alfred Hitchcock, the director. They say he had a nervous actor before the camera who kept blowing up. Hitch calmed him with a great line. "Relax," he said. "Only your whole career depends upon this scene."

But there was no wit and no comfort attached to my miserable first effort. I crept on stage in an apathy of embarrassment and muttered my words like an automaton that needed the oil can. The scene was too much for me, as indeed, any scene would have been too much for me at that time.

I repeated my fiasco in the evening and I was even worse, conscious as I was of my hopeless performance at the matinee.

My grandmother was brokenhearted. She averted her eyes as I stumbled over the ropes and flats backstage to seek out the corner that passed for my dressing room. I scraped off my disgraced make-up as fast as I could.

I wandered the streets of Kansas City for a short time that evening, but there was no solace in that city, which always offers various delights to the gay in spirit. Finally,

I trudged home to the boardinghouse and went quietly up to my room to hide my embarrassment under the covers.

Propped on my bureau was a letter in a well-known handwriting, in purple ink. I fingered it for several minutes before opening it, but after a while I concluded that it was a great kindness of Mum Mum's to send me a note rather than scold me in person. I opened my letter and read:

> My Dear Lionel: You must forgive your Uncle Sidney and me for not realizing that when Sheridan wrote the part of Thomas he had a much older actor in mind. We feel that we were very remiss in not taking cognizance of this—although we are both happy that you are not at the advanced age you would have to be in order to be good in this part.
>
> We think, therefore, that the play as a whole would be bettered by the elimination of the front scene and have decided to do without it after this evening's performance. Sincerely and with deep affection, your Grandmother,
>
> Mrs. Drew.

Since my debut, most performances of *The Rivals* have gone on without the front scene. I seem to have killed it for good. Or perhaps directors have been worried lest I come back and play the part again.

At any rate, so far as I know, I am the only actor who has ever been formally canned from a play by his own grandmother. I claim another distinction: I was overjoyed.

I had always been taught to call at Mum Mum's room to say good night, and now, knowing that I would not have to play the hateful role any more, I did not hesitate to knock at her door.

Mrs. Drew was sitting before her fire having a bit of crackers and cheese for supper. On the table she had a small glass containing her dram of rye whisky, just a warming soupçon which she liked before bedtime.

She looked up at me with brimming eyes and opened her arms. And then her expression changed. She saw I was almost laughing.

"This is odd, sir," she said. "I find the occasion rather distressing, but here you arrive garlanded in smiles."

"Oh, well, you see, Mum Mum, it's just that I agree with you so completely. You and Uncle Googan are quite right. Entirely right. The play will be much better with the elimination of the front scene. You mustn't mind me at all."

"So. Well, dear boy, what would you like to do then?"

"Perhaps I could paint scenery. Or would you rather send me home?" I offered.

"We'll keep you around," Mum Mum said. "Perhaps something will come of this after all. I am forced to remember that your father was not so distinguished an actor either when he first started out."

And so I remained with the company. My chief usefulness was a hearty performance as Ganymede for Uncle Googan, who required frequent refreshments in the form of Manhattans and Martinis, which I ran for or prepared when commanded.

Ever since that sweating and screeching debut in Kansas City I have had a blanket aversion to acting. Not to any one bit of acting perpetrated by me, but to all acting perpetrated by me. Ethel, as I have said, understood the theater early, realized the value of being an actress, and I have always been both willing and happy to take acting seriously as applied to her, or, indeed, to anyone else. This is not false modesty. But it is a fact which I might as well establish now in this wayward chronicle that I never considered myself cut out for the priesthood, as it were. The reason I worked in the theater was that I had nothing else to do, and the reason I worked in motion pictures was that I had nothing else to do.

Anyone can be an actor. And if you need five dollars you can even be an author.

4. *The Sword Swallower*

ONCE I asked a sword swallower how he learned to swallow swords. I put my query respectfully because I considered this gentleman my superior as an artist, and he was certainly a better entertainer. Indeed, come to think of it, there are undoubtedly Indian-club jugglers, ladies who go over Niagara Falls in barrels, and side-show entrepreneurs who are *greater* artists in their fields than, say, even Piotr Ilytch Tchaikovsky or Anatole France in theirs. At any rate:

Question: "How do you learn to swallow swords, sir?"

Answer: "You swallow a sword. If you live, you are a sword swallower."

I think that is about the size of most things that people accomplish; excluding, perhaps, embalming and bookkeeping, which may be arts at that for all I know. In the main, I suggest, your artist of any kind becomes an artist by trying it and surviving. This is absolutely true of actors, a profession wherein the mortality rate is fortunately extremely high.

After my disaster with *The Rivals* I was let alone for a while, it being conceded in our acting family that Jack and I were abnormal sprouts, slow to blossom, but eventually due to floriate by the nature of our seed pods. While we could, Jack and I exerted ourselves to stave off the day.

We had a preference for *dolce far niente,* but we tried almost everything else.

Between the ages of fifteen and twenty I reluctantly appeared in some plays. Perhaps there is a record of all of them in aged and forgotten playbills, but I hope not, and I shall make no effort to unearth them. I was sent on the road, and my earliest efforts are not worth mentioning except to report that I regurgitated my sword at every opportunity and that I did survive.

Finally, during a period in which, in spite of all exertions by my family and some fainthearted gestures by me, I happily failed to obtain employment as an actor, I persuaded my betters that I should be enrolled at the Art Students League in New York to become a famous painter. This enterprise lasted for three years, during which time I painted copiously, if not industriously, and colorfully, if not successfully. This was what I wanted. The only thing that prevented my becoming a good painter was sheer lack of talent.

At this art school there occurred an incident which sums up my entire life. My whole existence, as I have mentioned before, has been a series of undeserved promotions. At the art school it was like this:

I was applying myself to the rudiments in the class of the celebrated John Twachtman alongside of Clarence F. Underwood, who later became the boss magazine-cover man, and Ferdinand Pinney Earle, who also became renowned for his brushwork. We were surrounded by as effete and arty an atmosphere as any Bohemian could wish: beautiful women, pretty girls, girls in mink, splashes of color, easels, smocks, and intense young men destined to become famous.

Mr. Underwood, I distinctly recall, was employed on a delicate Ethiopian head, which he was modeling with precise definition and vast care.

Ferdinand Pinney Earle was doing something or other, but whatever it was was not important enough to prevent a conversation with me. This led into an argument. I don't know what the argument was about. It doesn't matter, but the argument became loud and bitter and led to blows.

In those days it was my habit to fight people at the drop of a hat, and an unconscionable number of hats were dropped in my presence.

Earle was twenty pounds heavier than I but just as willing to trade licks. We fought all over the place. We crashed into easels, scattering color like an explosion in a paint factory. Girls huddled and screeched. Clarence F. Underwood sought safety on a high chair, clutching his Ethiop to his bosom.

Ferdinand Pinney Earle gave me a terrible shellacking. He flattened me and blasted me and took my face apart and blacked my eyes until the thing was over and the tottering warriors were led apart to recuperate in a saloon.

There, of course, we met, shook hands, congratulated each other, applied unguents to our noses and steaks to our eyes, and quaffed a number of bottles.

Smocked girls acted as couriers, reporting to us at the bar that the class was now closed and that Mr. Earle and I had been exiled from artistic society.

Later, when we returned to school, the young lady who presided at the reception desk regarded us with a discouraging eye.

"Mr. Twachtman's class is a shambles, gentlemen," she told us. "I don't know whether they'll ever get it back in shape again. But I do know, Mr. Earle and Mr. Barrymore, from what I have been hearing in words no lady should have to listen to, that if they ever start that class again they will not have either of *you* in it."

We retired to the bar to think that over.

Members of the life class came in from time to time and agreed with us that it had been a lovely brawl, well worth the price of admittance. But they also agreed with the receptionist that Mr. Earle and Mr. Barrymore had been declared null and void so far as Mr. Twachtman was concerned.

We sat around that bar for several days. The dilemma was a sentence of death to Ferdinand Pinney Earle, who saw all his hopes of becoming an artist vanish. It was a fate worse than death for me. Not only were my hopes of becoming an artist evaporated, but I perceived that, unless I could grasp a brush in my hand quickly, I would have to succumb again to the family trade of acting.

Finally a fellow artist came in with a gleam of hope in his eye.

"I think, men," he said, "that if you will go to a friend of mine who is a friend of the *maître* of antiques, and will bespeak yourselves solemnly and repentantly and politely, that he will have you admitted to Kenyon Cox's class."

This was *the* Kenyon Cox, the master himself. I had never thought seriously that I would be admitted to his class under any conditions, but this was a desperate predicament. We agreed to try it. Our friend uttered one more piece of advice:

"When you get in," he said, "do not know each other. Sit far apart. Do not quarrel. Be very quiet indeed."

And that is how it came out. We applied, humbly, and

were admitted. We forgot each other's presence. We sat apart. It was like getting promoted from Sophomore to Junior for fighting in lecture hall.

As I was saying before, this kind of unmerited promotion has followed me all my life, and, praises be, seems still to be in effect.

As for Ferdinand Pinney Earle, I met him many times after that engagement in Twachtman's class. He never failed to say, with politeness typical of the Nineties: "Barrymore, you gave me quite a lot of trouble."

This was good manners indeed, for he had thrashed me.

Soon after this incident, however, it became apparent that for fiscal reasons it was necessary for me to abandon my true love and go to work. You must not think that either the name of Drew or Barrymore was sufficient to get me onto a stage. They were not sufficient. It was difficult for me to find a job as an actor on account of my inexperience—no record of good parts, no notices, none of the hallmarks by which producers judge a newcomer.

In the end it was McKee Rankin who employed me.

Rankin's first name was Arthur, but he had dropped this shortly after going on the stage. At the age of twenty-one, he was acting important roles with Mum Mum's stock company at the Old Arch Street Playhouse in Philadelphia. Afterwards, he essayed starring roles of his own, married Kitty Blanchard, who was a popular actress and dancer, and became an actor-manager.

Rankin had three daughters: Phyllis, who married the late Harry Davenport; Gladys, who became Mrs. Sidney Drew (Uncle Googan), and thus was my aunt-by-marriage; and Doris. Doris became Mrs. Lionel Barrymore. But at the time of which I write she was a little girl.

McKee Rankin and Kitty Blanchard were billed always as "Mr. and Mrs. McKee Rankin," and enjoyed considerable success. In 1874–75 they played in the old Union Square Theater stock company in New York in the first production of *The Two Orphans*. But their principal play was *The Danites in the Sierras* by Joaquin Miller. Their tours in this play, which were highly successful, also included London, which appreciated the Rankins almost as much as we did.

There was one remarkable scene in that play, one which I suppose could not possibly be played before a modern audience, but which God knows was high theater at the time. The situation was the old one about the woman who hides the fugitive. The posse, or the soldiers, or whoever it was, enter her home and question her.

"Is he here?" they demand.

She takes a noble stance and says "No."

The posse leaves. She then advances to stage center, throws one hand across her eyes and the other up, and declaims:

"God forgive me—my first lie!"

The Danites also went well in London, in spite of an interesting first-night fiasco.

In London there is, or was, a costume company known as "Nathan's," patronized not only by actors but by swells who obtained there on occasion the cutaways, formal attire, toppers for Derby time, and other paraphernalia of the upper crust. And so "Nathan's" was better known in England than Western Costume Company is here.

One of the curtain lines of the McKee Rankin play called for a dramatic bit in which an actress points to a man and declaims: "You—you—you—are Nathan!"

The British howled at such American naïveté.

One of the plays Rankin did with Nance O'Neil was *Magda,* known as *Heimath* in the original German, which was for some time in the repertoires of Modjeska, Duse, Bernhardt, and Mrs. Pat Campbell. I appeared as Max, a pretty good part too, not that it mattered a whit. I was grateful to McKee Rankin for my little job and for making it possible for me to eat. My wardrobe in this production was more important than I was, it being absolutely authentic. We obtained it from a costume company which had got hold of it from a Minneapolis lieutenant who had been an officer of the precise regiment I was alleged to represent. If I did nothing else right, I modeled that officer correctly. I am certain it was the only correct costume in the play.

I was in a number of the Rankin plays, enacting any part that was not nailed down. During this time some of McKee Rankin's precepts and instructions apparently rubbed off on me, or were assimilated by osmosis, because I gradually got better parts and began to feel more at home on stage.

In Minneapolis, for a quickly rehearsed engagement, we presented our interpretation of *Oliver Twist.* I was not taking my work seriously at the time and spent as many hours as possible smoking in the alley with Rankin—such time as he could spare from his admiration of Nance O'Neil, who was with the company, and who was distinctly worth admiring.

It turned out that I had been assigned to play two parts in this production, the roles of Joey and of Toby Crockett. Being a reasonably quick study, I got up in my lines in a night or so, but for one reason or another we never went through a complete full-dress rehearsal. We went on cold, and did all right, too, until as one of my scenes loomed before me I realized to my horror that Toby Crockett and Joey were both supposed to be *on stage at the same time.*

I was already on as Crockett. Joey was supposed to enter and I was to hold a conversation with him.

I looked around helplessly, peering through the wings for Rankin, but Rankin was peering at Miss O'Neil, and I was left to play a scene with myself, two parts at the same time.

There was a window, left center. In my extremity, I used that window. I walked over to it and addressed Joey through it. Joey answered me—in another voice. It was a ventriloquist act, pure and simple. I mumbled and muttered and somehow got away with it.

As a matter of fact, McKee Rankin was so pleased with the expedient—which also saved employing another actor—that the scene stayed in the play that way. I did my ventriloquist act, without being detected, in every engagement after that. But this is a talent which, perhaps unfortunately, I have let fall by the wayside.

During this time my roommate and companion in the bars, where we repaired after work for intellectual fraternization, was Frank Butler, who later became brother Jack's partner in a number of interesting escapades. He was a tall man, almost handsome, who would have been obese if he had ever had enough to eat.

I first met the interesting Mr. Butler when he was performing as an actor, but his real talents lay elsewhere. Frank was a newspaperman of buoyancy and talent and a wassailer of gaiety and charm; as an actor, his distinction resided only in the overpowering fragrance of barleycorn which his movements wafted toward the audience. It was claimed by some that half the men in the first three rows always departed in the direction of the bar after being tantalized by Butler through the first act.

Attractive as it undoubtedly was to have this aromatic fellow on stage, even the tolerant McKee Rankin finally concluded that the dramatic unities were suffering from alcoholism. He was compelled, most reluctantly and politely, of course, to dismiss Frank. This was a calamity.

Butler felt extremely low about losing his job. Indeed, so did I, for reasons of friendship and also for economic considerations. I believe I was making possibly as high as thirty-five dollars a week at the time, and this was hardly sufficient to support us, let alone buy us our few moments of solace at the bar.

After examining the matter carefully for some hours over various cans of suds, Frank and I reluctantly agreed that it would be necessary for him to forget the theater at least temporarily and return to the newspaper business.

We attired ourselves in the best we had and together paid court the next afternoon at the desk of a city editor. I forget the name of the paper. It was one of the morning sheets in Minneapolis.

Frank and the city editor began to exchange professional reminiscences, disinterring the reputations of various newspapermen they mutually knew, while I perched on a desk and envied the easy camaraderie of this amusing way of making a living. While they talked, I observed that an onlooker was uncommon interested in what they had to say.

He edged closer and interjected himself into the conversation.

"Now, about that vacation I'm due," he said.

"Oh, yes, that," said the city editor.

"Well, we've got a replacement here. What about it?"

"Why not?" said the city editor. "Go ahead."

So the stranger walked out of the office on vacation and Frank Butler went on the payroll.

Frank emerged insufferably elated with a button-bursting strut. He had entered humbly to apply for anything that would provide eating money. He emerged a preposterous giant—with the title of dramatic critic.

His newly created eminence immediately launched a series of philippics against the McKee Rankin company. This daily spate of criticism was glittering and malicious and funny, but Rankin ignored it with lordly disdain. I thought it was hilarious until Butler took after me also.

The following week after we had opened at the Strand with a play in which I had merely the insignificant role of a flunky who makes one entrance bearing a tray, Mr. Butler let fly.

He wrote:

> Last night's performance provided as wretched an evening as these old eyes have witnessed since being compelled to see twelve men hanged in a row by a bungling sheriff. Of all the plays put on the boards in America yester-decade, this slow-footed and badly spoken entry by McKee Rankin must surely stand as the worst.
>
> Paradoxically, with every aspect at the nadir, one performance actually stands out more hideously than the rest. A deplorable young actor whose name I am

> able conveniently to forget, although it smacks of Barrymore, appeared only once in a figment of a role but enacted it so balefully that the audience was terrified all evening lest he come back on stage.

We lay abed late next morning having our coffee and reading "the notices." And that was the criticism my roommate read me, under his own by-line. It was one of the earliest poor notices I had. Possibly not the worst, but I have never had one so terse.

Mr. Butler's stay as a practicing journalist in Minneapolis was not long. He undertook to apply criticism to the town as well as to the theater. He wrote an article under the heading of "Five O'Clock" in which he described in polished periods the delights taking place in various parts of the world at that hour. He concluded his piece by asserting that, in contrast to the civilities being enjoyed everywhere else, nothing whatsoever was taking place in Minneapolis. Mr. Butler thereupon became jobless. I understand that in later years he published a volume of good verse and married a pretty actress.

In the year 1900 there was an extremely successful play on Broadway called *Arizona.* It was written by Augustus Thomas, who later played a highly important part in my life. In some textbooks on the theater I am recorded as having appeared in this play in New York, but unfortunately it is not so. There were, I will hazard, at least eighty-seven different road companies of this production touring the provinces, and I was obscurely in one of these.

I was twenty-two years old or thereabouts but I was cast as an old man. It was always my notion from the beginning that, if I was any kind of actor at all, I was a character actor. Character parts are more savory, more fun to roll under the tongue, and form such a perfect disguise that egress from the theater is often easier. As Miss Bette Davis, that intelligent young woman, once expressed it: "Anybody can play the part of a queen. The audience will believe what you do because nobody ever saw a queen."

Not even in my extreme youth, when, as a matter of fact, I was possibly handsomer than I am now, did I yearn to act romantic leads, clutching ingénues to my bosom and kissing them in the third act.

And so in one of the eighty-seven varieties of *Arizona* I played my old man all over the country and was content, gathering no fame, until that excellent actor and producer, James A. Herne, dropped in for a matinee performance.

He clapped a bemused eye on my ancient and was deluded by an impression that I was a good performer.

Mr. Herne came backstage to speak to me. He was astonished, he said, to discover that the portrayer of the septuagenarian was a moppet of so few unshaven summers.

"You had better come with me, Barrymore," Mr. Herne suggested.

Flattered but unambitious, I hesitated.

"I will give you more money," he said.

I accepted instantly.

James A. Herne wanted me for a small part in *Sag Harbor,* a production in four acts which he brought into New York for seventy-six performances at the Republic Theater on September 27, 1900. Thus, in spite of my disinclination for the theater and my diffidence about getting ahead in it, I made my modest debut on Broadway at the reasonably early age of twenty-two. The trouble was that Mr. Herne expected me to act my age, possibly one of the most difficult things a young actor ever does, and which I was entirely incapable of doing. Old men I could play. Young ones I could not play.

And so I did not burst upon New York with banners flying and tubs thumping, or win any of the acclaim which attended Ethel, who had already conquered New York and parts of Europe at an even earlier age.

This was, as a matter of fact, a year in which it would have been difficult anyway for a newcomer to attract much attention against the great names then heralded in the theater.

Otis Skinner was doing *Prince Otto*, Richard Bennett and others were performing in *A Royal Family* (no connection with a spoof many years later which entertained the Barrymores), Weber and Fields were working in their *Fiddle-Dee-Dee*, E. H. Sothern was reviving *Hamlet*, Belasco had *Zaza* on view with Mrs. Leslie Carter, Richard Mansfield was playing in *Henry V*, Maude Adams was to be seen in *L'Aiglon*, Sarah Bernhardt was appearing in repertory at the Garden Theater, and the wonderful Floradora Girls were responding sensationally to inquiries about there being any more at home like them.

Sag Harbor had the honor of opening the Republic Theater. It did well. It made William T. Hodge a star. As for me, I sneaked into town with the company, made my Broadway debut before a coterie of critics who were unanimously inattentive to my genius, and was dismissed after a few performances. I had a hand, then, in opening the Republic Theater, and I might have had the honor of closing it, too, some years later when I played there in *Peter Ibbetson*. But this time I had Jack with me.

Mr. Herne was one of the greatest actors that ever lived,

a great man in his own right quite aside from acting, and he was a kind man.

He had two daughters. He had to fire me not only because of my wretched acting but to fend for the honor of his family—which I left unsullied. But as I say, he was very kind about all this.

"Lionel," he said to me, "this is a disaster for which only I can be blamed. I have done you a disservice for which I hope you can forgive me. Due to my own ineptness, and for no other reason at all, you have been cast in an impossible part.

"Oh, you have created a brilliant role out of it, but it is of course not for you and gives you no scope whatsoever for your talents. I should be ruining your career, which is going to be brilliant, if I did not urge you at once to drop this very poor role and take a vacation.

"Yes, that's it, what you need is a vacation, my boy. You just take a vacation. Do not, I beg of you, hold this lapse against me."

And so I took a vacation. There was nothing else to do, since Mr. Herne had cut off my source of income. But I have never received such wonderful treatment as I received from James A. Herne. I should like to repeat the experience and get fired by that man all over again. Not even my grandmother was kinder.

5. *A Little Night Music*

I HAD REACHED Broadway, which is to say merely that I was unemployed there, but Ethel had conquered it. She had opened in *Captain Jinks of the Horse Marines* in our home town, Philadelphia, which had seen many Drews and Barrymores in its time and was not impressed, but when Charles Frohman brought the play to New York, Ethel became a star.

Jack was living at the Algonquin Hotel through the courtesy of its renowned manager, Frank Case, and was wearing good clothes through the courtesy of his uncle, John Drew, whose shirts did not fit him but could be shortened. I was, as I was saying, "at liberty."

But according to the historians, this era at the turn of the century was no great shakes in the theater. The critics were already looking back with bitter nostalgia to the glorious old days at Wallack's, and muttering of the fine achievements of Augustin Daly and A. M. Palmer as if we of the current crop of debutantes and young bucks were kindergarteners let loose in the halls of a profaned palace. It is true that Augustus Thomas and Clyde Fitch were on their way up, but their impact was not then impressive. The theater, everybody who knew anything said, was on its last feeble legs and would soon perish. I seem to recall seeing things like that in the prints very recently, a half

Spencer Berger Collection

Miss Ethel Barrymore

Spencer Berger Collection

John Barrymore, 1907

a century later. The theater, indeed, has been perishing since the days of Aristophanes.

What irked the critics was commercialism. The esteemed reviewers, especially the celebrated William Winter, attacked not only the producers but the audiences as well, alleging that the producers were venal moneygrabbers and that the public was vulgar. "Common tastes" and "animal appetites" were some of the phrases I recall that Mr. Winter applied. He said that the theater business had fallen into the hands of "moneygrubbing tradesmen who had degraded it into a bazaar."

I write these lines with a clear conscience and a superior smile. I had nothing whatsoever to do with the degradation of the American stage for quite a while. I was a free and untrammeled artist, out of work.

What chiefly inspired these spates of abuse heaped on the theater around 1900, and for some years thereafter, was the rise of the syndicates.

Charles Frohman and his older brother Daniel had come out of the West to acquire theater holdings and to build the queen of theaters, the Empire, in 1893, and they had established a virtual monopoly. Then came Klaw and Erlanger.

In the old, early laissez-faire days of the New York theater, the Rialto was bounded by Fourteenth and Twenty-third Streets. It required a good many years for it to shove so far uptown as Thirty-fourth and the Empire at 1430 Broadway. And in those days, the booking of plays and players outside New York was an informal and haphazard procedure.

The out-of-town managers, the often very distinguished out-of-town managers, came to New York in the summer to meet the Manhattan producers and stars. Their offices were in their hats, which they moved from bar to bar and from club to club for the conferences necessary to their business.

"Now, yas, yas, yas, I can let you have Booth," a New Yorker would tell a Detroiter, "but wait a moment, no I cannot, old man, he plays Chicago and then has to jump to Kansas City. But I can let you have Sothern for the week you require." Of course, I am putting into the managers' mouths the words Booth and Sothern probably said themselves, but I prefer to play safe because my fear of these great names persists.

And that is how the culture of the theater was brought to the American people. This informal booking went on all summer.

Klaw and Erlanger changed all that. Marc Klaw, who had been a lawyer in Louisville, Kentucky, and Abraham L. Erlanger, who had sold tickets in a Cleveland box office, joined up with C. B. Jefferson, the eldest son of Joseph, in the production of extravaganzas and musical comedies. They did reasonably well, I suppose, but they actually had little money when they went to the producers with an idea.

To a Detroit or Los Angeles manager they would say: "Why spend the hot summer in New York booking shows from producers' hats? Why not enjoy a cool vacation while we do it all for you?"

To a New York producer: "You really want to spend all your time in New York in the worst season of all? Let us handle your booking. We can do it—and for a starter we'll do it for nothing."

The suggestion was so obviously attractive that both

producers and managers agreed to it. Klaw and Erlanger, with Jefferson in the background, became a trust, a monopoly, almost overnight. They did not do business on a gratis basis after the beginning. They charged a commission to both producer and out-of-town manager. And they were soon in a position to dictate terms and bookings, to withhold play dates, to make or break great stars, on their own terms. The greatest monopoly in the history of the theater was formed in just this way.

Klaw and Erlanger were challenged later by three daring young men from Syracuse, Sam, Jake, and Lee Shubert.

The Shuberts invaded New York very literally on a shoestring: they were financed by a Syracuse haberdasher who backed them after they had shown talent and enterprise with modest stock-company presentations in Syracuse, Rochester, and Albany.

It was time for a challenge. Mrs. Minnie Maddern Fiske, in revolt against the system, was performing anywhere she could get a hall not owned by the syndicate. She would appear in anything from barns to skating rinks. David Belasco, when he found the doors of all Washington theaters closed to him, presented Mrs. Leslie Carter in Convention Hall under a leaky roof. It leaked on opening night, wetting, among others, Admiral Dewey and Secretary of the Navy Morton. Sarah Bernhardt sought refuge from the trust in a circus tent.

This deplorable situation, as I say, was attacked by the intrepid Shuberts. They leased the Herald Square Theater, declared war, put on cheap productions, and gradually acquired the Casino, the Princess, the Majestic, and the Lyric in New York, along with a magnificent chain of houses from the Atlantic to the Pacific. And they were soon in a position to make both producers and stars cry "Uncle" at their bidding.

But this, I think I can assure you, was not done by the excellent Shuberts quite in the spirit of chauvinism. They were not precisely St. Georges piously bent on conquering the monster. They were out to make money, and they did make money. But what they accomplished was healthy, as most free-enterprising ambitions have always been healthy in this country.

The Shuberts controlled a theater empire worth $400,-000,000 when they crashed in the stock market debacle of the late Twenties, but they have since recouped. Recently they purchased, in the biggest theatrical real-estate deal since Radio City Music Hall, the plot between Forty-fourth and Forty-fifth Streets, west of Times Square, acquiring the Shubert, the Broadhurst, the Booth, and the Plymouth Theaters from the estate of the late William Waldorf Astor for $3,500,000 cash. And from the top of the Shubert Theater, overlooking Shubert Alley of great fame, Lee Shubert today controls another empire from his twelve-by-twelve office. The Shuberts, Jake and Lee, are a $60,000,000-a-year brother act.

It was not thus when I met them. In 1901, Sam, Jake, and Lee, the sons of an immigrant peddler, were almost as virginal in pocket as I was.

I was sharing rooms in a drafty tenement on Thirtieth Street with Jack Gallatin, brother of A. E. Gallatin, the writer, and William Carpenter Camp, whose family had a fortune but kept him short of rupees most of the time. These diggings were known to us as "Running Water" because the bath tub always dripped—continuously, since we slept most of the day and the plumber could never get in to fix it.

I had made the rounds of the agencies and production offices one afternoon, offering myself as an actor, when on the way home to "Running Water" I paused at some blessed oasis for refreshment and someone said:

"Barrymore, a couple of newcomers from Syracuse are going to put on a show. Why don't you go over and see them?"

I gulped my lemonade and ran to the nearest exit, presenting myself somewhat breathless before Sam Shubert.

He was a small, harassed man and did not impress me. I told him I could act.

"What is your salary?" he asked.

I perceived that Mr. Shubert and I had an interest in common.

Up to this time in my career, actors of my stature who received fifty dollars a week were doing handsomely. Most of the time I had been delighted to accept thirty-five. But I thought, "What the hell, we'll give this thing a try," so I said: "Seventy-five dollars a week."

There was once, I am reminded, an impressive British actor who called on Arthur Hopkins.

"And what would your recompense be, sir?" Arthur asked.

"Why, I am accustomed to being paid at the rate of two thousand dollars a week," said the actor.

"Oh, I am so sorry," said Arthur. "All we have left is a bit part. It's the part of a butler. It pays twenty-five a week."

"I'll take it," said the actor.

I was in the same position, but Sam survived my vaulting request. Possibly he thought he was getting Ethel.

"This is a dressy part, you know," he said.

Having little more to wear than the threads on my back at the moment, I shrugged.

Sam shrugged back at me. Possibly he thought he would acquire along with me the wardrobe of John Drew, the most impeccably-attired gentleman of the theater. At any rate, we shrugged ourselves into a deal for me to appear in a play called *The Brixton Burglary*, a farce in three acts by Frederick W. Sidney.

We were to go into rehearsal at once and open in Albany.

I ran afoul then of the toughest stage manager in the world, Mr. Ben Teal. He frightened everybody, lashed us, derided us, and was particularly astute with cutting remarks about my acting abilities. Some of the people couldn't take it and dropped out, but I reasoned that this experience couldn't be worse than starvation, so I endured.

We went up to Albany and registered at the Ten Eyck Hotel. I had to take Gallatin with me, as banker, to buy food and lodging, and William Carpenter Camp, of course, was on hand to provide the clothes. In return, by elaborate lend-lease arrangements, I supplied Camp with money when the company manager paid me.

With these informal arrangements of borrowed clothes and borrowed money, I managed to make my debut with the Shuberts.

We opened at the Herald Square Theater on May 20, 1901, and played for forty-eight performances, a good enough run. This was the Shuberts' first Broadway play and it is likely that on its success depended the founding of the theatrical empire now represented by the vast sums of money I enviously mentioned earlier in this chapter.

I was not, however, either a finished or a studious actor. In the back of my head—nay, very much in the front of my head—persisted the idea that I would eventually discover an escape from the family profession. I harbored delusions of accomplishing this through painting. Also, I became interested in music and began to take lessons. Not that I ever thought I could become a professional musician, but as an anodyne from acting and because I had heard some Bach, which revealed to me new experiences and inspired an interest in the piano.

I was thus, in spite of the terrible man Ben Teal, cavalier about attending rehearsals and about giving the best performance possible to lure money into the box office for Sam, Jake, and Lee.

Once I skipped an important rehearsal entirely, stayed home in bed at "Running Water," and was awakened late in the day by emphatic pounding on the door.

I released the latch and crept back between the covers.

Sam Shubert entered, under the influence of a mastodon rage, and began to berate me.

"What in the hell's the matter with you, Barrymore?" he said. "Get up! Get out of there! Come to work! How do you ever expect to amount to anything lying there stinking in bed?"

He then pleaded with me to be a better boy, and it astonishes me to recall this scene. That was the great Sam Shubert, the founder of the syndicate. It was as if Louis B. Mayer had to rout me out of bed today.

There were good plays on the boards that year, all of them enacted by people of character who held the art of the theater more in respect than I held it. *Diplomacy,* the Victorien Sardou drama which Maurice Barrymore had taken West when he was shot in the shoulder, was revived by C. F. at the Empire with William Faversham, Guy Standing, and Margaret Anglin. Nat C. Goodwin was playing Shylock in *The Merchant* at the Knickerbocker, and David Warfield was on view in *The Auctioneer* up the street at the Bijou. Maude Adams appeared late in the year in Barrie's *Quality Street,* and Booth Tarkington's *Beaucaire* was seen at the Herald Square with Richard Mansfield.

I applauded them, but I knew very few of them, for the Theater did not seem to be my way of life at this time. During my long months of happy unemployment I played baseball when I could, became a dilettante in painting, and made an approach to studying music.

As a musician, I claim a certain distinction. I once met Tchaikovsky. Tchaikovsky came to this country in 1891 and, indeed, opened Carnegie Hall. I was thirteen years old then, and my father had a dog named Belle Clyde.

I had been bidden to go to the veterinarian's one afternoon to fetch Belle Clyde, who had come down with an ailment, and to meet Maurice Barrymore at the old Plaza Hotel, then a red brick building. Belle and I naturally found our way to the gentleman's café for our rendezvous with Maurice, and there we met a friend of my father's, a doctor.

"What are you boys doing here?" he asked. "Step up to the bar and have a drink."

So Belle and I stepped up to the bar and had ginger ale on the doctor. Presently a gentleman enveloped in a beard and a fur coat entered, greeted the doctor, had a drink with him, and the two of them spoke together for some minutes in an odd language that I could not understand. I was presented but did not get the name of the furry gentleman, who soon departed.

Not so very many years ago, as the crow flies, I met my medical friend as we were coming out of Carnegie Hall, where we had just heard a performance of the Sixth Symphony, to my mind the best thing that Tchaikovsky ever wrote.

"Barrymore," the doc said, "it must be a source of satisfaction to you to remember that you once shook the hand of the great man."

I muttered and looked at the doctor much as to say, "What in the world are you talking about?" He then explained to me that it was Tchaikovsky I had met in the bar, with Belle Clyde.

Great artists, I apprehend, cannot always be distinguished, or appreciated, by their looks. Debussy once said of Grieg: "From the front he looks like a genial photographer and from the rear he resembles a sunflower."

Debussy also hung one on Mendelssohn, who, he said, "was pretty good, but he always reminded me of a talented attorney."

My interest in music, which in recent years has excited the curious to speculate about whether I perform on a tuba or jew's-harp and to wonder if the incredible report is true that I can actually read notes, began at an age so early that I cannot recall it. I can most certainly read notes and, upon occasion, put them on paper out of my head; I make elaborate gestures toward playing the piano and, when my house is empty of housekeepers and spies,

I perform for my own amusement and astonishment upon an oboe. But all these pursuits are decently practiced in privacy and I do not have my picture made while I am engaged in them.

At some period in my extreme youth, I recall, I used to go with my father to the house of Thomas G. Patten on Eightieth Street, a spacious mansion wherein I could gaze on a number of paintings of the kind popular then—Arabs and sunsets, and a handful of probably spurious Corots. Mr. Patten was my father's brother-in-law, a circumstance of relation which was arrived at when Maurice, after my mother's death, married Mamie Floyd and Thomas married Henrietta Floyd. Thomas had a player piano which amused and then interested me. I heard Bach's fugues for the first time. I discovered that I could make shift to imitate playing certain simpler passages by placing my fingers on the keyboard and going along with the mechanism.

By the time I was in my early twenties, I had mastered the trick of playing modest tunes, what with a little coaching here and there, mostly of an informal kind, and eventually I set about trying to learn something. One of the teachers with whom I worked diligently for several years was the excellent Mrs. Agnes Morgan of New York. After that, between and, in fact, during plays, I attacked the theory of composition and of harmony under various masters, one of them the distinguished conductor and composer Henry Hadley.

Henry Hadley was a Lambs Club friend. Late one night, Lou Payne, who later married Mrs. Leslie Carter and is now an actor in Hollywood, Willie Camp, and I were at the club, broke, posted, and thirsty. It was near the end of a long summer of unemployment for all of us. We were looking for new arrivals who might take pity on us with a collation.

Mr. Hadley entered.

"That ought to be good for at least three drinks," I whispered to Lou. We approached and made pleasantries.

"Why, delighted, sir, thank you very much, yes, I believe I will join you in a small drink. You know my friends?"

Victor Herbert entered.

"Might be good for a couple more," whispered Payne.

He was indeed, but Hadley and Herbert soon brushed us small fry politely aside and began to discuss music.

"What are you doing, old man?"

"Why, rehearsing another operetta," Herbert said in his Irish accent.

"Tell me about it," Hadley urged.

And so we repaired to a table where Mr. Herbert could tell Mr. Hadley about his operetta. Herbert handed Hadley the complicated orchestral score. Hadley read it as easily as you are reading these words.

"Wonderful, old man, wonderful. I wish I could hear this. I wonder now—there's a good piano upstairs."

So upstairs we all went. There was a handsome grand there, which we soon covered with drinks, sandwiches, and music.

Hadley began to play. But Herbert's attention was directed to a strange object under the piano.

"Looks like a cello," said Herbert. "By gad, it *is* a cello. Now I wonder—"

The cello was Herbert's own instrument, as you know. He had come to America as a cellist. But this cello was a *particular* cello, as it turned out. It belonged to Willie Jefferson and was a gift from his father—Joseph Jefferson himself. And it was a genuine Stradivarius.

Willie always claimed he could play the cello. I never heard him. Perhaps he could. Just being Willie Jefferson, of course, was enough, without having to play anything.

Victor Herbert extracted the instrument, tuned it, and was delighted with its mellow tone. He was astonished when he discovered that it was a Strad.

And so, between free drinks and sandwiches, Lou Payne, Willie Camp, and I listened to *Kiss Me Again*, played by Victor Herbert and Henry Hadley. We were the first persons in the world to hear it.

The production of this famed operetta came off in due time. The angel of the show was Felix Isman, who was, although I naturally did not know it then, the current husband of the lady who became my second wife.

I do not recall whether Willie Jefferson recovered his Stradivarius or not. The latest report I have on that good companion is that he is living stylishly in Honolulu and that he owns an enormous double bed over which he has a chinchilla spread.

I began at once to see a lot of Henry Hadley. I consulted him at the club from time to time about musical problems that were too deep for me and he kindly advised me. He gave me books to study, examined my efforts, and suggested that I come to his apartment occasionally for musical sessions.

In order to facilitate this, I moved instanter into a Carnegie Hall studio, where Hadley himself had quarters, nudging as close as possible to the master. On appointed days I would turn up for my lessons.

Invariably, Hadley would meet me—at whatever time of day it was—elegantly attired in a brocaded dressing gown. He would send for coffee and cigarettes, and we would begin to peruse some effort of mine or some composition that I needed to understand.

"Well, yes, yes, yes, now, let me see—let me see," Hadley would begin.

At precisely this moment there would be a knock on the door. It never failed. There would be a knock on the door.

A smick-smack and enchanting blonde would enter.

Hadley would say, "Ah, yes, yes, yes, my dear, and have you met my young friend Mr. Barrymore?"

He would then fix me with an eye. A pleading eye. The eye said: "Are you going to be such an oaf as to *sit* there, my dear fellow?"

So I would gather my sheaves of music and depart.

This always happened. I would leave in disappointment (and envy) for my own small diggings upstairs. My brother, who was at extremely loose ends those days, often came in at unusual hours seeking either a dinner or a night's lodging. He was living as best he could, and it was this era of his life, I suppose, that gave him that cactus toughness which enabled him to endure so much. Jack was, indeed, like the century plant, all bristles and cactus until it unexpectedly flowers.

Being relatively wealthy at the time, I could afford a room with a private bath. One evening, Jack appeared loaded to the eyes with liquor—with which indulgent friends must have plied him; he could not have bought it himself—and decided that a cold tub might put him in shape.

He removed all his clothes and hopped into an icy bath.

This did not seem chill enough for his needs, so he opened the window.

"Be about your affairs, old man," he called to me. "I shall lave me and depart ere fifteen minutes have transpired."

I left for the evening and was detained by certain interesting matters until past four in the morning. As I prepared for bed, I was startled to see Jack's clothes still on the chair where he had tossed them.

I opened the bathroom door. There he was, sound asleep in the tub of cold water, with the window open to a New York winter.

He felt fine when I awakened him and did not suffer a sniffle.

But back to my music: it began to look, finally, as if I would never master the theory of harmony. I required a good, patient, and preferably free teacher. But what little learning I have, caught up with me by accident, like everything else in my life.

During *The Mummy and the Humming Bird,* a play I worked in for Charles Frohman, I was an organ grinder—and, indeed, the amount of real music I knew at that time was about that of an impresario with an ape on a string. My role required me to go back and forth under the stage from time to time to make various entrances. To do this I had to wend my way through the members of the orchestra, who would be employing their time at cards or dice.

One evening I fell into conversation with an ancient German who was on his way for a drink of water.

"By the way, sir," I asked him, "do you know where I might get some lessons in harmony?"

The old man answered quietly:

"Well, I give lessons in harmony."

And there I was, stuck with it. I had to take him on. And it was one of the most fortunate things that ever happened to me. My aged musician was known under the remarkable name of Richard Klugscheid (literally translated "Klugscheid" means "clever and wise") and he had been in the first violin section of the old Philharmonic.

He became my teacher, not part time, but for life. I owe that delightful old gentleman countless, endless hours of pleasure and excitement. He taught me music and how to enjoy music. And he was so kind, so wise, and (of no interest to the reader but of vast importance to me) so inexpensive.

Somewhere along the line, between the ages of twenty-five and thirty, I began to compose things for my own amusement. I never thought of having anything published, or of hearing my "works" performed. Indeed, I felt then precisely as I feel now: I have, by your leave, composed a few things which have been performed in public by good orchestras led by distinguished conductors, but I take *music* seriously, not myself. If suddenly I were to begin to feel cocky, all I should have to do to disabuse myself of the nonsense would be to imagine what would happen if one of my pieces came to the attention of Brahms when that gentleman was in a bad mood.

I shall have something more to say about music later on in this confession. At the time of which I write, my early twenties, baseball and the admiration of such giants as John L. Sullivan and Fitzsimmons were also important.

6. *Dinner Was the Main Thing*

My skill as a baseball player was announced in Detroit. I was working there in McKee Rankin's company, making my perishable contributions to the drama in some small part, and Willie Collier was appearing in opposition to us in another theater. It was the habit of the actors to meet at various restaurants and bars after the evening performance to discuss the state of the nation, and those of us who were young and without funds attended these sessions studiously, receiving drinks and suppers in return for our attentions.

My baseball-playing prowess was announced by me. It was in the middle of the winter, which seemed like a safe time to propose myself as a wonder on the diamond. Willie Collier was a great ball player in fact. After four drinks I was a great ball player, too. I was a crafty and powerful hitter. I smacked 'em ahead of or behind the runners as ordered from the bench. I slid bases with spikes which threatened to amputate the opposition. In sum, I was obviously a good deal faster, smarter, and braver than J. P. Wagner. I said so.

In the chill of a Detroit winter, when a young actor escaping from the drafts in his frayed garments sought only a sacerdotal Tom-and-Jerry or so and indulgent companions to listen to his brags, it naturally did not occur to me that any person alive would lend serious ear to my baseball fantasies. But among those in the restaurant that night was a fellow named Van Rensselaer Wheeler, a fine baritone.

Later in the year, as madding spring arrived with hopeful chirpings of birds and bill collectors, I was in the Lambs Club in New York suffering from a chronic condition. I was broke and posted. Willie Camp, my wardrobe, was with me, also in hunger. We were sitting around like a pair of crows on a fence with eyes cocked, hoping something would turn up, when in walked Van Rensselaer. He shot a look at me and said:

"Now, there's a ball player. How about it, Barrymore, how would you like to come down to St. James for the week end?"

I would have gone to Zanzibar for a blue-plate. I forgot about being a ball player and went out to Long Island to eat the ducks, and anything else they had in the pantry.

They fed me, but they also put me in right field. First thing I knew, a fellow smote a ball. I looked up and to my joy saw that it had been hit so far that no fielder would be expected to catch it. Nevertheless, I ran as fast as I could and as far as I could and turned. And there it was. That ball was coming at me like a planet bent on collision. I stuck up a glove and caught it.

I examined this ball in astonishment until yells from the crowd reminded me I was supposed to do something with it. Throw it toward third was the proper caper. I leaned into the throw and let fly. The players had tagged up after the catch, a man had started from third, where my ball did not go, and was on his way home. My desperate, badly-aimed toss went into the catcher's mitt on the first bounce.

For some reason, possibly a bit of strategy by a pitcher who hadn't had a chance to observe the new hitter in action, I was given a base on balls the first time up. The second time up, I was hit, and thus took my base. The third time up, the bases were loaded. It was a dead-eye sinecure that I was not going to get walked.

"I don't care," I mumbled to myself. "If this fellow does hit me and kill me it will be a good thing. At any rate, it will save me considerable personal embarrassment."

By this time I was welcoming death.

In this mood I cut at the ball and knocked it over center field for a hit that was by the mercy of God a three-bagger.

I was a big man. I really was. I know what it feels like. No man or boy who has ever knocked in three runs need wonder how the mantle of greatness comforts the shoulders. I am certain that no conqueror, no king, no admiral in the moment of victory as the enemy's fleet sinks in smoke and disaster, ever feels better or greater.

I stayed on for the rest of the week, then stayed for a month, then stayed for the greater part of three years, off and on, playing on Willie Collier's baseball team and occupying the third floor chamber next to the bathroom.

All around Long Island at that time were actors and athletes and acrobats. They all played ball and they were good at it. John Kernell, one of the fine comedians of the day, was one of our supporters. When not watching ball games he would hire a buggy, put two cases of beer in it, start out across Long Island, finish the beer, then follow the empty bottles back home. But Bill Gray, one of our team mates, could run the hundred in ten flat.

Willie Collier owned the uniforms and the grounds, so of course he pitched. Between games, we acted, putting on plays on the Island to raise a bit of cash; indeed, for one production which we presented up and down the North Shore, the company cleared a total of twenty-five thousand dollars. Or so I was told. If I had ever at any time laid hands on even a part of such a staggering sum, it is a certainty I should never have continued to be an actor.

In addition to the gentleman sports, actors, and gymnasts with whom we competed, one of our chief rivals was the insane asylum team. Actually, their nine was composed chiefly of nurses. But I remember the awesome moment when Willie Collier, having been dusted off twice by a vicious pitcher who threw fast balls at his head, stalked toward the box with fists cocked for action.

"I wouldn't do that if I were you, Willie," the umpire's quiet voice said. "That pitcher is a schizophrenic who thinks he is Attila the Hun." Willie retreated.

In the summer, Tony Farrell had a restaurant down on the shore which was patronized by the fancy. We repaired frequently to this kindly spot, allowed ourselves to become swozzled, and sweated it off the next day at the ball park. Or we swam. I was a stout fellow in those days, as we all were, convinced that we possessed inexhaustible natural resources within us for any contingency or any abuse. Young men, I believe someone said, are handed double-barreled shotguns in their extreme youth and don't know how to use them; years later, when they learn how, their aim is bad. It is still a wonder to me that any young buck of enterprise, with juice in his veins, manages to survive at all. At any rate, during one of these summer frolics at Easthampton I was nearly drowned and another young man risked his life for me.

I was with Jack Gallatin and in the exuberance of brisk water and hot blood, I swam out too far. I was caught in a sea puss, frighteningly far from shore, and I bellowed for help.

On the beach was a young fellow who had been married only three days and he did a gallant thing. He started after me. He left his girl and swam into an ugly sea to try to save a drowning man he didn't know.

I struggled, swallowing brine, going down and coming up. So far as I am concerned, the legend that your entire life passes before you as you drown is nonsense. I knew that I was drowning and I didn't expect to get saved, but when I saw that good man coming after me, I gave it all I had. My rescuer wasn't a skilful swimmer and was having his own troubles, but he kept coming.

Just before he reached me I got a foot on firm ground, enough to balance with, enough to keep my mouth above water and get some breath. I was safe then, I could have come in by myself.

The bridegroom put an arm under my shoulder and we fought our way back to the beach, whereupon, of course, we were pounced upon instantly by life guards and other heroes who had watched the entire episode without doing anything.

My first impulse, when I had got my breath, was to uphold my own esteem, to reveal that I had reached a foothold and saved myself before my rescuer grabbed me. But some blessed instinct saved me from this dishonorable action. The gentleman had risked his life for me, he had meant to save me, and he *thought* he had saved me—and boys, was he a hero to his bride! I thanked him profusely.

To my dismay, I have lost that man's name. I have

never told the story before, but if, perchance, he reads these lines let me thank him again for risking his life for me.

Those indeed were the days, grand days for young men, with everything in its proper place, no war or threat of war, and great men to admire. John L. Sullivan and Bob Fitzsimmons, for instance. I was knocked out by both of them.

Sullivan enjoyed frequenting the popular bars in order to create imaginary disturbances by pretending he was drunk. Having swaggered and bully-boyed about the place, announcing that he could lick any man in the world—which he indubitably could at that time—he would show his skill and timing by knocking the hats off his friends' heads. He used me as his model one memorable evening.

I was wearing a flat hat, a hat so flat that it fitted right down on top of my pate, with no protruding crown, and this deceived Sullivan. He hit the hat all right, with a mighty right, but it stayed on and I went down with it, and out.

When I came to Sullivan glowered at me.

"Trying to go fancy on me, are you, Barrymore?" he accused.

I was in no shape to dispute him. If he had put any steam into the blow, I wouldn't be here to tell about it today. There are stories told about how the stalwart Barrymore used to box with John L. Sullivan in his youth, but these, I regret to say, are akin to certain other tall tales and embroideries about the Barrymores. I never sparred with John L. Sullivan. My youth was not distinguished for intellect, but I had more sense than that.

Fitzsimmons laid me low at the Berkeley Hotel. I was—as who was not?—his worshipper and fan and had taken care to make myself known to him for the privilege of shaking his hand and being greeted by him in public.

On the afternoon of the tragedy, I was wearing my new and excessively fancy vest and drinking martinis at a table in the hotel bar. Fitzsimmons came in, creating a stir, and paid me the compliment of joining me.

The theme of his conversation piece that afternoon was science and the ease with which a man could be rendered unconscious by a scientifically placed blow.

"You can do it with a finger," he said.

Most of us were ignorant of judo, and though none would have challenged Fitzsimmons if he had proclaimed that he could topple the Flatiron Building with a left hook, we expressed a certain amount of skepticism about this statement.

"With a finger," said Fitzsimmons. "Takes only a light tap, correctly applied. Like this."

He leaned forward slightly and flicked my throat with his index finger.

The martinis came up and I went down.

Bob Fitzsimmons was a good man and a gentleman and he was extremely regretful about the matter. So was I.

I knew another great champion well and used to work out with him at the gym. This was William Muldoon, who toyed with me. We wrestled for form and for exercise, not for falls—and if you have seen Argentine Rocco and Gorgeous George, the Great Atlas and the various Barons and Lords of the current television circus, let me promise you I was not at all like them. Muldoon took me on because he was a friend of my father's and because I was willing.

Indeed, Muldoon once appeared with Maurice on the stage. Maurice conceived the notion that it would be a fine thing for Muldoon to play Charles, the Wrestler, in a production of *As You Like It.* Madame Modjeska was taken aback by the notion at first, but when she saw Muldoon she consented. Maurice took great pains with his scene with Muldoon, cooking up a fancy-hold match in which Muldoon was to make a bridge and Maurice was to jump on him.

They revealed this act in Chicago. Muldoon made his bridge, and Maurice jumped. But the big scene was stolen by a voice from the gallery:

"Hey, Billy, throw him up here!"

But I would not have you think that my little friends and I were so devoted to the professional muscle as all this no doubt sounds. We became aware that there had appeared in the little magazines a new kind of poetry, blank of meter, free of convention, as different from traditional poetry as "Nude Descending the Staircase" was different from Watteau's landscapes. At this time, the time of the Long Island ball-playing enterprises, Maeterlinck was at the crest of his popularity, and the master had recently published some verses of his own which Jack Gallatin, Willie Camp, and I found unbearably obscure and far from solving any of life's problems for indigent young men.

We recited this poem to each other, examined it from various angles and from various stances, and confessed that while it was unquestionably a nosegay of pretty words, it seemed to lack sense.

"I think, gentlemen, that we should write a poem ourselves," I said.

"Forsooth, indeed, pray why not?" said Gallatin.

"I shall bed me with the muse," I said, retiring to a corner, from which I emerged shortly to borrow paper from one and a pencil from another.

After a proper interval of gestation, I emerged with a five-line epic which Gallatin and Camp hailed as a masterwork.

But I advised caution.

"We will not say I wrote this," I warned. "No one will respect such a misbegotten work of art. We will say instead that we have translated this thing from the French. All chi-chi things are translated from the French, as you know. And we will admit that the translation isn't excessively skilful, asking pardon for any technical deficiencies."

We revealed our poem to the Long Island literati and baseball-playing fraternities the next day and it met with considerable success. It was solemnly examined by poets and writers. They seemed to discern depths of meaning in it.

But neither then nor now did my five lines mean anything at all. Nothing. Here is the proof. Here is my poem:

> The curtain of my soul is drawn,
> Its essence flows at will to distant verdant fields;
> Oh, river of my anxious, tortured soul,
> Thoughts soar on up and up through Zada's realm;
> My soul, my soul, alas my soul!

As I have been indicating, these were careless days. Now in retrospect it seems to me that they were perhaps endowed with a certain raffish, callow charm. Even the exigencies of poverty and the bleakness of days and nights when I fretted and connived to lay hands on a dinner or a new coat appeal to me now as being either outrageously comic or pathetically tender.

But over it all was the specter of economic insecurity, and this is the one thing that looms up solemnly at all times. No matter how roguishly you wag your finger at it, there it is, and it is painful. Those of us who have known it and survived to acquire warm beds of our own and three meals a day eventually are inclined, as I say, to make jests about it in mellow years and to look backward with an affectionate eye. But in the watches of the night, if we have not turned out to be either fools or hogs, we know compassion—at least for ourselves.

There were, indeed, members of the Drew-Barrymore tribe who were exceedingly prosperous. Uncle Jack was the First Gentleman of the Theater and was handsomely paid for it at the rate of seventy thousand dollars a year. Maurice became a matinee idol and was rewarded. Ethel was a star and made money. And all of these kinfolk were both generous and kind. But it was a characteristic of our family to let each other alone.

A few years ago, a close friend of Jack's, Ethel's, and mine spent an evening with the three of us and afterwards made a statement.

"You Barrymores frighten hell out of me," he said. "You are so *polite* to each other."

After my mother's death when I was fifteen, Ethel was the only member of the family who managed in any way to look after any other member. But Ethel, bless her, was always on hand when the chips were down.

7. *Three Curtains Fall*

WHAT SECURITY the young Barrymores could lay claim to resided in Mrs. John Drew.

Our affection for her was warm, though tempered sometimes by the kind of respect with which one makes his manners to Constitution Hall or the Bill of Rights. We lived in her home, we went confidently to her for advice—or money; we took her scoldings as our due, and we were immeasurably proud of her. Mum Mum was, it goes without saying, a magnificent actress and a bravura person in her own right; she was also a grandmother. I have to this day a special understanding with men and women who were fetched up by their grandmothers: I am convinced always that they are ladies and gentlemen.

I saw my grandmother for the last time at Larchmont when I was nineteen, in 1897. She was then burdened with seventy-seven years, more than seventy of them passed in the theater, the last fifty of them as a star and manager on the American stage. But she was rich only in tradition and personality and her family was scattered. It had long ago ceased to be necessary to maintain the Twelfth Street house in Philadelphia, and indeed Mum Mum could not have maintained it in her last years. So she spent her last days in a boardinghouse at Larchmont with Jack. To the last minute, it never occurred to her that she had retired.

She was confident that she would be on stage again next year.

I had heard casual hints that Mum Mum was not as vigorous as usual, but in our family we have always tried to conceal our ailments from each other and from the world with the same touchiness with which we defend our private sins. My grandmother regarded illness as a kind of gaucherie, as a combination of social and professional error which no well brought up Drew would permit. But on this visit I found her in grave pain, although she gallantly and lightly denied it, and so I did not annoy her with my personal problems. To amuse her we talked instead about Ethel's success and about how far theatrical people had come up in the world during her day.

Ethel, at eighteen, had played with both William Gillette and Sir Henry Irving in London and was, at the moment, by far the most incandescent beauty in the town. She was reported to be engaged to any number of British swells and scions, including Laurence Irving, son of Sir Henry, and Gerald du Maurier. She had cabled her father announcing her engagement to Gerald.

"Congratulations," Maurice replied.

A few days later she cabled Maurice announcing that her engagement was broken.

"Congratulations," Maurice replied.

Another great gentleman whose name was linked with Ethel's was the Earl of Devonshire and Ava, about whom I could tell Mum Mum a tender and ironic story.

Ava was the handsomest man in London, much handsomer than any actor, possibly the handsomest man that ever lived. He was a soldier and a brave one, but he was as distinguished in the boudoirs of London as he was in the battles of the Boer War, in which he was eventually killed.

After his gallant death, there began to appear at soirée after soirée and party after party innumerable lovely women in deep mourning. Some one would inquire in surprise:

"*You* in mourning, my dear? I didn't know. A relative—?"

The pretty would drop her eyes and murmur the magic name:

"Ava."

It got so that no one could say the name seriously.

I was happy that these things amused Mum Mum because her doctor told me that she had not long to live. Mum Mum, of course, disagreed with him.

"The typical nonsense of his deplorable trade," she would say. "There is nothing the matter with me at all. I am merely resting between plays. And I must be up soon for a new rehearsal."

Jack was very young at this time, turning handsome, and he had enterprises of his own which could have engaged him pleasantly, but never once did he leave his grandmother until he had rubbed her feet, tucked her in bed, and said good night. Then he would stay with her until she fell asleep. No matter how Jack Barrymore behaved later, it is good to remember that he did these things when he was a boy.

I stayed at Larchmont as long as I could, but being in my usual state of indigence, I was soon forced to return to New York to seek some kind of employment in order to eat, in the theater if absolutely necessary. Jack remained with Mum Mum, and one evening he saw her gently to bed and kissed her good night for the last time.

With the death of Louisa Lane Drew, whose home had been the only home Ethel, Jack and I had ever known, our only link with stability and security disappeared. This was harder on Jack than on Ethel and me. Ethel had already arrived, was a celebrity and a star. I had been for some years on my own, but Jack had been Mum Mum's favorite, had lived with her and depended upon her.

My mother and father, affectionate and generous persons though they certainly were, were actor and actress on the stage, traveling, living in hotels, spending money when they had it, mockingly enduring near-poverty when they didn't. The rearing of offspring was not their forte. They did what they could with what they had, which is all that anyone can ever do.

When my masters, the psychologists, the psychiatrists, and the learned reporters who attempt to explain everything about everybody from the dream-books, apply their techniques to John Barrymore, I make the simple suggestion that they remember that his grandmother who reared him and adored him died when he was fifteen. Jack never felt safe anywhere after that.

Georgie Drew, our mother, had died in 1893 while Jack and I were at Seton Hall. Ethel was at Notre Dame, but when Georgie fell ill and failed to recover from a trip to the Bahamas, Maurice was on tour, Uncle John was in Europe, Mum Mum was on the stage in Boston, and the only possible member of the family who could take care of the invalid on the necessary trip of recuperation to

California was my sister. Ethel was fourteen. She left school and went with our mother to Santa Barbara. There Georgie was briefly happy, renewing a friendship with Modjeska, but there she died; and on Ethel's inexperienced shoulders fell the entire burden of making all the arrangements. She spent eight days in a day coach, having not enough money for a berth, as she brought our mother back home.

Maurice died in 1905 after an illness that endured for two wretched years. He had achieved his pinnacle with the part of Rawdon Crawley in support of Mrs. Fiske's Becky Sharp, earning the praise, even, of the redoubtable William Winter. He had, indeed, seen all his children on Broadway, for Jack and I had arrived there—hard on the heels of the parades of praise that welcomed Ethel's appearance—and I can suppose, now that I like to think of such things, that he was proud of us. As for that, of course, I cannot take oath because all the Barrymores in my ken were, and are, desperately embarrassed about saying anything complimentary to each other's faces. There is on record only one boast about me by my father:

A friend complimented him on the birth of his first son.

"Yes, I'm proud of him," said Maurice. "The newspapers always accuse me of taking things from the French. This is one time they cannot say that."

I saw him for the last time in Amityville. I had gone up to bid him good-by for the time being because I was heading West to take part in some dramatic enterprise having to do with making a living.

In his last years my father had taken it into his head that whatever I did I was pulling something. He regarded me with the baleful doubt of a man who thinks another man is setting out to engage in shady card games or in the robbing of orphanages.

"Where did you say you were going?" he asked me suspiciously.

"West, and then on to San Francisco."

"You are a God-damned liar, Lionel," my father said. "Everyone knows that San Francisco has been destroyed by earthquake and fire."

What prescience, what flash of occult illumination inspired that remark I cannot pretend to know. I can only vouchsafe that Maurice Barrymore said it one tense day in 1905, shortly before he died. There had been no earthquake, no fire, in San Francisco. That great tragedy came a full year later, in 1906.

Maurice's funeral had been held in New York by the time I reached Chicago, hurrying back from San Francisco. It had taken me two days to reach El Paso.

It was, of course, Ethel who took Mum Mum's place as the family bulwark, who looked after her father in his illness, and who buried him.

I think it is true that Maurice Barrymore's collapse, following Mum Mum's and his mother's death, had a lasting effect on John Barrymore. I believe that Jack was haunted, in those dark moments which come to all men, by the fear that he too would collapse; and I have been told that it is psychologically sound that the thing you most fear is precisely the thing that is most likely to happen to you.

8. *We Didn't Want to Act*

EVEN BEFORE THE deaths of Mum Mum and our parents, Jack had made irresolute but sincere motions toward escaping from the theater. Like me, he wanted to walk, not run, toward the nearest exit.

My brother's real and earnest and lifelong ambition was to be a painter. Like me, he made his bid early and failed. He even went so far, once, as to persuade Maurice to put money for lessons in the hands of the Art Students League; but eager as he was to learn and to escape, trapping Jack Barrymore in a classroom was like tethering a he-fawn in a cell. He broke loose in one day and never returned.

Jack reported this to his father in trepidation, but that most unusual of parents merely smiled and said:

"Boy, what defeats me is how you happened to go to class for even one day."

But for some time after that Jack studied under George Bridgman, who took a special interest in him, challenged his undeniable talent, and gave him friendly help far transcending mere class work.

He learned fast, by that baffling process of his own which always enabled him to master techniques when he was interested in them. Jack shared with his father a Flaubertian passion for techniques. He never took acting seriously—until he had to do it. Then, out of unsuspected resources of observation and knowledge would come, as

Spencer Berger Collection

An early photograph of Lionel Barrymore

Museum of the City of New York

Lionel Barrymore as The Dragoman in *The Fires of Fate*, 1909

if on the spur, the bagful of tricks that are the equipment of a studied craftsman. For instance, it was neither whim nor accident that Jack was known for astonishing get-ups and make-ups in the theater and in motion pictures: he *knew* make-up, technically and expertly and soundly. And he understood this art far better, of course, than the artificers who merely applied the tufts and the paints.

He knew what made automobiles run. He was fascinated by automobiles and therefore he learned about them. I have seen him confound and embarrass expert mechanics who undertook to instruct the actor about his own car.

Jack took little interest in music and so, naturally, he avoided knowing anything about it. But even as a boy he proceeded to know all about all artists who worked in pen and ink. He collected—when he was in pocket—the works of Italian masters, and he could identify at a glance even the most obscure artists in this field.

And so, when he announced himself as an artist, he did not venture into a field in which he walked as a stranger. He knew a great deal about art and artists and he learned quickly. It is a fruitless but interesting speculation to wonder what might have happened had the family bane of acting not magicked him away from the easel and onto the stage.

Jack had, at that, the experience of getting paid money for two of his pictures. The fee was five dollars for each. As the result of a recommendation from Ethel to Cissie Loftus, who bespoke his skill to Daniel Frohman, Jack was commissioned to do a poster for E. H. Sothern's production of *If I Were King*. The poster was a good one and was revived along with the play, for years afterwards, to the great pride of all Barrymores. Jack also sold a sketch of a hangman walking along a road, carrying a stick which casts a shadow behind it resembling a gallows, and above the road are the faces of men and women he has executed. This macabre thing was doubtless inspired by Jack's admiration for Beardsley. He was astounded to discover that Andrew Carnegie had purchased his drawing for ten dollars, of which Jack received five.

Both of us at about this time were artist's models, a facet of the Barrymore careers which I believe is little known.

Jack fell in with a spare and hungry artist named Rip Anthony who resided at the old Aulic Hotel opposite the side of the Herald Square Theater on Thirty-fifth Street. Jack posed for this artist, who was very good, as a matter of fact, although always hungry, in return for lodgings on various bleak nights. He was limned as all sorts of figures and persons, from dying members of the Seventh Cavalry in Custer's Last Stand to a Roman matron grieving at the tomb of her son.

I too was immortalized in paint. I knew Augustus Thomas, to whose house I went as often as possible for dinner, and there I met a hero of mine, Frederic Sackrider Remington, that extraordinary draftsman so well-known for his paintings of the West.

A new drawing of his had just appeared in print which I had admired and envied, so when I met him at dinner I told him so. It was a dramatic painting, showing a pioneer with mouth twisted in agony as he died scratching at a water hole.

As I talked I did what people attached to the theater usually do. I twisted my mouth and imitated the character dying at the water hole.

"Say, you can do that?" said Remington. "Old man, would you mind dropping by some time? I could use you."

I dropped by as fast as possible and posed for Remington. None of my portraits is recognizable, unfortunately, unless by some staggering leap of the imagination you can find me in the persons of some of the Indians and old settlers, cavalry officers, and pioneers whom Remington painted. I am usually perishing violently with a big grimace.

In this respect, my brother and I in these early years practiced similar techniques: we associated with friends who had no more money than we had and we placed ourselves in the way of meeting people who might be charmed into purchasing food and drink. Rip Anthony and Jack, indeed, used to engage in a special chicanery when they were hungry.

Anthony, who was tall and spare, with a pointed black beard, a man who could appear as distinguished as a cardinal when he wished, would enter some hotel, usually the Aulic, take a table, and lie in wait for someone who might buy a drink for the privilege of taking part in a conversation. If this failed, Jack would join him, and Anthony, in a voice loud enough for the waiters to overhear, would cordially invite him to dine. They would take a table, and bread and butter would be placed before them. This would instantly disappear into Anthony's pockets, and the two would sit for a while as if waiting for guests who were tardy.

When no guests turned up, the pair would move on. But for the sake of their reputations, Anthony would leave a message:

"If Mr. Frohman and Mr. Jefferson come in and ask for

us, please tell the gentlemen that we have gone on to Delmonico's."

The crumbs and butter pats thus pilfered from hotels made good breakfasts for Jack and Anthony the next morning.

Jack occasionally picked up a farthing or so by peddling a drawing to a clothing firm. He was also, most briefly, employed by the New York *Telegraph,* which commissioned him to make a picture of the Duchess of Devonshire. Jack accomplished this in less than thirty minutes by being careful to follow the lines of Gainsborough's well-known portrait, and was told that his work of art was no good.

Jack tells in his *Confessions of an Actor,* which he published in 1926, how he then went to work for Arthur Brisbane on the New York *Evening Journal.* Mostly he did conventional newspaper work, line cuts of conflagrations, murders, and dahlia shows. But he finally began to appear on the editorial page with illustrations of the sayings of the great Brisbane himself. Jack was an admirer of Doré. His works were steeped in allegory and gloom and usually matched Mr. Brisbane's pronouncements.

He then began to do the drawings for the verses of Ella Wheeler Wilcox, and this was an extraordinary combination. Mrs. Wilcox was a sunny poetess who wrote of love and buttercups. One morning, to her bewilderment and horror, she looked at her paper to discover that one of her bonniest poems had been illustrated with a dire picture of a hanging. She called Brisbane in outrage.

"Don't let that dyspeptic old pessimist illustrate anything of mine ever again," she warned.

Brisbane sent for Jack, warned him, and dispatched him

to the Hoffman House to make his peace with Mrs. Wilcox.

His diffident tap was answered by Mrs. Wilcox herself. "I am Mr. Barrymore," said Jack.

"Why are you here, boy?" said Mrs. Wilcox. "Was your father afraid to come?"

The two then had a long talk during which Jack confessed his shortcomings. One of the reasons, he said, for the dankness of his drawings was that he had never learned to do feet and always required long grass to hide them. Mrs. Wilcox was taken by the young man, called up Brisbane and insisted on having John Barrymore illustrate all her works from then on.

Jack was fired from the *Journal* when he did a picture showing how Paul Leicester Ford, the novelist who wrote *Janice Meredith,* was shot and killed by his brother Malcolm. Jack had come in late, as usual, too late for his picture to be reproduced carefully. It came out badly, a smudged botch, which particularly annoyed Mr. Brisbane. He had composed a savage editorial on the crime, referring to details "which the picture on this page illustrates." But all the picture proved was that Jack Barrymore had spent a late and entertaining night.

Brisbane sent for him.

"Barrymore," he said, "you were an actor before you came here?"

Jack confessed that he had been on the stage, if you could call it that.

"Well," said Brisbane, "could you go *back* to acting, do you think?"

Jack had neither the conviction nor the confidence that he could. But Arthur Brisbane cast his die for him and Jack reluctantly returned to the theater.

At the outset of my reluctant theatrical career, it struck me more than once, especially when I was hungry, that I was getting more than mere co-operation from the New York managers in support of my belief that I wasn't an actor. Jobs were uncommon hard to find, but because I was in favor of food and drink, I had to go after them. I asked everybody for work and presented myself as a seasoned and accomplished player who could be trusted with important parts.

But instead of becoming anything like a Broadway fixture, I became the out-of-season, or road-show Barrymore. If anybody wanted an actor to play the split week in Elmira, I was the actor for that part. It began to look, very ironically it seemed to me at the time, that I not only couldn't succeed at the first thing I wanted to do—at painting—but that I couldn't even make my way in the family trade, which I didn't want. But being in it, I was for it, and I did the best I could.

Aside from this resolution, which I cordially invite you to accept as proof that I have character, I found it a good deal pleasanter to cling as long as I could to the environs of The Players, The Lambs Club, the Algonquin Hotel, the art galleries, the concert halls, and the good restaurants wherein conversation could be bartered for food and drink. Most certainly I wanted to paint, or to do something (I was not sure what) about music, but it became sharply clear that it was time to do something serious about acting too.

As time passed it also became clear that I was batting my head against doors that seemed to be held by Fate itself, with the producers in cahoots. Apparently, I never would have got both feet across the threshold of Broadway if that remarkable sister of mine had not gone to work.

Ethel has always been in a position to hand De Lawd a ten-cent seegar and call for a miracle.

She was on vacation in Paris with Charles Frohman and Charles Dillingham the summer of 1901. The meeting which concerned me took place, I presume, at one of those restaurants, probably at Armenonville in the Bois, where C. F. would go to fill himself with pastries, watermelons, oranges, ices, pies, cakes—mounds and pounds of anything sweet. Ethel astutely waited until Frohman was in his happiest mood, which was when he was fed, and propounded a question:

"What are you going to do about Lionel?"

There wasn't anything for C. F. to do about Lionel, no reason why he should do anything, but under the influence of Ethel and the desserts he assumed that there was.

"So," he said, spooning at a pie, "I will give him something to do. I will put him in a play."

Thus I became a Charles Frohman actor principally so that Charles Frohman could keep Ethel quiet and have a pleasant evening eating in the Bois.

The play was *The Second in Command,* starring a relative of mine, Mr. John Drew. In it also were Guy Standing, Lewis Baker, and Hassard Short. It played seventy-six performances in New York, long enough to give me a thorough introduction to Charles Frohman.

Frohman was a small, round man whom Billie Burke once accurately described as "solidly rounded like a top, always spinning from one project to another, walking up and down rapidly as he talked, nodding, jabbing with a pudgy forefinger, leaving sentences trailing in his wake, but sometimes snapping them like a whip, with sharp pungent twists of tongue."

C. F. controlled the great Empire Theater in New York, among others, theaters in London, theaters everywhere; he was a theater trust in himself, often producing as many as four or five plays on Broadway at the same time, delegating authority with the precision of a corps commander. But he directed his players himself. How he did this is still a vast mystery even to those who worked on the stage for him: his muttered and mumbled instructions were delivered as confidences; they were casually vague references to the business at hand, never precise instructions about going there and standing here. But through some kind of telepathy he made you know what he wanted, and what he wanted was invariably correct and dramatic and in good taste.

I think he despised words because he thought so fast that words tripped him like stumbling blocks, but when he wished to express himself he could do it—if you were onto the hang of Frohman rhetoric. He would say, for instance: "Nazimova is a murderess. She poisons her husband because she's in love with a nigger." This meant that C. F. was getting ready to produce the play *Bella Donna.*

He himself liked to act, liked to read his plays to his actors, choking with emotion and shedding tears over the sad scenes and punching out the comedy with a fat finger.

All great plays, he said, "are written backwards because every great play is a solution to some human problem," which, I suggest, is a wise observation. But Frohman dealt in simples. He would also say: "The public is like tired children at the end of a day. They want a Cinderella story."

He liked writers "because they are so like actors except for a sense of humor. They always expect anything and everything from their works. If the roof should fall in during the production of a writer's book, I would not put it past him to think that the catastrophe was a stage effect, quite worthy of his book."

He liked to tell about a production of Bret Harte's novel, *Sue,* at the Garrick in London in 1898. It was a special production for an audience of two—Bret Harte in a front seat, Frohman in the rear, and unbearable tension backstage as Annie Russell, who played Sue, and Guy Standing, who wore a beautiful spangled uniform and was himself such a handsome dog that all women fell in love with him, and the rest of the cast, prepared to go on for this audience of one world-famous author and one world-famous producer. Miss Russell was most affected of all, and as the curtain fell at the end of a scene, she flung her hands up, screamed, and fainted.

It was a real faint. It had nothing to do with the book or the play. But Harte commented:

"Great scene, great climax, real acting. Just right."

Frohman was tireless and tactful in behalf of all his players, settling every problem for them from where they lived to how they acted. He was the best I ever knew at the gentle task of soothing the nerves of a worried and nervous actor. He was working once with a young man of undeniable talent who kept fiddling with things, throwing his arms around in large, nervous gestures, and chewing up the scenery in sheer despair and fright. C. F. let him alone until he had massacred the scene a dozen times, then he said, very quietly:

"Now, let's hear some of the play. We know you can act, but nobody will expect acting of that sofa you have been pushing around."

It settled the fellow and he went on to do the scene simply and right.

If this gives a picture of Christlike patience by C. F., I have painted the scene out of kilter. C. F. did for a fact perform deeds of kindness and thoughtfulness for his people, but know the truth: he counted it as money in his pocket. The actor always thought it was out of the greatness of his heart when Frohman was generous, and Frohman let him think so and made him think so, but it was because of the great returns that Frohman expected, though they might be planned for two years later.

I have come to the conclusion, anyway, that there are few nice fellows who cast their bread on the waters unless they have shrewd hopes that it will come back at least crullers.

My Uncle John Drew was, it goes without saying, a great man to be on stage with. I have heard, as you have, of the many tricks he was supposed to have played, to the distress of fellow players—like pinching Billie Burke's elbows in *My Wife,* her first American play—but he never inflicted any of his japes on me, and certainly he did not pinch my elbows. He was like the urbane captain of a ship. He had a certain type of scholastic humor and irony in him off stage, but before an audience he preferred workmanship. His point of view was that from the time the curtain goes up until the time it goes down is the time you are out there making your living.

Uncle John was a far better actor than he ever got credit for being because he made his art look so easy. Believe me, and I prayerfully ask you to believe me, it is not easy. It is a hard thing to be good enough in any department at all to make people want to see you again. Uncle John, like most actors, made out that it was a casual matter, but neither he nor anybody else holds that thought when he is out there working.

But Uncle John, as I say, made it appear easier than most, so easy that he never appeared to be acting. As one young lady drama critic put it: "John Drew doesn't act, he just behaves."

As I learned then and there you cannot go far placing your faith in audiences or in drama critics either. Audiences, beyond any question, are the ignorant Igorots of the world. No player worth his salt regards audiences as anything but a kind of enemy, an enemy for which he has no respect.

There was a typical, gushing Boston lady who told us she liked So-and-So, the actor, "because he is so witty." She only knew him on stage, of course, where he recited funny sayings. Actually, he was a dull clod who read his lines like a parrot. He happened to be blessed with a witty author. It is a strange and of course fortunate thing for us who earn our living from audiences that they are so gullible, endowing the actors with all the spiritual and mental qualities of the parts they play. To repeat, never trust an audience—but I'll get back to Uncle John.

He went, naturally, to the greatest tailor in the world, Pool, and to the greatest bootmakers in the world, Peel, of London, and Asamonte in New York. Asamonte, who will not mind my guess that he is about eighty-five years old now, made shoes for the artists and players of his era and held that no performance worthy of comment could be given save in his footgear. When Bobby Reed, a great artist, and I went to see Asamonte about fitting us with some of those remarkable boots, Bobby harassed the fine craftsman by pretending that his boots didn't fit.

"Nothing a-matter with da boot," yelled Asamonte, "maybe something a-wrong with-a your foot."

"I will have to go to Camay to get fitted," needled Bobby.

"Camay! Camay!" screamed Asamonte biting his thumbs. "I'm-a gonna tell-a you something. You know da Fanny Dav-na-port?" said Asamonte. "I make the shoes and boots for da Fanny Dav-na-port for twenty year. One year she marry theese McDowell, and she go to Camay for boots. Next-a year, da Fanny Dav-na-port, she die."

But Uncle Jack did not depend upon nine tailors and a bootmaker. Indeed, although his reputation as the glass of fashion entertained audiences and entertained him, in the long run this renown compromised his recognition as a fine actor. In one of the plays I did with him—it might have been *The Second in Command,* but it doesn't matter—he wore only one suit. We were on tour with this production when the lead of the local stock company dropped around to the theater one afternoon to pick up his mail and just "happened" to prowl into Uncle Jack's dressing room—for the plain purpose of examining the wardrobe of the great New York Beau Brummell.

His eye clapped on the one suit hanging in the closet

and when he saw it he gave probably the best performance of his untalented life.

No player could have put more disdain into his "Ha!" and into his sneering gesture as he walked away.

With the exception of Uncle Jack and myself, the entire regiment of *The Second in Command* had been played by Englishmen in the original London production. John Drew was, as a matter of routine with him, brilliant, but I was in a role in which it was difficult to make comparisons. So nobody knew, and nobody took pains to try to find out, how good I was or wasn't in this play. I was acceptable, and they let it go at that.

Of course I knew by now what I should do on stage. James A. Herne had told me when he released me from the cast of *Sag Harbor* that some people have the faculty of being engaging and young but that I should never do anything but character parts. I agreed with him completely, with no regrets, believe me, for the hero boys. But it was all I could do for some time to get any kind of part on any stage, let alone the characters and villains I thought I could perform with more gusto and more good will.

9. *The Mummy and the Humming Bird*

WHEN THE SUMMER came on and Ethel went again to London and Paris for the season, I was an actor who had played a part in a Broadway show with no more acclaim than the well-known but anonymous George Spelvin, and no provisions had been made for me as C. F. and Charlie Dillingham planned their next season. Ethel thought it would be a good idea to sew another one up for brother, so she approached C. F. again, reminding him that she had a relation named Lionel who was an actor.

"All right, Ethel, I'll do another one," said Frohman. "I have a part for him. We'll give him a go."

I cannot, of course, be sure what Frohman & Co. expected. It is possible that C. F. thought, when he handed me the part of Giuseppe the organ grinder in *The Mummy and the Humming Bird*, that I would blow higher than the Tower Building and that he would thus be rid of me. I ascribe this possible feeling to C. F. because this was my own reaction when I saw the part. In sober recollection, however, it seems more likely that for some reason, probably Ethel's assurances, Frohman must have thought I could perform it.

I saw both the difficulties and the possible rewards of this role as soon as I laid eyes on the script. Any mime with vision enough to identify a billboard would have seen them, for here was a character, a lusty, gusty, emotional, sentimental, and salty Latin, a Sicilian with the smell of the streets of Mistretta or Castrogiovanni on him, with a bandanna and a knife and a rolling eye.

I had never had a part before that even remotely appeared to be so alluring or so challenging, but as I sat in my room poring over the fine lines, muttering the words to myself, I felt suddenly as if the Holy Ghost had again descended upon me and assigned a composition that only Rembrandt could accomplish. In situations like this, you perceive what a shame it is that you don't know Rembrandt better.

I did not have the technical equipment to play the part of Giuseppe. I did not know how to grind an organ, let alone know how a man would act who did know how to grind an organ.

Seeking help, I trudged one damp night to pound on the door of George Barnum, who had played with Ethel in *Captain Jinks of the Horse Marines,* because he was the kind of actor who would know how to act anything, and because he was a good man who liked to help the meek in experience.

I showed him my part.

Barnum fixed a shining eye on it at once. "Good," he said. "You will kick the daylights out of it."

"I would if I knew how to do it," I said.

"You are fortunate, youngster, you are besplattered with luck. You have come to the right place. I shall show you. But to begin with, we shall call in the excellent Ralph Delmore, who will demonstrate the Italian palaver to us."

Ralph Delmore, like Barnum, was a skilful and astute

actor. Moreover, he was of Italian descent, his real name being Donnarmo. The notion amused him and he consented to join Barnum in the experiment of turning Barrymore into an actor.

These gentlemen took me in hand like a pair of rooster owners training a cock for battle. Night after night we yelled at each other over the cacophony of the Casino Roof. Barnum eventually fetched in a real Italian organ grinder whom we watched and imitated and screamed at, using him deliberately as a model.

But chiefly, I imitated Barnum and Delmore. I saw clearly what had to be done: Barnum and Delmore were to play Giuseppe and I was to be their mouthpiece.

This resolution—or this discovery of how to play a part—opened up instantly a vista of tremendous possibilities in my entire future. This set me on the course that I have followed since in every part I have played. From that moment on I always had from two to four other people in consultation when I undertook a role; although, of course, it goes without saying, more often than not my professors didn't know they were being consulted.

In short, I went on stage with the conviction that I was a composite of George Barnum and Ralph Delmore playing the part of Giuseppe, the Sicilian organ grinder. I did it the way they would have done it. I was aware of it when I was acting and I did not forget what I was trying to accomplish as the character and the scenes developed.

In support of this approach to creating a role, if we may be studious for a moment, I might suggest that the more good acting you have seen, the better you will be in your part. In the arts, in any art, great things have been accomplished for so long, for so many years, that it is impossible to do more than take up where somebody else left off. We are fortunate that we have the great works to start from. And so, if you are an artist and there is another artist who has done well the kind of thing you want to do, invoke him; sit at his feet; *call him up*.

The better you have observed a plumber walk into a room with his pockets sagging and his feet heavy, the more you have noticed where his eyes go first, the better you will be able to act like a plumber if you are lucky enough to get such a good part. If you do not know a plumber, then consult what social connections you have and try to meet one.

Charles Keane, the artist, used to say: "Always keep a sketchbook in your pocket. There may be a fellow on the bus, with his pants falling in folds in just one particular way, in a way that will never happen again. Get it down. Put it down now or you will never have another chance."

You may, to be sure, recall that Jefferson or Booth did such-and-such a thing in such-and-such a way, and you are permitted to say "I will be like that," or you may find your tutor in Baron Michele Leone, who wrestles extravagantly in the Olympic Auditorium in Los Angeles. I observe the Baron over television. His rages and despairs are wonderful and real to see when he has lost a decision or a crotch hold. Of course, his tempest would be just as hot over a spoiled plate of polpetti: the Latins are probably the ultimate in actors. They are acting all the time, and yet they aren't. You might say, in passing, that when a gentleman sits on a hot stove and arises suddenly clutching his backside, he is acting. But then he isn't, either.

You can learn something from him though. Anything that happens is grist to the actor's mill.

Many actors, I suspect, will make believe that they are not aware of the ideas I have just set down. They speak occultly and importantly of "schools" and "techniques," but in their hearts they do not mean a word of it.

I worked with Barnum and Delmore every night for more than three weeks. It was an intense experience in observation, not based on scholarship in books or on formal study of the Italian language, or of Italian folklore. If Barnum and Delmore, or the organ grinder who was our model, were late because they had their own affairs to attend to, I was there ahead of them and waited their pleasure. They could not escape me. As the role developed, I not only included Barnum and Delmore and the organ grinder in everything I did but every Italian waiter I had ever held intellectual conversations with in Plavano's table d'hôte, over which I lived, or any other greasy-spoon establishments I could recall.

I became so Sicilianate that it was alleged that I wafted the odor of garlic for three city blocks.

I had thought (now that you have learned to act we will go on with the story), I had thought that Charles Frohman and John Drew would be astonished by my sudden virtuosity, or by my synthesis of Barnum and Delmore, when I finally revealed my full-flavored Italian before their eyes at dress rehearsal. I even ground the organ correctly. But they accepted my thumb-biting fellow calmly and with no surprise. I can't explain it. It turned out that they would have been surprised if I hadn't got away with it, a thing which is still a matter of mystery to me.

The round Mr. Frohman was as serene as a custard at that important dress rehearsal when I unveiled my Italian. I was not.

At the end of one of my scenes, which built to a crescendo of emotion, I had to take a knife from my belt, kiss it fiercely, and cry:

"Vendetta! Vendetta!"

Then I was supposed to collapse sobbing into a chair as the curtain slowly descended.

I threw all the organ grinders who ever blessed a knife into that sequence and hurled myself, spouting real tears, toward the chair.

I missed it completely.

No one laughed as Frohman raised his pudgy hand and said quietly:

"Now, I'm glad you did that tonight, Barrymore. Because you will never do it again."

I assure you that I did not do it again. In all subsequent performances of *The Mummy and the Humming Bird* I took careful aim.

This was the play, of course, that marked the turning point in what up to now we might by courtesy call a career. It established me as an actor. The red apple from the family was on my dressing table opening night, and the applause was good.

John Drew, who was the star of this piece, took it in good heart. To a friend who asked after his health at The Players a few nights after we opened, he replied:

"Well enough, thank you, considering that every night I have to play second fiddle to that preposterous nephew of mine."

The critics, of whom I shall have more to say later, not

all of it in admiration, were kind to us. In comparison with the swifter pace of modern reviewing, I think this cutting from the New York *Daily Tribune* of September 5, 1902, is interesting. Here it is:

THE DRAMA

HOW MUMMIES ARE MADE MEN

The Empire Theatre opened last night with John Drew and his company in the first American production of Isaac Henderson's play, "The Mummy and the Humming Bird." To make a mummy out of Richard Carvel and the rest of those heroes who owe their stage existence to Mr. Drew would seem to be no small task. Yet Mr. Drew achieved it. He made such a good mummy, in fact, that one could identify it on first sight. Without even removing the wrapping one said, "Ah, here they all are again! Mr. Drew, is it not?"

But soft, a word or two about the play. The mummy is an English scientist so wrapped up in his science that he leaves his young wife without those attentions young wives are accustomed to receive, preferably from their husbands. She tries—she really does—to induce him to abandon the laboratory for loving, but fails. So she resorts to the friendship of an Italian—a dashing Italian—author, nicknamed by the mummy the "Humming Bird." A young Italian organ grinder then comes along, and by signs and vigorously suggestive speech in his native tongue tells the mummy he is in England to avenge himself on a fellow countryman who had seduced his wife. He recognizes his man in the Humming Bird's picture. The mummy wakes up, and engages him as a valet.

The young wife, who is charmingly unsophisticated, even for one so young, then goes off alone at night, after a stormy scene with her husband, to the Humming Bird's apartment, where she becomes greatly surprised at what the latter suggests to her and is stoutly protesting when a knock is heard. It turns out to be the knock of the mummy, who has been connected with events by the blood-seeking valet. The young wife hides in the bedroom, and the mummy enters. The mummy, with charming self-restraint and the most polished of manners, then proceeds to set a little stage and enact a little play, with a keenness worthy of Sherlock Holmes and a sense for theatrical effect that would do credit to that gentleman's dramatizer. He gets his wife out of the bedroom and home unknown to the Humming Bird, he has lots of fun noting that wicked man's embarrassment, and he finally waves in his face (or, rather, writes on his engagement calendar), the vendetta of the organ grinder. Then he goes out, like a true gentleman, with a polite "Good night."

But the next act! We haven't had much comedy yet this season, to be sure; there have been so many comic operas. And it is seldom safe to predict what the season may bring forth. But the first scene of the fourth act of "The Mummy and the Humming Bird" is surely the drollest up to date, nor does a dip into the immediate future promise anything to excel it. It is so very droll it were a shame to describe it. It must be seen to be enjoyed. Suffice it to say, some men are born humorous, some men achieve humor, and some men have humor thrust upon them. In this act Mr. Henderson belongs to the last class.

John Drew played through the part of Mr. Drew, alias Lord Lumley, alias the mummy, with ease and mastery of the stage situations. It must be said in justice that it was a thankless, often impossible, part, as written, to make a vital character of, and that John Drew is quite as pleasant a person to watch performing as a live mummy.

The one vital character in the play was the organ grinder of young Lionel Barrymore. In his single short scene he exhibited a burst of genuine passion that was good to feel, for he made you feel it with him. He should in the future prove worthy to carry the family name into the casts of far better plays than "The Mummy and the Humming Bird."

10. Escape by Boat

We were in good company in 1903. Marie Dressler was starring in a comic opera called *King Highball* and Lillian Russell was singing "Come Down, My Evening Star" in the Weber and Fields comedy, *Twirly Whirly*. This production paid us an interesting compliment in November by inserting a burlesque called "Humming Bird and Onions." I doubt if I ever enjoyed any performance on the stage more; myself a composite of Delmore and Barnum in Giuseppe, I could now run over to the Music Hall to see this synthesis buffooned—a triple-plated satire that one was, to be sure.

The Frohman office presented Ethel in *A Country Mouse* (Harry Davenport was in this one too); Mrs. Pat Campbell in *Aunt Jennie,* and later in *The Second Mrs. Tanqueray;* and Tyrone Power (father of the current movie star) in *Ulysses.*

My next play was *The Best of Friends,* a drama in four acts by Cecil Raleigh, with Richard Bennett, Tully Marshall, and—Ralph Delmore. This time I could not go on as if I were Ralph Delmore acting a piece on the stage, because there *he* was on the same stage. I had to work up my own character, and also for the next Frohman play *The Other Girl,* a comedy in three acts by Augustus Thomas. This was quite a play, with an extraordinarily skilful cast, including Drina De Wolfe, Elsie De Wolfe, Richard Bennett, and Ida Greely Smith.

The Best of Friends played 65 performances, but *The Other Girl* stayed on for 160, occupying successively the Criterion, the Empire, and the Lyceum Theaters.

So now, at last, here it was. Nudged by Ethel, favored by C. F., taught by Delmore and Barnum, I had—to put no false modesty on the matter at all—got both feet firmly planted on Broadway. One good show will put you there. Three in succession constitutes an endowment policy—until your first failure.

I was now in a position to command a decent salary and to wear decent clothes and to eat three times a day, every day, all of which I did. It had taken an unconscionable time, of course, for I was twenty-six years old, had been attached to the theater since I was fifteen, and was only now beginning to make my living. I could have set up for a fairly solid citizen, I suppose, except for the fact that I still regarded acting precisely as I had regarded it from the beginning, as the family trade which I wished to escape at any cost.

I do not suppose that the sons of Delmonico or of Escoffier, if such there were, were enchanted by the glamour of being cooks when their fathers broke them into the profession as dishwashers. Neither Jack Barrymore nor I, even when we plucked the first grapes, wanted to be actors. We wanted to be artists of another kind.

Suddenly, also, I wanted something else.

Doris Rankin, who worked with distinction in *The Copperhead,* in which I played years later, was not an actress then. She was the young sister of my Aunt Gladys, Uncle Googan's wife. She was sixteen years old, and I had known her, I suppose, since she was a child of three. She was McKee Rankin's daughter and had of course been in and around the theater all those early years when Rankin worked for Mum Mum and when I worked for Rankin. I suppose, also, that I had not taken a good look at Doris until she became sixteen.

Harry Davenport, the late Harry Davenport, who gave everybody a lesson in acting every time he stepped on stage or before a camera, owned a farm upstate somewhere about that time. He was married to Phyllis Rankin. I visited him one week end, and there was Doris.

At this point I must beg forgiveness, perhaps unnecessarily, because I doubt if there are any in the audience who even half expected that your Uncle Lionel had it in him to spin a love story. Indeed, my collaborator in this work, a large and determined man with the heart of a Borgia and the curiosity of a postmistress, has both badgered me and plied me with cold beer in heroic efforts to make me out a romantic fellow, all to no avail whatsoever. I would play the part with enormous good will if I could, but James A. Herne discovered many years ago that I am miscast in these roles.

Let us say: we fell in love. We said, I suppose, all the sincere and foolish things that the young and in love always say, but that was a long time ago, and I am not sure that I would remember them for you even if I could.

We were married at St. Xavier's Catholic Church on Sixteenth Street, New York, in the presence of and with the approval of most of the Rankins and Barrymores who could attend. This I remember precisely: before the ceremony was over, it occurred to me bleakly that this nice girl, only sixteen, hadn't the slightest idea what she was getting into, taking on a partner such as I.

We were not settled in our housekeeping arrangements before I began to mumble again about the Fate which made me earn my bread as an actor. Jack, of course, was muttering the same complaint, meantime supporting himself in Chicago as a musical comedy comedian—and good, too—under the management of Mort Singer. Very soon, of course, Jack did *The Fortune Hunter* and was on his way, reluctantly, as an actor.

When I spoke of these things to Doris, she, being young and just married, easily found herself in enthusiastic agreement with me. Indeed, she went even farther than I went.

"I think I should quit the stage and go to the Art Students League again," I would say.

"Why go there?" Doris would reply. "Go after the real thing. You've been to the Art Students League. Go to Paris."

I found myself instantly convinced. I supported this conviction by declaiming, too, that American art was no good and that the only place in the world to come by civilized and modern instruction, plus good conversation, was in Paris.

Some sums of money had come my way in the theater, but I had of course saved not a farthing, and the prospect of spending three to four years in Paris without any source of income whatever was disconcerting even to Doris and me. It was necessary, I saw, to acquire a patron, to convince someone who had access to cash that it would be a good thing for the arts all around if Barrymore retired from the stage and was supported for a spell in France.

There was only one person in the world who might

undertake such a supporting role for me and that was, naturally, Ethel. I cozened her.

I did not, of course, suggest to Ethel my distaste for the theater. To doubt the sacredness of the theater arts in the presence of Ethel Barrymore would have been comparable to the impiety of demeaning Holy Writ in the presence of a nun. Instead, I tried to make it plain that my departure would be an ultimate *benefit* to the stage. I did not tell her that I would engage never to go within two blocks of a theater again as long as I lived if I had my way about it, but dilated with all the conviction I could muster on the proposition that I was plainly not much good as a mime, had great and unexplored talents in other directions, and might surprise everybody after all and amount to something if I were financed to a chance in Paris.

We sat up all one night talking about this. I wore her out. I told her that I wanted to borrow enough money to go to the Art Students League again.

"Well, why that?" Ethel said. "You went there. Why don't you do it right and go to Paris?"

"I don't have enough money."

It was very late. Ethel undoubtedly said it to get rid of me. She said:

"All *right,* I'll lend you the money."

And do you know what I did then? I took the money and went.

We sailed on some unpretentious craft with no magnums of champagne spilled and no shouts of encouragement from the Rankins, the Drews, and the Barrymores. Most of the clan were, of course, applying themselves industriously to the family trade. When they heard about my enterprise they bobbed their heads knowingly over another one of those curious escapades Lionel was always getting himself into, and predicted freely that not much good would come of it.

For my part, I rejoiced because I had broken loose from the stage at long last. I considered it a complete, logical, and irrevocable break. My passage was a bill of divorcement which meant freedom to work at what I wanted, my opportunity to *obtain*.

As the little boat pulled out of New York Harbor with my girl and me aboard I knew, certainly, that I had acted on the stage for the last time.

11. Paris

JEAN-PAUL LAURENS had a beard like Plutarch. He wore an ancient and threadbare frock coat whose seams and edges were crusted with green mold and on his head an enormous cylinder of a top hat. Around his shoulders he draped a knitted shawl. He loved to go to funerals.

I used to watch him, an impressively tall and solemn man, but obviously taking great pleasure in the occasion, as he attended obsequies at a fashionable church across the street from the Deux Magots, at St.-Germain-des-Prés. It was the notion of some of my boisterous contemporaries of this oasis that Jean-Paul Laurens especially enjoyed the funerals of other painters and that a dead march for a critic was an ecstatic experience, but this jackanape opinion, of course, was no doubt a libel.

Laurens had painted the astonishing and beautiful "Death of St. Genevieve" on one wall of the Pantheon, a magnificent work, with figures so lifelike that you could reasonably expect that at any moment one of them would get up and walk away. On another wall was a decoration by Puvis de Chavannes, with angels floating through the air—everything flat and frescoed, unrealistic, but just as magnificent as Jean-Paul Laurens' work.

I would stand in the middle and wonder: which is the better? I never found out. What makes any work of art great or greater than another, is, of course, the sixty-four dollar question, and has been the question all of my life. All you can say is: they are both great, and you pay your respects to each and hope that you can learn a little something by looking.

I looked at Jean-Paul Laurens' works with admiration and awe and upon him with awe and terror. I was registered at the Académie Julien, where he taught, but it was a long time, several months in fact, before I risked consignment to hell and damnation by appearing in class with a painting for him to criticize.

He would enter the crowded studio followed by a fellow who lit his cigarettes. Laurens would puff and merely say "Merci," never "Merci, *monsieur*."

First the master would look at the model. Then he would jab a fierce eye at the drawing—and then he would turn slowly and look at *you*.

Any student who underwent this experience would devoutly wish he had had the ordinary good sense to cut his throat that morning while shaving.

Jean-Paul Laurens, of course, was not our daily instructor. He came on Saturdays only, probably being paid a franc a year as a token for his condescension. By Saturdays, we were expected to have something on our boards, something that filled the board. It was the rule that you started at the top, putting a head there, and brought the feet down smack to the bottom of the paper. You had to fill it up, large.

I attended the daily classes, wherein we were taught the Laurens methods, but on Saturdays, when he was due to criticize, I absented myself.

One day he came on Wednesday and there I was, with some mess on my board. Jean-Paul Laurens approached with his interpreter. He was always accompanied by this man, who spoke seven or eight languages, and if you were English or American he spoke to you through him, with a certain contempt, no matter whether you understood French or not.

He looked at the model. He looked at my drawing. Then he looked at me.

"Ha," he said. "Who are you?"

I told him.

"You have been working here?"

"No, monsieur," I said, in an effort to escape.

"Ha," he said. "Then you have been working in your *chambre,* in your room, no?"

He was puzzled but he was canny. He hadn't seen me before, I had said I hadn't worked there, but he saw that his precepts had been followed. He said "Ha!" once more and walked away.

In this school, no one said you were good. No one said you were bad, either. You paid your money and you came to class and sketched and learned, or you stayed away. Anyone could enter. It was up to you. Indeed, Paris, all Paris, is like that: I suppose it is one of those places that depends largely on you and what you bring to it. You are let alone in Paris and if you are interested in something you probably like it. Among other things that I liked in Paris was the fact that the Barrymore name meant not a ha'penny to anybody. No one regarded me as an actor or as a scion of a family of actors.

Nor, for that matter, did names of considerably more scholarly distinction make an impression. In one of our classes, taught by Marcel Bachet, was young William James, who had recently been a stroke oar on the Harvard crew. He was visited one day by his uncle, Henry James, who made a noble entrance attired in a frock coat and a top hat.

Forty pairs of eyes glared at him. In this class you didn't do anything so bourgeois as wear a top hat, or any kind of hat, for that matter. The class squalled as one man:

"*Chapeau, monsieur, alors, chapeau!*"

And Henry James doffed it, humbly and quickly.

"Yes, sir," he said, and took off the hat.

We had, of course, a few queer ones, men of great talent, perhaps, ahead of their times, perhaps. There was one, a mysterious fellow with a strained, handsome face, like Baron Michele or Edgar Allan Poe. He did those *numero cinquante* torsos, huge things, with heads jutting out of collarbones, much in the manner of the current Salvador Dali. He was referred to in the class as "Whistlaire," and of all the students there, he was the only one Laurens was ever nice to. But he was too poor to buy a drink, so he kept to himself proudly and we never knew him well.

I studied also with Richard Miller, who had to run his studio under a subterfuge because of the rule that if you had a school in Paris it had to be a French school. He took in a partner, therefore, one Carré, a Frenchman, and himself became "Millaire."

"Millaire" had a studio at the end of the rue Boissonnade where he painted by artificial light—because, as some painters do, he liked it: he got the results he wanted that way. One evening, late at night, I had to take something to him, some package which I was delivering merely as an errand boy, and as I came into his studio he was at work on a portrait of his wife.

It was an astonishing, beautiful thing under his white

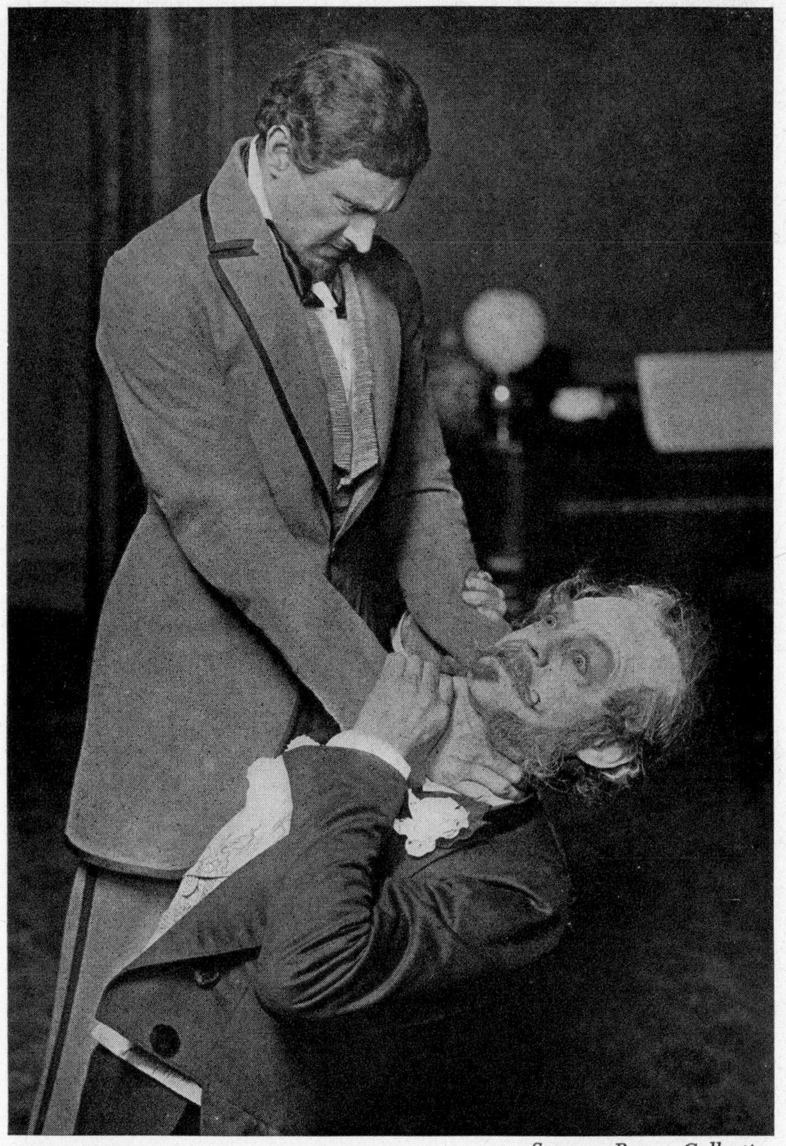

Spencer Berger Collection

John and Lionel in *Peter Ibbetson,* 1917–1918

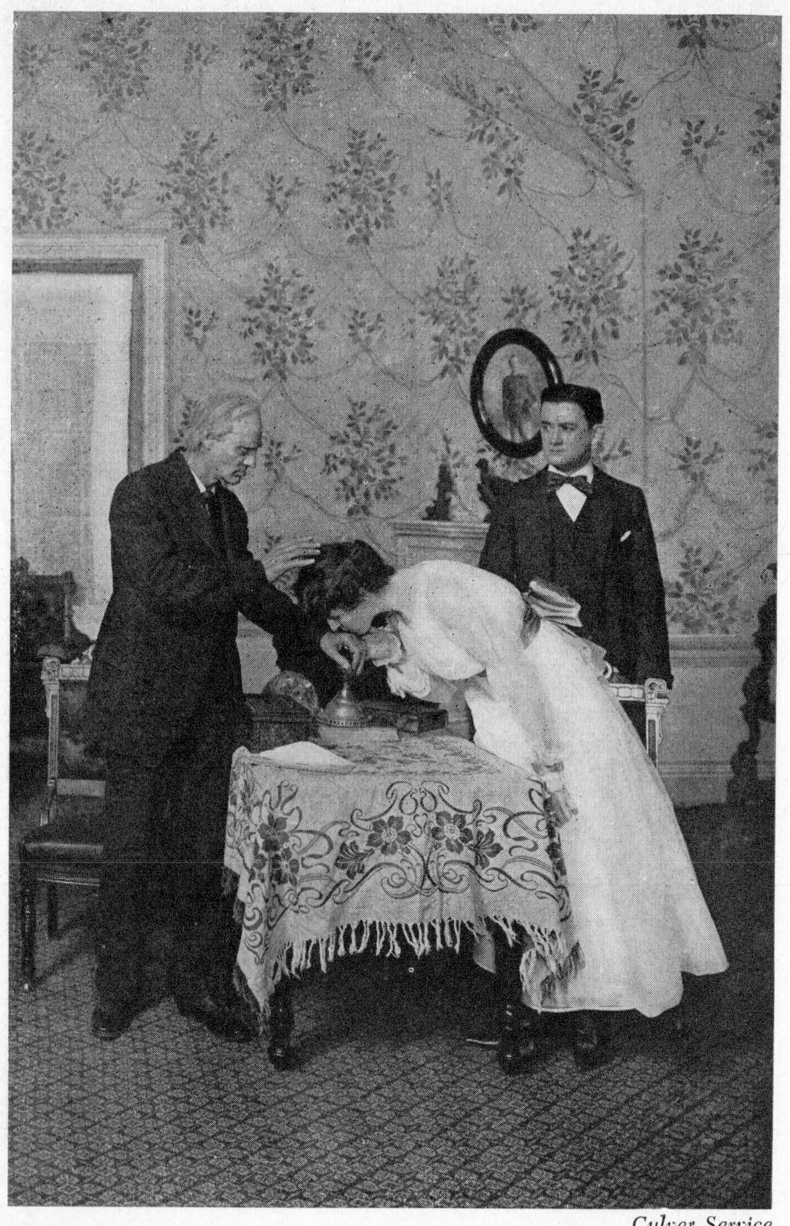

Culver Service

Lionel Barrymore and Doris Rankin in *The Copperhead*, 1918

lights, late at night in Paris. Miller was painting one of the loveliest pictures I have ever seen. Let me tell you a story about it.

A few years ago I was loaned by Metro-Goldwyn-Mayer to David O. Selznick. No money changed hands between David and me because my salary was paid by my own studio, but David thought that he would do something for me at Christmas time because I had worked for him. He had Stendhal, the art dealer, telephone me.

"Selznick says he wants you to have anything in my gallery for a present," Stendhal said.

"I wouldn't think of it," I said.

"Then I think I'd better come out and show you a few things," Stendhal said.

So he did. He brought out two things, one a bronze statue by Remington, naturally a priceless thing; the other, an oil painting.

I declined the statue, though this was hard to do. But I accepted the painting because it was Miller's portrait of his wife, the picture he was working on that night when I was a student in Paris.

We lived first on the sixth floor of a house on the rue Bonaparte. I had to go out to the fortifications to see the agent and sign for this studio, and when I rapped on the door out stepped a gent in what I thought was a bathrobe.

"Oh, beg pardon, m'sieu," I said, "so sorry to disturb you in your bath."

"This is not a bathrobe, this is a Greek costume," he said, wrapping himself up togalike and striding impressively away. I then recognized him as Raymond Duncan, brother of Isadora, who to this day, I see by the papers, appears in public wrapped in his robe and his philosophy.

As I waited I heard the high strains of an aria from *Carmen.* I inquired about that when I was let in and discovered that this was the house of Mme. Emma de Roquer, better known as Emma Calvé, who was famous for her *Carmen.*

The auspices seemed extremely good for a young artist, so I signed up for the quarters in rue Bonaparte.

Our rooms cost us one hundred and thirty-five dollars a year and were no bargain. We were artistic but uncomfortable. When we complained to the landlord that the walls sweated he looked at us with Gallic contempt.

"But of course, monsieur," he shrugged. "Of course the walls sweat. You have a fire!"

We did not stay there very long. All told, I suppose, we occupied a half dozen residences in the Latin Quarter, acquiring various places which I thought would enhance my opportunities as an artist. One of these was a studio over a printing office which had unusual advantages in low prices and high lights. We moved in, delighted.

At nine the next morning we discovered why the price was so modest and why *monsieur le propriétaire,* a gentleman named Duval, had been glad to have us. All day that ancient building shook and echoed with the *thumtiddywumptumpclangwumpthump* of the presses.

But after a while neither Doris nor I minded the noise. It would have taken more than a mere French printing press to disturb us or to interfere with my pursuit of Art.

After a few weeks, M. Duval called.

"Everything satisfactory, monsieur?" he inquired, anxiously.

"Wonderful," we said.

Monsieur looked doubtful.

"You are sure?" he asked.

We were sure.

He went away, a puzzled man.

A few months after that we went to Barbizon, where Millet had painted "The Angelus." If Jean-François Millet had painted a masterpiece there, I could at least try something, so with adieus to M. Duval, we closed the flat and departed.

When we flung open our door on our return, Doris gasped. Indeed, so did I.

Where we had enjoyed a large, bare room with the bed behind a curtain on a string, there was now a Swiss chalet. I do not exaggerate. Our apartment had been redecorated, elaborately and expensively, to resemble a Swiss chalet. There it was, stairway and all, complete and beautiful.

Behind us trotted M. Duval, *le propriétaire,* rubbing his hands and looking anxiously pleased. We were good tenants, had not complained about the printing press noises. He had rewarded us.

Robert Henri, the artist, said something about his studies in France which didn't apply to him but did apply to me. "I spent five years of useless industry in Paris," he liked to say.

I have been asked, and I suppose I shall continue to be asked, whatever became of all the pictures I painted. After all, in something more than three years a man gets a lot of paint on canvas, good or bad. I most certainly used up a vast amount of paint but I never finished anything.

Indeed, few men students at Julien's ever completed a picture. At the end of the week when we had done as much as we could with the current project—torso, nude, bowl of apples, whatever—we scraped off the paint, cleaned up our palette and brushes, and tried to get ready to learn something new on Monday.

It was quite different with the girls, and there, I suppose, is one of the fundamental distinctions between men and women as artists of any kind. The women carefully packaged up their little canvases and took them home. I suppose today there are thousands, maybe millions, of wretched oil paintings in sitting rooms and attics all over the country, all painted by women, all referred to as, "Oh, just a little thing I did when I was studying in Paris."

I think I can speak authoritatively for the other male students but for myself I can be precise: I have no paintings to show because I never finished any.

Here is another thing: nobody composes anything, or pretends to finish it as a work of art, if he is studying that art. The only persons who insist upon completing and finishing up their student efforts are the damn fools who never get anywhere at anything.

We started out blocking in hands, arms, torsos, things that didn't move, which were like casts, and possessed only two or three values. Our teachers took the same attitude that James McNeill Whistler once took when he went down the line with a group of students.

"And with whom have you studied?" he would ask.

"With So-and-so," a girl would reply, naming some celebrated teacher.

Whistler went on down the row, asking the same question. He came to the last girl.

"And with whom did you study, my dear?"

"I never studied with anyone," she said.

"You couldn't have done better," said Whistler.

Our teachers made not even that comment unless you were a terrific shark. And then, come to think of it, they didn't say anything either.

Their attitude was like that of the great music teacher Leschetizky. Years ago if you studied piano you eventually went to Leschetizky. He would say:

"Well, now, play anything of your own. I will sit here and listen."

The student might say, "I will play von Weber's 'Invitation to the Dance.'"

"Remember, then," Leschetizky would admonish, "that you are giving a concert and that you come in with your white gloves."

The poor student would sweat it through. Leschetizky's comment would be invariable:

"Well, it was very good, but perhaps you forgot your white gloves."

In short, I cannot recall that anyone said one kind word about my painting in Paris. It consoles me, though, to recall that I never heard any kind words about anybody else's art either.

Actually, there were no classes, as we are used to formal classes in algebra or basket-weaving. You paid your money, you found a place, you sat down and worked. The various students went their way, not getting in each other's hair, not congregating at some favored café for song and drink, as the fiction writers would have you believe. Every time a new student came in, it was required that he buy everyone else a drink, but conviviality went no farther than that.

As I bought my drink for my first class, one old student told me the facts of life.

"You want to remember this, Barrymore," he said, "because it will be the only day in your life here that you will be noticed."

He was right.

During my time in Paris, Maurice Utrillo, whose mother was one of Renoir's models, was starving and brawling in Montmartre, his genius unrecognized. I never met him for the reason that you do not seem to meet anybody in Paris that you ought to meet. Hollywood and Paris, oddly, are alike in one particular: in the popular mind, they are Bohemian villages in which everybody is supposed to know everybody else. They are not, of course, because they are sprawling communities of vast distances in which you can be as lonely as you can be, say, in the Congo or in Chicago.

But Utrillo was doing his amazing street scenes, peopled by his amazing people. His windows were lopsided or upside down. In one of his paintings I recognize Utrillo himself being taken off to jail, an occurrence familiar enough to him. Of course, though, those lopsided streets and lopsided persons look more like streets and people than anyone else could paint them. Van Gogh, for instance, paints a wheat field and you note, if you examine it, that nobody else could have painted wheat so *unlike* wheat; and yet, there it is, precisely like wheat. And so I reluctantly canonize both Van Gogh and Utrillo.

Gertrude Stein was there then and I knew her, but not well. Picasso was there and I saw him, sometimes at the Café du Dôme, where Montparnasse and the boulevard St.-Germain come together. The men who were known, who were doing things, were Lucien Simon, André

Dauchez, Prinet, and Le Sidaner, all great, all magnificent artists. They were the big noises so far as our art schools were concerned. They were among the fine painters whose works we looked at and sneered at and went away from wishing we could do a fiftieth as well.

Monet and Manet had come into their own when I was in Paris. The Impressionist School was the thing in those early days of this century. We had fled from vulgar and untutored America to learn from the better European school—so we thought—forgetting, of course, that this same European school had been spat upon and derided only a few years ago.

Manet, Boudin, Jongkind, Monet, Pissarro, Bonvin, Daubigny, to name the handful of impressionists responsible for the great new movement, the "light-seeing" movement, had not been able to make a living in Paris. They had to flee to Belgium and to London. In London, they were influenced by Turner and Watts and Constable, and they learned to paint beautifully. But in the beginning, the impressionists whose works command thousands and hundreds of thousands of dollars today were starving to death and feeling lucky and blessed if they could get as much as two pounds for a picture.

Émile Zola took their side in *Le Figaro,* and lost his job as a critic as a result. Alphonse Daudet, Théodore Duret, and Arsène Alexandre supported the movement, but even these great names and powerful propagandists were not enough. No public salon or even semiprivate gallery was open to them, they enjoyed no sales, and saw only the bleakest outlook for the future.

Had they painted with light itself they would have been denied a public, for the bourgeoisie hated them with a bitter, diabolical virulence. On the surface of water, on rivers or seas, they painted the wind-driven *frisson,* reflections of limpid skies, and the trembling drops of sea sprays on the edge of froth-whitened waves. They did these things beautifully, but their landlords evicted them.

When a few of them got together in 1874 to show their works at Nadar's Gallery—Boudin, Bracquemond, Cals, Cézanne, Colin, Degas, Guillaumin, Renoir, La Touche, Lépine, Monet, Berthe Morisot, Pissarro, and Rouart—both press and public attacked their art as idiotic cartoons. They said these painters were disloyal to the country's tradition, that they were trucklers to foreign ideas, and that they were unworthy of any kind of respect.

We forget these things. Like other Americans I had come to Paris to soak up enlightenment from this enlightened race who were ever in the front row applauding the new and the best in beauty and art. It was a shock to discover that the French are so much like ourselves, coddling their own brand of Puritanism and resisting the experimental like any first family of Philadelphia, Boston, or Charleston, and hooting from the gallery. For my own part, I did not follow any particular "school" or worship at the feet of any particular master's easel, nor do I think I do now. It goes without saying, however, that we are all of us today in a sense impressionists, at least influenced consciously or unconsciously by impressionistic art.

The reaction of those early men to the scorn and intense hatred which greeted their works was philosophical. Take the story of an Edgar Degas painting. During his hand-to-mouth days when he was happy to beg a nod from an art dealer on the street, Degas sold a painting for five hundred francs and was glad to get it for eating money. Years later the same painting–not a bit better–was resold in Philadelphia for one hundred thousand dollars.

"And how do you feel about that, Monsieur?" some one asked Degas.

Degas shrugged. "Like the winner of the Grand Prix, I suppose," he said. "All he ever expects to get is his bag of oats."

I have been, of course, canonizing the impressionists. In all good will I have to decline to make the sign over the modernists. I can't stand them. I despise them. I agree with Mr. Sargent, who said he liked representative things, things that *look like something*. Few of us, on the other hand, can fail to appreciate such great men as Van Gogh and Gauguin. We appreciate them, of course, for their color. As for Van Gogh–why indeed should I imitate a fellow who draws even worse than I do? If I could imitate the color those gentlemen achieved, that would be surpassingly wonderful. But what have they got? I don't know. I like Renoir but not Matisse–but Renoir, to be sure, is not a modern. Grant Wood is as good as anyone when he wants to be, and we might say the same thing of Thomas Hart Benton. It comes again, I suppose, to that baffling, beautiful enigma which casts a glamour about all art: which is good, better, or best, and why? *Quien sabe?*

You will, like me, disagree with your most respectable friends and even with "all the learned and authentic fellows" about art of any kind. You will say: "How can So-and-so say such a thing, how can he hold such an abysmal opinion? He was my friend until he said that." And so it always goes. It is a mystery and a dilemma more enchanting than a haremful of ladies each more amiable than the next.

I found in Paris, as everyone always finds who investigates these mysteries, that art pays no attention whatever to countries. You will find great artists in Phoenix or Moscow or Tulsa or Copenhagen or anywhere. Art is a gypsy, paying no attention to nationalities.

I am convinced, though, that most artists of whatever caliber or whatever genre, from my sword-swallowing friend to the great sonnet writers to the great painters, have often excelled not because they waved their integrity at the world like a flag and demanded freedom to work as they chose but because they accepted the restrictions and requirements of their day and did the best they could. Take Meissonier. Meissonier, among other things, was a brilliant illustrator. He worked in the days before the photographic halftones, which meant that he had to put his drawings on a wooden block supplied by the publisher. The publisher consulted his own problems, not Meissonier's, and gave the artist odd-shaped or elongated blocks which he had selected because they fitted his pages or his space limitations. Whatever it was, Meissonier had to draw his pictures on these blocks of pear wood.

When the drawings appeared critics applauded Meissonier for his compositions, for his daring and genius and startling perspective. It was, of course, the very oddness, the very limitations, which had inspired Meissonier to create his fine compositions, and so this I think is a highly moral anecdote. More often than not, I am convinced, the best thing you can ever do is to do with what you have.

At any rate, these considerations of art aside for the moment, we lived in Paris during that time and it was great. Those were, I suppose, the golden years, the last years when anybody was safe anywhere, when people rocked on their front porches at ease in the evening untroubled by threats of war, speculations about Hell Bombs, Kinsey Reports, the night sweats of Sigmund Freud, or the curses of Karl Marx. Even hereditary monarchs felt reasonably secure. Doris and I were happy, I with my escape from the stage and my adventures as an artist, she with being young and being in Paris and with various experiments she conducted with fish and sauce over her small stove.

I am sure I did not know precisely where I was going, or exactly what my ambition was supposed to be; a condition which is one of the bonuses of being young. I heard of new successes by Ethel, who was ever Onward & Upward, and I learned that Jack had begun to have triumphs of his own on the New York stage. Uncles Googan and Jack proceeded as usual on their merry way, and all of this seemed to me quite enough distinction for the tribe. Moreover, the checks from Ethel came regularly.

We consorted with various artists and writers and explored Paris. After poking about and being misdirected dozens of times, we finally found the house in which Balzac died. In the middle of the garden there was one of those senatorial statues of Gambetta in bronze, but Doris cut a quick eye around and said, "Look over there," and over there was a modest bronze tablet, no larger than Major Doyle, the midget. "Honoré de Balzac lived and died here, dates so-and-so-and-so," was all it said. And that was all, for France's greatest writer. After his death, we learned, one of his unpublished manuscripts was found. It had been used to wrap up beans.

At 23 rue Boissonnade, one of the many places we lived,

we knew an interesting woman named Mildred Aldrich. She lived with her sister and wrote pieces, a weekly letter, for a Boston paper. Eventually she and her sister quarreled and they parted. Mildred went out to one of the little towns in the environs of Paris and leased a cottage for $137 a year, four acres and a house.

Mildred knew, of course, that there was a war on, for this was 1914. But war was something a proper Bostonian lady ignored, so Mildred pretended it didn't exist until the morning of September 6 when she rose to greet the French dawn at 2 A.M., and walked straight into the Battle of the Marne.

Out from Paris came Papa Foch's taxicab army and from the fields of the Marne the wounded streamed in. Her small cottage was soon a hospital. She stayed on and nursed them, and later wrote a famous little book which you probably know, *The Hilltop on the Marne*.

She was still there, in the same cottage, years later when I went over to Paris to do a picture, *Enemies of Women*, and I went out with an old friend of hers, William Thompson, to have tea in her garden. When we left to go back to Paris I realized it was a final good-by for Thompson and Mildred. I went ahead and sat in the car, not looking back at these two old people making their irrevocable farewell, and we drove on into Paris together, not looking at each other or saying anything.

But Doris and I were in Paris long before World War I. We were there, indeed, when Blériot flew the Channel on July 25, 1909. We did not see him do it, worse luck, but I recall seeing him and he looked exactly like Jerry Colonna.

Since there was no graduating class to march with, no

diplomas to be got, it was a question how long I was to stay in France and study to be a painter. No one said, "Barrymore, you are pretty good now, you ought to sell something." The French never say that. The French, to repeat the theme of a discussion a few pages back, never said anything good about any artists. Not one of theirs ever obtained without sustaining the vastest, bitterest roasting imaginable. I reiterate that the inhabitants of the City of Light are as chary of their praise and as suspicious of the new as any codfish village in Massachusetts. It was not remarkable, then, that they did not hail me as a genius with a paint brush. I left Paris with no idea whatsoever how good I might be, but I privately suspected that I was no Rembrandt.

When Ethel was married to Russell Griswold Colt, thus giving notice that she intended starting a family of her own, it seemed only appropriate and decent that I cease being a remittance man. Doris and I sailed back to New York. I had no notion of returning to the stage from which I had been happily absent for almost four years.

12. The Ash Can School

I WAS IN for a shock. While I was in Paris admiring the salon-keepers of the Beaux-Arts and the lighting effects of the impressionists, a new exciting masculine school of painting had been created in America. Its impact tumbled me over, as it did everybody else who came in contact with it.

The new school was "The Ash Can School," sometimes called "The Revolutionary Black Gang." As the derisive appellations suggest, Americans were at first appalled by the new thing. They were not perhaps so violent as the French were in their attacks against the early impressionists, but nevertheless they took a sneering stance and tried to stone it to death with epithets. What had happened was important and revolutionary for sure, because the new school made the first break for freedom from the influences of three hundred years of European art; but at the same time it was very simple. All the Ash Can School had done was decide that it was a good idea to paint the life that they knew best. That was all. They invented no techniques, presented no new theories. Simply, they began to paint America.

Of course this startled America. Most of us to this day persist in regarding art of any kind as having something to do with the dead. Deceased poets, deceased novelists, deceased painters are our gods. We decline vigorously to accept either the beauties of morning light in our own backyards or the glories of our everyday language.

George Luks, Maurice Prendergast, Everett Shinn, John Sloan, Arthur B. Davies, Ernest Lawson, William J. Glackens, and Robert Henri painted street scenes, prize fights, saloons, and people as they saw them in America. I realize—to repeat—that this sounds like no revolution at all today, but that is because we are now familiar with the works of these fine artists and with the works of others who followed them. In 1909, their realism, their preachment of art and drama in everyday life, was overt rebellion against the sentimentalism which marked American painting and against the classic, cheesecloth, studio art of Europe.

As I returned to this, I was in the position of the wealthy Philadelphian who took his ulcer on the grand tour to have it treated by the most celebrated and most expensive physicians of Europe. He wound up in Vienna in the office of the most renowned medico of all who gave him a thoughtful examination and sent him home.

"My dear sir," he said, "there is only one man in the world who knows how to do anything for your peculiar ailment. He is Dr. Thimgymaquack of Philadelphia."

It was to this excitement, then, that I returned. New York had grown and expanded. It was bigger and noisier and lustier than ever. The Ash Can School was the thing, and, for that matter, the modernists had furtively arrived also. They were secreted in Alfred Stieglitz's Photo Secession Gallery. There the select folk and the critics caught their first glimpses of photography regarded as art, and as abstract art, and of the paintings of Matisse and Picasso.

It was not much later, February 15, 1913, to be exact,

that we had the historic Armory Show at which Matisse, Cézanne, and Lehmbruck were unveiled, along with Marcel Duchamp's "Nude Descending the Staircase," to astonish and delight city editors and women's clubs. But this was a little later and at the time of which I write, the time that was important to me, the Ash Can School was the school that made the impact.

I brought myself up to date in these matters as fast as I could, eyes popping; and finally got around to some consideration of the Lionel Barrymore career as a professional artist. It seemed to me, with all these great things going on in the galleries, that I had nothing to show anybody and that my most cunning expedient was to break in through the medium of magazine illustration. Almost anybody, I was sure, could do that.

With this in mind I toiled over my drawing board preparing a handful of sketches which I could show editors as samples of my art, and sought an opportunity to make my debut under the most impressive circumstances. Naturally, as you quite understand by now, that meant Ethel.

My sister was already a big star indeed. She was the fashion. I believe she had already said "That's all, there isn't any more" in the play *Sunday,* and with or without that phrase she was operating far uptown from me in the carriage trade set.

Ethel knew Charles Belmont Davis, brother of Richard Harding Davis, and to him she spoke impressively about her talented brother, Lionel the artist.

"Why don't you take some of your work down to *Collier's?*" said Davis. "I know the art editor there. I'll speak to him."

I did that. I wrapped up my works carefully and went

hopefully down to the *Collier's* office. I arrived at the reception room, sent in my name, and sat down to wait.

It was a large room decorated with pictures. I had a long wait. To pass the time, I walked up and down the hall examining the paintings.

There was a Shinn. A Glackens. Another Shinn. A Luks, a Sloan, a Baylinson, a Henri. The walls were covered with the works of these artists.

I went up to the girl at the desk.

"The paintings," I said, "they ran in the magazine?"

"Oh, yes," said the girl, "those are illustrations we used."

"I mean those"—pointing—"those Shinns and Henris, those Glackens and Luks. I mean those."

"Why, yes," she said. "Naturally. Those fellows come in all the time. They work for us."

I thought that over.

"Where is the men's room?" I said.

The girl waved a hand. I grabbed my sketches and departed. On the street I found an ash can and stuffed in my drawings, tamping them down. This was as close as I ever came to intimate association with the Ash Can School, and it was as close as I ever came to being published by a magazine. I never went back to *Collier's* or to any other publication.

I will confess something. In any discussion about art I always become inarticulate—but in my heart I think I know more about it than anybody. I will reveal myself in true colors at last. I am an appreciator, a member of the most important clan in the world. As great as Beethoven and Wagner were, they were great because they *were*. So it is with appreciators, and we are a great bunch of people too; proud, no doubt, and exclusive, no doubt, but we insist that we are great folk.

As an appreciator I know this, that there are degrees of rotten eggs, but no degrees whatsoever in fresh eggs. They are fresh or they aren't fresh. A picture by Robert Henri or John Sloan is a good thing, a fresh egg; and in comparison with lesser works, the difference is as the difference between the poles. It just is, and there you are.

I find it a handsome thing to know that I am an appreciator and accountable to nobody. As such, I don't hesitate to say who I think is a fresh egg and who's a rotten one, and if you disagree with me I am astounded and embarrassed by your ignorance and your lack of good sense.

Of course, as Whistler said, "So do the donkeys know what they like!"

13. D. W. Griffith

THE YEAR WAS 1909. A decision had to be made, but I did not make it. The Lord God, I have finally learned—or some of his instructed representatives on this odd planet—makes the decisions, and most of us, no matter how fatuously we believe in our own brains and our own will power, are not sharp enough to estimate the possible outcome. We had to eat, and so I returned to the stage.

I cannot say that I was desperately cast down about not making out as a painter. Neither Jean-Paul Laurens nor Richard Miller, nor, indeed, anybody else, had ever predicted that I would succeed as an artist; and most certainly I had daubed no canvases that even in my own eyes were any good. I had pursued this art as a young fellow might pursue a marvelous girl, with flanking movements and hopeful gestures, but never winning enough encouragement to make fulfillment seem possible.

I did not want to return to the stage, but it was something I could return to. This changed my whole life, of course.

The play was *The Fires of Fate*, a drama in four acts by Sir Arthur Conan Doyle, produced by Charles Frohman in Chicago. We had a reasonably good run but the least said of this play the better, especially since I cannot remember much about it. The show came on to New York and ran for twenty-three performances, but without me.

I had joined Uncle Googan and Aunt Gladys in vaudeville.

The Drews were starred in a Keith and Proctor production, a one-act play, called *The Still Voice*. The author was Aunt Gladys, and *The Still Voice* had to do with some rich people who had purchased a painting of Christ. From this painting, which hung in the library, came a voice which said things that needed to be said to that family, New Testament things.

We went all over the country with this play. My only objection to it was that it was too good for its audience and was consequently not understood. Of course, my criticism here is nonsense because no one more intelligent than a calf expects anything from audiences.

Shortly after *The Still Voice* I was again in a familiar fiscal condition. I was empty in pocket and in need of employment. Perhaps I might have caught on again on the Broadway stage, perhaps not. At any rate, nothing rewarding was offered me and I had heard at the bars and at The Players of a new thing, motion pictures, for which an actor could work anonymously at easy hours and low pay. The movies were in low esteem in 1912, little more than nickelodeon performances, one-reelers with no sense of direction and certainly no art. I went down to 11 East Fourteenth Street to call on D. W. Griffith, whom I had met at lunch, and offered myself as a motion picture actor.

Griffith was not encouraging.

He looked me up and down, peering over that fine, cantilevered nose of his, and he said:

"I'm not employing stage stars."

"I am not even remotely any such creature," I said. "I will do anything. I mean absolutely anything. Believe me, I'm hungry. I want a job."

I think it must have been reasonably easy to perceive that I was sincere.

"All right," said Griffith, "we'll put you on. You be here tomorrow afternoon at two o'clock in a dress suit."

I had to borrow the dress suit but I was there on time. My pay was ten dollars a day. That is how I made my debut in motion pictures.

At about the same time two girls, one in New York and the other in California, also made their bows with Griffith and the old Biograph Company. Their arrival on the scene was not only important in the history of motion pictures but was personally important to me. One was Mary Pickford and the other was Anita Loos.

Terry Ramsaye, the great chronicler of motion picture history, tells the story of their debuts at entertaining length in his *A Million and One Nights*, but, in brief, they were like this:

Gladys Smith was Mary's real name. Along with her brother Jack and her sister Lottie she worked as a small child in Chauncey Olcott's *Edmund Burke*, but she was always hopeful that one day the lightning might strike and she would get a job on Broadway.

This seemed pretty much out of the question, since the Smiths played the provinces and came no nearer to Broadway than the small theaters of New Jersey; but the story goes that Gladys Smith, then aged sixteen, stormed across the river, fought her way into a David Belasco rehearsal, walked out on stage while the great man was in a bad temper, and so impressed him that he gave her a job then and there. Knowing Miss Pickford and Mr. Belasco, I find the tale entirely credible. Belasco was himself as dramatic as any actor; he was "on stage" at all times. The abrupt appearance of a curly-headed, appealing little girl would have inspired him to change moods and play the gracious maestro. Besides, he *needed* just that girl. In fifteen minutes, Gladys Smith had a Broadway part in *The Warrens of Virginia* and a new name, Mary Pickford.

Her approach to D. W. Griffith was almost as abrupt and just as appealing. After the Broadway engagement, the Smith family found itself on the shoals, and it was up to Mary to go out and find a job that would buy groceries. Like me and like other actors hard pressed around the belt, Mary went down to 11 East Fourteenth Street.

There was a receptionist in the front hall. In the offices of big agents, managers, and producers, there is always a receptionist. She is no ordinary person. She is a kind of actress herself and she has been cast for her ability to read one line and one line only with cold, haughty conviction. This line goes:

"Mr. High Brass is not seeing actors today."

Mary heard the line, but this time the receptionist looked up and caught the full impact of the Pickford charm. Miss Pickford, even today, could eat a porterhouse steak at the Stork Club and at the same time make you think of a waif in a snowstorm.

The receptionist ad libbed a line which was not in her script. Possibly she thought she was taking her job in her hands. The fact is, of course, that the whole motion picture industry depended upon what she said next.

She said: "But wait a minute. I shouldn't do this, but—"

Griffith did see her, and it was precisely as it was with Belasco: in fifteen minutes Mary Pickford had a job. Her job was a part in *The Lonely Villa,* a melodrama.

The lady has been extremely profitably employed ever since.

Anita Loos was the daughter of R. Beers Loos, a California editor and play promoter. His shows were the heart-stopping melodramas of the old tent-and-sawdust school of acting, from which, indeed, had sprung the great David Belasco himself. Little Miss Loos, then sixteen, was not an actress but wanted to be. She felt thwarted because her father did not put her on to love and suffer under canvas for the West Coast. Her frustration inspired her to write a story (another example of the theory that all writers are hams and would never write a word if they could act). She innocently sent her story to D. W. Griffith.

It could not happen today. No studio today will even open an envelope containing an unsolicited story, but in that era a motion picture producer would read anything and probably make a picture of it. Griffith read *The New York Hat,* liked it, bought it for fifteen dollars, and that was Anita Loos' debut in motion pictures. Lest anyone confuse the lady's great talent with someone else's, Miss Loos is the same who later wrote that sociological document, *Gentlemen Prefer Blondes.*

The New York Hat was one of my first films. I acted in it opposite Mary Pickford.

Several other well-remembered actors arrived in motion pictures that year. James Kirkwood, who became a star, found his way to 11 East Fourteenth Street by accident while Mary and Griffith were shooting *The Lonely Villa.*

Griffith looked up and saw Kirkwood, and whether he recognized him as a stage actor is doubtful; what he saw, undoubtedly, was merely the right-sized man to break down a door.

"Not in my line," said Kirkwood.

"Easiest thing in the world. Try it," Griffith argued. "Anyway, when you put on a muff nobody will know you."

Kirkwood shrugged and did it and thus launched a new career. He brought on his friend Henry Walthall, who arrived protesting, but stayed to become the famous Little Colonel in *The Birth of a Nation.*

Mabel Normand came to the screen the same year from posing for fashion pictures, and met a young fellow all of us liked but whom we ignored when he tried to tell us and D. W. Griffith how to make motion pictures. His idea was to have a lot of pretty girls and a lot of policemen running around. This was Mack Sennett. It took him quite a while to get started, but start he did, and Mabel Normand was his star.

There were also the Gish sisters, Lillian and Dorothy, Alice Joyce, Georgie O'Ramey, Louise Vale, Louise Orth, Jack Mulhall, Thomas Jefferson, Franklin Ritchie, Lily Cahill, Donald Crisp, Dorothy Bernard, Edwin August, Alan Hale, Mae Marsh, and Florence Lawrence. None of our names was known then to the public. The star system had not been invented. Florence Lawrence was, actually, the first motion picture star, but only because she was billed as "The Biograph Girl." Her name was never used. Mary Pickford became known as "Little Mary," not as Mary Pickford in those days. It is an odd thought in passing that she never appeared in any of D. W. Griffith's truly great pictures. She had gone on to glory and more money before he made them.

My reception at Biograph was cordial enough, although there were a few uncomfortable moments of suspicion when I first entered the men's dressing room.

"Who's the new man?" a fellow said.

"That's John Barrymore's brother."

"Never heard of him. Is he an actor?"

But they let me hang around.

I was in all kinds of pictures. Griffith, with his remarkable cameraman, G. W. ("Billy") Bitzer, who had to work with a bicycle lamp on his camera to warm the film and prevent static, shot fast, a picture a week at least. It seemed to me that I spent most of my Biograph working hours taking part in battles.

We engaged in one particularly fierce campaign with a troop of National Guard Cavalry working as Confederate soldiers. Their orders were to make a gallant charge to rescue Mary Pickford as the Union Men, including me, crept up on a cabin. Griffith, be it noted, was from Kentucky and contrived to have the Confederates win as many battles as possible.

This was an unusually desperate and heroic engagement because as the day wore on the cavalrymen hit their bottles with increasing thirst, and lined up for the charge propped on their horses like plastered owls. Light was fading rapidly and Griffith was in a hurry to get the last shot on film to save employing everybody for another day's work.

He assigned ten of us to death scenes, giving us numbers which he would call out to signal our demises.

The charge came, finally, with the "Southern" troops roaring, lurching, and falling off their horses. It was a terrifying maneuver. Griffith called my number and I died like a dragon, clutching my throat and gasping horribly. I staggered under the eaves of the cabin, near a corner, kicked convulsively, and expired. It was a performance that would have pleased Fred Remington. My object, though, was to fall in a corner where the horses wouldn't step on me.

The other Union gentlemen caught on and did the same thing. We fell in a heap and died en masse, a pile of corpses under the eaves as the horses thundered around us.

Griffith made more noise than the cavalry. He worked us over in his excellent and blistering rhetoric but he had to call us back for another day's work. We had to do it right the second time, and a horse's hoof missed my face by a twentieth of an inch as I perished miserably out in the open.

Most of us performed literary as well as acting prodigies for Biograph. Mary Pickford wrote *The Awakening, Caught in the Act, The Alien, Granny, Lena and the Geese, Fate's Decree,* and a number of others. I myself wrote dozens of screen plays for Griffith. They were called "scenarios" then. One of my stories was produced under the title of *The Tenderhearted,* and concerned a butcher boy.

This boy, whose name was Joe, worked for a meat cutter in Port Jefferson. His job was to go over the island taking orders for meat. He used to pass an old lady who lived on Middle Island, a terrible dump, and this old lady kept a cow. Every day when Joe passed her place he took pity on her and gave her a bit of beef, and she would give him a drink of milk. She died eventually, and when her will was read it was discovered that she had left fifty thousand dollars to Joe, who immediately bought the butcher shop.

Griffith couldn't eat alone, always asked some of us to join him in the Fourteenth Street restaurants, so one day as a conversation piece and with an eye peeled for a check, I told him the story of Joe the butcher boy.

"That's a picture," said Griffith. "We'll rehearse it this afternoon."

And we did.

"Here, Bobby," Griffith called to Bobby Harron, "you get on the wagon and be the butcher boy."

We shot and finished that picture before I wrote it but I was paid twenty-five dollars.

I am not certain whether the Museum of Modern Art has respectfully salvaged a print of this contribution to literature or not.

Under Griffith the motion picture was beginning to show vigorous signs of becoming a complex and artful way of telling a story. At this time, mind you, there were only one-reel comedies and dramas. It was thought inconceivable that any audience could sit through a longer show than that, a consideration which, worse luck, was quickly abandoned. Stories were developed on such elemental lines that most companies kept on hand large rolls of stock titles, ready-printed and available for insertion. They included such labels as *Love at First Sight, Confused, Two Days Later* and, of course, the classic of all time, *Came the Dawn.*

Griffith drove his actors to get what he wanted. Hard-bitten players like me he largely let alone, but when he worked with his younger people, especially the Gish girls, he directed them minutely in every gesture they made, from the lifting of an eyelid to the correct way to scream. But he abandoned stage conventions to widen his view and he did the unheard-of thing of changing his camera setup in the middle of a scene. This is routine today, of course, but it was a startling thing forty years ago.

Griffith gave the screen its first idiom and articulation. Up to this time the cinema had barely been able to recite the alphabet; now it acquired grammar and punctuation. Now, and notably in *The New York Hat,* Griffith used cutbacks, close shots and sharply edited scenes instead of the conventional forms of the stage. He showed actors' faces in close-ups. And so it came about that through my usual habit of serendipity I had stumbled into a classic: this was one of the films that heralded motion pictures as a serious medium. *The New York Hat* is on view today at the Museum of Modern Art in New York for those who approach it with proper respect.

In giving the screen its new grammar, Griffith was assisted by another pioneer whose name should be marked in great letters in Hollywood's hall of fame. Billy Bitzer invented the close-up and the fade-out while experimenting with a camera in his own basement. In fact, according to Mrs. Bitzer, who graciously made some of Billy's unpublished memoirs available to me, he actually discovered Griffith.

Billy was busy photographing "off color" pictures when "Larry" Griffith arrived at the old studio. These "off color" pictures, considered very naughty for the times, went so far as to show a girl disrobing down to a pair of tights. Their most interesting action occurred when the lady would be overturned in a chair so as to show a flash of her petticoats, possibly even the edge of her pants.

David Wark Griffith was not in these pictures, but was employed as an extra in crowd scenes, and Billy photographed him. Bitzer was immediately scolded by the executive department for showing this extra as if he had four arms.

Billy, who was sure of his photography, interviewed Griffith and learned that the young actor was deliberately making jerky movements because pictures in those days jerked on screen and he thought, of course, that was the way he was supposed to act.

After teaching Griffith how to act, Billy's next chore was to introduce him to direction. He broke down a story for D. W. into five parts and wrote them down on the back of an old laundry card, specifying "Heart Interest," "Drama," "Danger," "Comedy," and "Rescue." From then on, Griffith took things into his own hands—and every motion picture made since that day has stemmed from the principles laid down by Bitzer and Griffith.

Mrs. Bitzer, who now lives in New York—Billy died in 1944, aged seventy-three—tells me also that Billy put up the seven thousand dollars which enabled Griffith to finish *The Birth of a Nation,* an investment which netted Billy two hundred thousand dollars which he promptly lost. All told his contributions to motion pictures are so considerable that every actor in Hollywood should rise up every morning and bless the names of D. W. Griffith and Billy Bitzer.

I knew D. W. Griffith well and I liked him. He was from Louisville, where he made his start on stage as a boy by working in stock companies. His father was Lieutenant Colonel Jacob Wark Griffith of the First Kentucky Cavalry, C.S.A., who when he was badly wounded for the third time in battle found himself unable to move, with a cavalry charge coming up. The Colonel commandeered a buggy and led his regiment to a victory. Possibly the memory of this fantastic exploit had something to do with D. W.'s fondness for cavalry prowess in his pictures.

Griffith had been known as "Lawrence" Griffith on the stage, where he was not an enormous success, and he wrote short stories and a few plays under that name. He was about thirty years old when he came to Biograph.

Griffith did everything. He preceded Hollywood in everything that has been done since. It is an abiding mystery and a scandal to me that an ungrateful industry has not raised a statue to him ninety feet tall at the intersection of Hollywood Boulevard and Vine Street. This statue should be of solid gold.

After the discovery that California, and particularly the undeveloped crossroads of what eventually became Hollywood, provided more reliable sunshine even than Jacksonville, Florida (Florida almost got the studios), motion pictures gradually moved West. Griffith began to spend half the year in California after 1910, and all of us wanted to be taken along. I was not invited and it was not the proper thing to approach Mr. Griffith and ask him for a trip. I connived.

We were making pictures at Coytesville, and were having most of our meals at a restaurant which I believe was called Rambeau's. Minnie Maddern Fiske learned I was with Griffith, who she probably thought was some obscure manager. She remembered something favorable about me from the old times on Broadway and it occurred to her that I could do a part in one of her plays.

Now Mrs. Fiske hadn't seen me for years. I was twice as big as when she had looked me over in *The Mummy and the Humming Bird,* or whatever it was she remembered. In short, let's face it, I was fat. I knew it would never do for Mrs. Fiske to clap eyes on me but it just occurred to me that her interest might be a good thing.

I arranged with her agent to have the lady put in a call for me while I was eating at Rambeau's with Griffith. I also arranged to have Griffith sit near the telephone.

At the proper time the telephone rang, a waiter answered it, and came over to me.

"A Mrs. Fiske wants to speak to you, sir."

"So? *What* Mrs. Fiske wants to speak to me?"

"Mrs. Minnie Maddern Fiske, Mr. Barrymore."

"Oh, in that case all right." So I went to the telephone. I made the conversation long—and loud.

"Why, yes, indeed I would. Work with you? Delighted. I'm sure I'd like the play. Why, yes, Mrs. Fiske. Yes, I could start at once. Shall we meet and talk it over?" And so on. I performed this scene so that Griffith could overhear every word; indeed, the exigencies of the timing played so patly into my hands that Griffith could also overhear some of *her* conversation.

Griffith came to the point immediately, just before a forkful of spaghetti touched his mouth.

"How would you like to go to California, Barrymore?"

I waited until he had masticated so that I would have no rival for my reply.

I said I would like it. And I stayed away from Minnie Maddern Fiske. She would have been horrified. As I say, I knew I was too fat for her but I could be a character in pictures very nicely.

14. Hollywood, 1913

WE DID NOT go to Hollywood, although, contrary to some current journalists who take the stand that Hollywood does not actually exist, being merely a state of mind, there was such a place then. There had been such a place since about 1876. It had nothing to do with motion pictures or the theater. It was founded by Horace Henderson Wilcox and his wife Daieda, who were Methodists and Prohibitionists from Topeka.

Mr. Wilcox had been a shoemaker and undoubtedly a good one, for he had made enough money to take part in the California real-estate boom of '76 which was set off when the Los Angeles Chamber of Commerce, through broadsides and prayer, dazzled the Southern Pacific with the project of negotiating the Tehachapi Pass and burrowing a tunnel through the San Fernando Mountains. It hardly seemed worth while at the time because Los Angeles was a brawling pueblo of a mere 7,000 souls, few of them worth saving; but this railroad exploit set off the whopping enterprise that created the astonishing city, brought the movies to Hollywood, and marked its effect for better or for worse upon all of us to this day.

To begin with, the valley which Hollywood and most of the studios now share was the home of saber-toothed tigers, imperial elephants fifteen feet high, vultures larger than condors, eagles, wild turkeys, rabbits, and the Cahu-

Culver Service

Irene Fenwick and Lionel Barrymore in *The Claw*, 1921

Spencer Berger Collection

Lionel Barrymore and Pauline Starke in *Women Love Diamonds.* M-G-M, 1927

enga Indians. Proof of this can be found in the La Brea Tar Pits wherein the wretched bones of these beasts and Indians are still antiseptically preserved. It seems appropriate that they were the forerunners of our town. We can only hope as time and history pass that the skulls and tibia of certain saber-toothed gossip columnists and perhaps the elephantine hides of a producer or so will become likewise embalmed.

The first white man to find what is now Hollywood was Governor Gaspar de Portola, subdivisor for the King of Spain. The Royal Governor, according to the records, took one supercilious look at the vermin-ridden, rabbit-fed Indians, and hurried away. He sought greener fields to carry out his twofold assignment, which was prophetic: his job was to spread the Gospel and to grab real estate, the twin projects in which Southern California still excels. He fled, ignoring the opportunity to name the region "Cahuenga," which is what Hollywood ought to have been called in honor of its first subhuman inhabitants.

When Horace Henderson Wilcox and Daieda Wilcox came on the scene with their Arabian horses "Duke" and "Royal" they bought up 120 acres of land from John Bower for $12.50 an acre. There were a few people here ahead of them: Christian Duen, a Danish sailor; Herman Newman, a German; Ivar A. Weird, a Dane; and José Mascarel, a Frenchman. They owned and farmed the land which now constitutes Hollywood.

Horace and Daieda wrote back to Topeka and urged their Prohibitionist friends to come on out; and they did, and bought land, preferably from Horace. The Wilcox ranch itself centered upon what is now bounded by Hollywood and Cahuenga Boulevards, and the boundaries were marked up to a few years ago by the pepper trees they set out.

The Wilcoxes eventually died broke and land-poor, and left no legacy to Hollywood save only their name on one of the principal streets, and the name of the place itself. And the origin of that name is in dispute. The California Historical Association believes that Mrs. Wilcox named her ranch after a farm owned by a friend in New England. Another theory is that she mistook the Tonyon berries, which are still prevalent in the hills, for genuine holly. At any rate, a place name that has attained connotations as gaudy as any in the world, from Babylon on, was the whim of Daieda Wilcox, Kansas Prohibitionist.

Faye Thomas Frederick, a teacher at the Selma Avenue Public School in Hollywood, says that the main social organization of the town during the Wilcox era was the Hollywood Club, and that its principal entertainment was a May Day fete. In 1909 the Hollywood Club's innocent celebration was drowned by torrential rains and the revels were canceled at considerable financial sacrifice. The Prohibitionists hurried home to steam their feet and ward off colds with foot baths and hot toddies and never again emerged in the public eye. I think we can suggest with some certainty that Hollywood has not been the same since.

We made pictures not in Hollywood but on a vacant lot at Pico Boulevard and Georgia, on any other vacant lots from which we could dispossess the small boys, and principally the streets of downtown Los Angeles. Canvas dressing rooms were ranged around the edges of our own lot.

One of the first problems that smote Griffith when he came to California was the scarcity of cheap actors for mob and crowd scenes. There had always been no lack of hungry ones in New York. Here he was forced to make overtures to the Oliver Morosco stock company, offering small sums for the daytime services of the Morosco people. One of the Morosco players was a girl named Marguerite Marsh, who was working in a musical number, *My Gal Irene*, with Charles Ruggles. Marguerite appeared in the picture *The Mender of Nets*, among others, the first year, worked with us again when Griffith trekked out the second time, and produced her little sister Mae, a school girl, who refused to be chased from the lot.

Finally somebody said, "Get a look at the kid. Just like Billie Burke." That started Mae Marsh in pictures.

We lived where we could, in rented rooms or in hotels which took an indulgent attitude toward the poor, and we congregated at the Alexandria Hotel bar which was in unintentional competition with the Hoffman House for the free-lunch patronage of motion picture actors. There were lush weeks when, having succumbed to steady employment, I earned as high as one hundred and twenty-five dollars, but most of the time I did not get that much money. Griffith himself was paid seventy-five dollars a week at this time with a percentage guarantee of only two hundred dollars. (It has been estimated that he *spent* thirty million dollars producing his great spectacles over the years that followed.)

I played, let us phrase it, several important parts in Griffith's *Judith of Bethulia*, the first four-reel feature made in America, with Blanche Sweet and Henry B. Walthall. This picture was modeled on the four-part technique

Griffith invented for his previous *Pippa Passes,* and was actually the front runner for his masterpiece *Intolerance.* I am, therefore, proud to have worked in it; but beyond recalling that Harry Carey was crucified upside down and that I appeared more than once in various disguises, I do not remember much about what I contributed to this work.

Among the people who consorted around the free lunches at the Alexandria and the Hoffman House were Wallace Reid and Henry King. Wally's father had been a ten-twent-thirt actor, but naturally, we made out that we recalled him as a distinguished ornament to the stage.

"Yas, yas, yas, remember your father exceedingly well. Played a split week with him somewhere or other. Yas, yas, yas, you will have a beer, won't you?" Actor talk. Broke actor talk.

I went back and forth a number of times and made an enormous number of pictures. I am, it suddenly occurs to me at the age of ninety-seven or whatever it is, a pioneer and possibly a kind of landmark in motion pictures. I was here long before a number of people, including Douglas Fairbanks, came out and had their careers and finished, and I am still here. I do not know why a statue to *me* has not already been erected in honor of my good works and durability. If this notion strikes my admirers as sound, which it is, I will be happy to contribute a modest sum. The statue should be, of course, recumbent.

At about this time, which I believe after thinking hard must have got us up to about 1913, I had a major quarrel with Harry Carey, who had become enchanted with the geranium and citrus-growing prowess of the Southern California climate and declared his intentions of homesteading. I dissuaded him from taking over for a pittance the property which is now the site of the Beverly Hills Hotel.

Donald Crisp, a prudent and astute actor who undoubtedly held onto the first dollar he ever earned, did invest in real estate and make money. He got hold of a piece of undeveloped property out in the ranch regions which he turned over for eight thousand dollars, a pretty profit. The property is now the locale of the Taft Building in the heart of Hollywood, probably worth eight million dollars. I had nothing to do with such enterprises or investments and have never had anything to do with them all my life, worse luck. In one way or another I earned enough—well, not enough, but sufficient—for the exceedingly simple requirements of my life. These requirements hinged around a little night music, a little painting, a good deal of beer, and escape from the rigors of acting on the stage.

If this smacks of a certain raffish charm and even of artistic integrity, I encourage you to accept it as such. It was not always charming. It was often hard and uncertain and disillusioning, and it was always insecure. I had, however, my interest in music and this had begun to take increasing importance in my progress through this odd vale. I had been, let us presume, well grounded in fundamentals by my various teachers, the cheap and free ones, and I had begun by now to set down on paper certain fugitive fugues and scherzos which went through my head. I was not and never have been an executant at the keyboard or the pipes or the strings, although I make shift to play them, and I was and am appalled by men who can perform. Imagine the deadly hours, the sheer brutal toil, that the poor wretch of a concert star endures—a

Rubinstein, an Iturbi, or a Heifetz. Iturbi once said that if he failed to practice his regular stint of eight hours a day he knew the difference at his next concert; if he worked only six hours a day, the critics knew it; and if he were indolent and toiled only four hours a day *everybody* knew it. They are marvelous, these great performers, and I am very sorry for them.

By 1914 or thereabouts Jack had become a celebrated light comedian on Broadway. He had appeared in *The Fortune Hunter, Believe Me, Xantippe, The Yellow Ticket* with Florence Reed, and in other plays which had both established and dissatisfied him.

The influence that dissatisfied Jack with his performances as an amiable comedian was one man, Ned Sheldon. Ned saw, and was the first to see, the depths and possibilities of Jack Barrymore as an interpretative dramatic actor. You must understand the real intelligence of that perception because, aside from the irresponsibilities that marked all his appearances, his drinking, and his other eccentricities, Jack did not then have a full-rounded voice and his diction was slovenly. Ned Sheldon saw through to something, the real something, whatever that something is when we consider genius, and he set about to develop it in Jack.

I suppose there has never been a more beloved man in the theater than Sheldon. He came to Broadway fresh from Harvard, with a degree from "Prof" Baker's renowned theatrical workshop in one pocket and a hit play, *Salvation Nell,* in the other. *The Nigger, Romance,* and *The Princess Zim-Zim* followed, but brilliant as Sheldon was in his own work, his great bountiful gift was human kindness. He advised the rich and the wretched, counseled the talented. He was the theater's acolyte and its people's priest. I think there is hardly a worth-while person in the theater of his time whose life was not touched, and improved by the touch, of Edward Brewster Sheldon. Certainly, his association with Jack was fateful.

Possibly it was part of Ned's campaign that caused him to travel in Europe with Jack the summer of 1914, when there was already turmoil brewing between Jack and his first wife, Katherine Corri Harris. No doubt influenced by Sheldon's pleas for more serious work, Jack returned to New York and did *Kick In* for Al Woods, a melodrama. This was considered a remarkable choice, vaulting a very light comedian into serious acting. Of course, Al Woods knew what he was doing, and the play—and Jack—were highly successful. He and Ned began to consider even more thoughtfully the problem of discovering for Jack the challenging plays he really needed. They found one in John Galsworthy's tragic *Justice*, which John Williams produced, and which revealed for the first time, in my opinion, the true powers that were in Jack.

Ned now began to talk about *Peter Ibbetson*. Indeed, he spoke of *Peter Ibbetson* to me too, in long conversations we had in his apartment. I was naturally glad to take Jack's work seriously—at last—but I was far from taking seriously any suggestion that I return to the stage.

"And you must play in this too," Ned would say.

"Ah, yas, yas, yas, indeed. Pour me one," I would say. I was happy. I had steady work in motion pictures. I had music. I could look at pictures and even paint a few. I had discovered that I enjoyed etching. I could finger the oboe a little. I could put down in notes the music I liked to invent, and on special occasions I could induce good musicians to play this music. Why indeed should I return to the rehearsals, the disappointments, and the nervous hard work of the stage?

I would nod my head and agree to appear in *Peter Ibbetson,* but of course I did not mean one nod of those nods. I doubted that Jack himself would do Ibbetson and, as a matter of fact, I had sound reasons to doubt that there was even such a play from the George du Maurier novel.

I was to find that a promise to Ned Sheldon (God rest him well) was no light thing, even when made with a bow over a beer. We did Ibbetson, Jack and I. For the brothers to undertake it at all was remarkable enough, but the truly remarkable part about *Peter Ibbetson* is not this. It is an authentic miracle that Du Maurier ever wrote the novel and it is an even greater miracle that Constance Collier ever produced it as a play.

15. *Dream Sequence*

SINCE WE ALL are descended from a number of kings and queens whether we like it or not, possibly any one of us could call a monarch cousin with as much propriety as the Du Mauriers, provided, that is and of course, that we are amused rather than abashed by the purple chip in our great-great-grandmother's woodpile.

George Louis Palmella Bussin du Maurier was the grandson of Mary Anne Clarke, who was born about 1776 and who was the intimate friend of the Duke of York. His mother was Ellen Clarke, who married Louis-Mathurin du Maurier. Daphne du Maurier in her fine book *The Du Mauriers,* published by Country Life Press, tells how Lord Chichester came to Mary Anne's home on April 1, 1809, to obtain from her certain correspondence signed by His Royal Highness and to arrange terms under which Mary Anne was to leave the country and enjoy a stipend from the Duke.

"If my mother has quarreled with the Duke, why does he pay us money?" young Ellen asked.

"Go look at yourself in the mirror," replied Lord Chichester.

He then turned to Mary Anne.

"Pray tell me, now," he said, "who *was* her father?"

Mary Anne, says Daphne du Maurier, yawned and wrinkled her nose.

"So many people at Brighton," she murmured. "And I have such a poor memory for faces."

But the most astonishing fact about George du Maurier was not his interesting ancestry. The astonisher is that he wrote a novel. Consider.

At the age of fifty-seven, George du Maurier had been for more than thirty years an enormously successful contributor to *Punch*. He was an illustrator (Thackeray's *Henry Esmond,* for instance) whose works commanded a national audience of delighted admirers. He had never written anything to give the slightest indication that he could produce a novel, let alone a novel which became immediately a best-seller both in Great Britain and America and, I think we can be sure, a literary classic of all time. This was of course *Peter Ibbetson.* To make matters even more astounding he at once followed *Peter Ibbetson* with *Trilby.*

As Deems Taylor puts it in his introduction to a Modern Library edition of the novel, "If *A Farewell to Arms* had turned out to be written by Charles Dana Gibson we should all probably feel much as George du Maurier's contemporaries felt about *Peter Ibbetson* in 1891."

Mr. Taylor's observation is, as Mr. Taylor's observations always are, an accurate stroke, for the Du Maurier pictures did indeed set the fashion for young females in England just as the Gibson Girl set the style here. They were giantesses. If you will examine Du Maurier's drawings of the Duchess of Towers in the *Peter Ibbetson* illustrations you will discover that the lady is depicted as ten heads tall. Peter himself, in order to top her, has to be eleven heads tall. But there were such creatures. Caroline Ticknor reports that when she went as a young girl with

Clarence King to have tea with George du Maurier, she was astounded and enchanted by his daughters in their tight-fitting jerseys buttoned up the back—perfect reproductions of the pictures she had studied at home.

Du Maurier contributed cartoons to *Punch* which were like this: A pretty girl and a young man are gazing into each other's eyes. She says, "I do not see the mote in your eye." He replies, "Ah, but I see the beams in yours." It was entitled "A New Adaptation from the New Testament."

I suggest that with a background of literary production no more impressive than this college-humor wisecrack seems to indicate, it is not a small miracle but a big miracle that Du Maurier turned into the author of *Peter Ibbetson.*

He once took a walk with Henry James in High Street, Bayswater, and offered to make James the present of an idea for a novel. He told him the plot of *Trilby.* Mr. James declined, telling Du Maurier that the notion was so good he could not think of depriving him of it; but as Deems Taylor says, about the most unthinkable literary project in the world would be to imagine Henry James writing *Trilby.*

Du Maurier went home that same evening, took a walk in his garden, worried his doubts, but sat down late that night and started not *Trilby,* but the first chapter of *Ibbetson.* Peter was of course himself, George du Maurier, as a small boy in London and in Paris. From whom Du Maurier drew the boy's uncle, Colonel Ibbetson, I do not know, but I eventually became him. In 1931, Deems Taylor wrote marvelous music and *Peter Ibbetson* also became an opera.

It is one of the great, unique stories. It is a story about

two lovers who become separated, and that, to be sure, has been done before, from Dante and Beatrice to Romeo and Juliet to Frankie and Johnnie; but in this story the lovers can meet in their dreams, and do, and so far as I know this is an utterly novel psychological idea.

What the modern Freud and Krafft-Ebing writing men would do with such a theme is horrendous to contemplate. It is also appalling to think what they might do with Gretel and the Witch, or with the Old Lady Who Lived in a Shoe, so let us not think about it. *Peter Ibbetson* was plainly improbable; but you believed it, and that was that.

Now that we have argued that it was extremely unlikely for George du Maurier to write *Peter Ibbetson,* we can examine the next improbability. This was that this strange novel in which we see Peter and his Duchess both in real life and in the dreams should become a play.

Constance Collier, who acts in motion pictures now with the authority of a marchioness at least, claims to be descended from Arabs and pirates because she is part Portuguese. She walked out of a London fog one evening, aged fourteen, onto the stage of the Gaiety Theater, and so impressed George Edwardes, the producer, that he made her in a few years one of England's leading musical comedy girls. She went on from there to Sir Charles Hawtrey and from Hawtrey to Sir Herbert Beerbohm Tree at His Majesty's Theater, and there she became a dramatic star. If Constance had not done these things, *Peter Ibbetson* would not have inspired a play for the Barrymore boys or a story for me to tell. She is a great beauty, but in one respect she resembles me: she has the fortunate faculty of emerging from curious and distressing situations somewhat better off than she was before.

At the beginning of World War I Constance had been critically ill and had lost all her money. She recuperated in France but eventually returned to London, where she took a small apartment in a hotel in Jermyn Street and made a habit of going to bed at nine o'clock. She had reasons to suspect that her brilliant career was ended.

But on an air raid night she recalls as "gloomy and sullen" she received a telephone call. It was from Sir Herbert. Sir Herbert was bored.

He said that he had engaged to be interviewed by a young newspaperman and that the prospect appalled him. Would Constance hop out of bed, join him at the Carlton, and be gay? Constance demurred, but no one demurred long with Herbert Tree, so she put on some finery and made her appearance.

The newspaperman was John Raphael, and Sir Herbert was as he had advertised himself over the telephone—bored and uncommunicative. There was a French woman present who spoke no English, and this made the party stiffer than ever. Tree would say nothing at all. What conversation there was took place between Constance and John Raphael.

Now, the upshot of that talk was that Raphael diffidently confessed that he had attempted to write a play from Du Maurier's *Peter Ibbetson.* He had written it years ago, had submitted it to every manager in London, and now brought up the subject as a kind of apologetic conversation piece.

Sir Herbert's comment, Constance remembers, was merely to the effect that "everybody had a skeleton in his cupboard," but having nothing else to talk about, Constance and Raphael pursued the subject and Constance found herself promising to read the *Ibbetson* play if Raphael could find a tattered copy and send it around to her hotel. The matter rested there, one of those matters that is awkward and usually best forgotten.

But this Ibbetson story had magic on it. A month or so went by, and Raphael did indeed send around a copy of his play. Constance, having nothing better to do than rest and pray during air raids, read it—and found it woeful. It was not "theater." It would not "act." Still, there was something challenging and odd in it, and Miss Collier thought that it just might be possible to rewrite *Ibbetson* into a piece that could be played on the stage.

It is appropriate that a Countess should enter the scene at this point. There is a Countess in *Ibbetson,* a very remarkable Countess. The real Countess who walks on stage now, briefly, was known as the Countess of Huntington, a British lady whose contributions to the war effort took the form of benefits for the wounded. She called Constance on the telephone and asked her to take charge of some side shows at one of her entertainments.

The idea did not amuse Constance. By now she had become so immersed in *Ibbetson* that she could think of little else. She found herself making an exceedingly bold request.

"If you will allow me to do exactly as I please and will give me a little money," she told the Countess, "I will arrange a performance for you that will exceed all expectations."

I offer the Countess of Huntington my blessings and my thanks, but she must have been a very innocent entrepreneur indeed. She went for it. She wrote out a check for five hundred pounds for a dream sequence, for a play that wasn't a play, and let Miss Collier go ahead.

Constance then rewrote every scene in *Peter Ibbetson.* She solicited Henry Ainley and Lilian Braithwaite and Owen Nares, collected a cast on the stage of the Vaudeville Theater, and astonished them all by announcing that they were to appear as characters in Du Maurier's novel. From Sir Herbert Tree, who had been annoyed both by John Raphael and by Du Maurier's story, she cajoled the use of His Majesty's Theater for a matinee on July 23, and she produced *Peter Ibbetson.*

Ibbetson made money for the base hospital at Étaples and that was the end of it in London.

Constance by now had been lucky enough to get some offers from Hollywood, and she thought arrangements could be made with the Shuberts for plays in New York. But she set sail for America with *Ibbetson* in her reticule and with *Ibbetson* on her mind and she called on exactly the one person in the world who could help her. That was Ned Sheldon, the man everyone in the American theater always called upon during his remarkable and—I pause to use the adjective thoughtfully and exactly—*noble* life.

Ned read the play, reached for his desk, seized a manuscript of his own, and tore it up. He had written a play called *The Lonely Heart* on the same theme as *Ibbetson,* but he decided instantly that *Ibbetson* was better. Specifically, he thought it was a better vehicle for my brother. But at that not quite good enough: Ned not only abandoned his own enterprise but patiently rewrote *Ibbetson* again.

Jack then took *Ibbetson* to Al Woods, who was celebrated for his productions of bedroom farces. I was not on hand at their interview, but it has been reported as follows:

Jack: "I have a play but I don't want you to read it."

Woods: "I just put up the dough?"

Jack: "That's it."

Woods: "What's it all about?"

Jack: "You'd hate it. But there's a big scene in which Lionel calls me a bastard and I knock him colder than a lobster cocktail. Matter of fact, I kill him."

Woods: "Great idea. Let's go!"

It is not to be supposed, of course, that Al Woods, an astute theater man, went into the production of *Peter Ibbetson* quite so casually as all that. He backed the play, presumably, because Constance Collier and Ned Sheldon and Jack Barrymore believed in it; but he did it chiefly because Jack said he would act in it. In the end, however, Woods lacked the necessary cash. Lee Shubert stepped in, skeptically, and became the producer. Florenz Ziegfeld loaned the special lighting stands to set up the strange effect of *Ibbetson,* and Maude Adams incredibly came forward to supervise those lights. It was Constance, with her great faith in *Ibbetson,* who passed these miracles.

In London, the part of Colonel Ibbetson had been expertly played by Henry Ainley, and this was the most exacting role, I suggest, in the show. It was a thankless role in which the old Colonel never for a moment excited the sympathy of the audience, and yet he had to be believable.

I had been contentedly working at the old Metro studios at Sixty-first Street and I was alarmed by the prospect of trying the theater again after nearly five years' absence. I did not want to act on the stage again under any circumstances, but I was in a predicament because of the facile nods and promises I had made to Jack and Ned over the beer. Moreover, when I essayed the role I could not get into the part. But Ned and my brother were elated with full-blown confidence, had great faith in me, and kissed me off with such lines as, "Oh, don't worry, old man, you'll be great on the night."

Jack himself, it turned out later, had misgivings of his own as he worked up his part. He pronounced that the wig he had to wear made him resemble a geranium. In strict accordance with the character of Peter as drawn by Du Maurier (it appears in all editions of the novel), Jack was fitted out with a beard. Jack admired the beard. He thought it kept Peter from being callow. But Beerbohm Tree killed the whiskers.

"Makes you look like a dentist, old boy, like a dentist," he complained. From then on, Peter appeared hairless.

Jack had other complaints. He objected to being romantic, and this was, indeed, an objection he voiced all his life. He was continually afraid of being dubbed a pretty boy, and possibly it is valid to suggest that in doing so many of the things that pretty boys should not do he was working out some embarrassed defense mechanism in his psyche. But let the head-feelers and couch doctors explain that one.

This was not, however, the major problem. The major problem was me. I found it impossible to realize the character I was trying to depict. I had no model. I had no experience to draw from. I had no friends, as in *The Mummy and the Humming Bird,* who could say, "Colonel Ibbetson is precisely like this. Look at him. Memorize him. Think about him. Now go and be like that."

I took what little comfort I could from Herr Kant's line, "Time passeth not," and so on, but so far as chronology was concerned with special reference to myself, I realized with horror that the dress rehearsal of *Peter Ibbetson* was virtually at hand. In my distress, I locked myself in various rooms in my attempt merely to memorize my lines, but always with the same result. I could not memorize them. I finally ran out of rooms.

One afternoon when I was hidden behind a piece of scenery during a rehearsal, I overheard a *sotto voce* conversation between Constance and Jack:

Constance: "But Jack, deah, the dress rehearsal is almost upon us and so far he has done absolutely nothing."

Jack: (Facial expression not indicated because of darkness) "Yes, yes, Constance, quite so. Well, perhaps that Personage you're always calling upon will be able to help us. Let us hope so."

Constance: "Personage I'm always calling on? Who?"

Jack: (In a whisper) "God."

That night, Sir Herbert Tree had sent tickets for Jack and me to see his opening in *Colonel Newcome*. I was against it, although not to attend was a rudeness. Jack was kind to me in my travail, but it was a charitable kind of kindness, not the kindness of confidence. Constance insisted that we attend, and Jack, I suppose, thought it didn't matter much since I would never be able to learn my lines anyway.

As my brother and I slid unhappily into our seats I held a newspaper in front of my face. Behind the paper I had my part, which I was still desperately trying to commit to memory. I was mumbling my own lines as the play began. But eventually, to my mixed rage and relief, Sir Herbert came on and I had, for the sake of manners, to lower my newspaper and attend his performance. We gave him the proper reception and I slumped back in my seat, wondering if arsenic would not be better than the rope.

It happened then. I realized clearly that here were probably all my Christmas presents for the rest of my life.

There was my Colonel, including make-up. Of course, it was Thackeray's Colonel Newcome that was being presented, but it was also Du Maurier's. There were little sounds, breathings, gurglings, that were exclusively the property of Sir Herbert's. And wrapped up in all of them, there was my own Colonel.

By the grace of God, with the assistance of Sir Herbert Tree, my happiness was unbounded. All I then had to accomplish was what a famous vaudeville entertainer of the time used to do when he imitated Grant, Cleveland, and Roscoe Conklin: I simply had to remember Tree as well as I could, let the chips fall where they would—and I suspected there would be plenty of chips.

I rejoiced, wordless, all through the after-the-theater supper with Sir Herbert, and at the rehearsal the next afternoon, the last before the crucial dress rehearsal, I, with the grace of the August Personage my brother had respectfully called upon, and with the assistance of Sir Herbert Tree, knocked the part of old Colonel Ibbetson for a row of Chinese pagodas. I really did.

Sir Herbert attended our dress rehearsal. He sat far back in the audience, and when it was all over I approached in some trepidation to pay my respects. He said:

"Congratulations, Lionel. Very good. Very good indeed. By the way, old man, I seem to know that old fellow of yours. I should say he must have been drawn from life?"

I muttered that it 'tweren't nothing and departed with hosannahs on my lips.

Our opening was, in the words of the trade, a smash hit. For once, with no reluctance, I applaud an audience. New York audiences are like London audiences in this respect: there can be no audience tougher if they don't like you, but there can be none sweeter if they approve. I think I should say, if pressed for the proportions of a successful play, that they go like this: one-third consists of the play itself, as written; one-third of the production; and one-third of the performance. In our instance, our God-given first-night audience was fully fifty per cent responsible for everything.

That God-given audience put up with things that would have been hooted off stage at an amateur effort in Alumni Hall in Oswego. Not once, not twice, but three times our scenery fell down in the same place, but there were no laughs. Our audience was always with us. It is still an abiding wonder, a truly thankful and great and special thing to me, even at this date, to recall that audience. I cannot recall it without emotion.

All told, *Peter Ibbetson* ran for nearly two years, counting the tour which Jack and Constance made with it. Jack was magnificent, and Constance Collier as the Duchess of Towers was magnificent. And let's stop kidding ourselves. I was good, too.

Even the critics and audiences understood that they had seen a great play and that it had been well acted. From *The New York Times* of April 19, 1917, we had this comment:

> Du Maurier's "Trilby" had scarce run its eventful course in Harper's Magazine and its memorable popularity was at high tide when a makeshift play was fashioned from its pages and exhibited with great success and profit on the boards of this country and England. But his earlier, rarer, and finer novel did not reach the stage until a quarter century after it was written, and, except for a single performance for a war benefit in London, was never presented to an audience until last evening. Then, at the Republic Theater, the play of "Peter Ibbetson" was given here, an interesting and ingenious play that catches something of the fine fragrance, something of the strange elation of one of the happiest stories ever told.
>
> It is appreciatively mounted and it is admirably played. There is Laura Hope Crews as Mrs. Deane, there is Constance Collier as that wondrous woman—Mary, Duchess of Towers. There is Lionel Barrymore as the loathsome Colonel Ibbetson, Lionel Barrymore, whom our stage has not seen in nearly a dozen years, returning to give a graphic and telling performance and share the honors with his brother John, who leads the company with his resourceful, finely imaginative playing as Peter Ibbetson. The reappearance of these two gave a special quality to the evening, and at its great moments the Barrymore-Drew box wept as one tear duct.

On April 22, again in the *Times,* there was a bouquet, signed by Alexander Woollcott:

> The performance at the Republic is an uncommonly good one. The central role is in the hands of John Barrymore—and his performance, while not yet as complete and perfected a thing as was his per-

> formance in "Justice," is none the less, by virtue of its finer moments, as lofty, imaginative and distinguished an achievement. . . . John Barrymore is playing well a role his father had long hoped to play.
>
> Then the production of Peter Ibbetson brings back Lionel Barrymore, appearing with his younger brother for the first time since the engagement of Barrie's "Pantaloon," at the Criterion in 1905—a dozen years in which he has done almost no work upon the stage. Lionel Barrymore's career began in the days of his distinguished grandmother, in the company of whose famous Mrs. Malaprop he made his first appearance. He is best remembered by this generation of playgoers for his work in Augustus Thomas's "The Other Girl," and for his exceptionally graphic performance as Giuseppe, the organ grinder, in "The Mummy and the Humming Bird," Mr. Drew's play of fifteen years ago. His most distinguished success was one in what are absurdly called "character parts," as if there were any other kind, and it is in such a part—the evil Colonel Ibbetson, artfully and richly played—that he returns to us, a most welcome prodigal of the stage. The greeting that awaited him must have warmed the cockles of his foolish heart. . . .

Ibbetson was played at the Republic Theater, where I had worked seventeen years ago for James A. Herne. He had told me then—as he gently set me at liberty from the cast—that I ought to do character parts.

16. Concerning Milt Shanks

BETWEEN 1917, when all the improbable circumstances of *Peter Ibbetson* brought me kicking and protesting back to the stage, and 1925, when by accident I escaped to California, it appears in the program that I worked in about a dozen plays. Some were good, some were bad. Sometimes I was a good actor, sometimes I wasn't. At any rate I do not propose to discuss them all; not, of course, in indulgence of modesty, but simply because I do not remember much about some of them, especially the ones in which I was terrible.

During this time Jack found his voice in his great plays, in *Redemption,* in *Richard III,* and in *Hamlet.* Ethel had already found hers and she continued and grew better. Both of them are known, I suppose, to almost anyone in America who ever went to a motion picture, but as great as the screen is or could be, and as respectable a medium for great expression as it is in the hands of directors with taste and sense, I have to say that if you have not seen John Barrymore or Ethel Barrymore on the stage you do not know them. I mean, and with no detour around Robin Hood's barn to reach the point, you did not know them for the superlative artists they always were. The difference between acting in motion pictures and acting on the stage is vast, as any tyro call boy in a neighborhood little theater can explain at length, and this is one phase of it: just as

Meissonier obtained *because* he had to create his art on odd-shaped blocks of pear wood, and just as John Keats contrived beauty *because* he was limited to fourteen lines in a sonnet, so does the theater make a triumph from its own limitations of proscenium arch and footlights, second-act curtains, and performances at 8:40. The screen, with its illimitable scope, and the theater, with its confinement, are—to rub the truism in—plainly not the same. Nor is the acting. Give motion pictures credit. They deserve it. But let's not confuse these two things which are not the same thing.

In Jack's instance an illustration springs obviously to mind. It was not his profile that made him great in *Richard III*.

Lest this be mistaken for a blanket indictment of motion pictures, let me have another go at it. Motion pictures can perform and do perform many things better than they can be performed on any stage by any actors. A coloratura can sing certain songs better than a basso profundo. I want to avoid a sharp letter from Eric Johnston.

The plays of my own which may be worth a look at were *The Copperhead, The Jest,* and *Macbeth.* I enjoyed one of Broadway's most thudding failures in *Macbeth,* but later on I shall manage to grumble a few words about it anyway.

One night early in 1918 Augustus Thomas missed the 6:15 for New Rochelle. Having nothing better to do he dropped in and saw the first act of *Peter Ibbetson,* then caught the 9:15 and went home. And here they are again, those agents of the Lord. I had not realized until I began to set all these words down about my behavings and misbehavings how precariously a man controls his own fate.

Upon grasping this, I hastily reread Ecclesiastes and confirmed my suspicion that all is vanity and nobody amounts to much.

Gus Thomas had written the play, *The Copperhead*, and John Williams was going to produce it. *The Copperhead* concerns the Civil War, and in particular a Pennsylvanian named Milt Shanks who was suspected of being a spy for the South and of having given information to the Confederates which caused the death not only of some of his friends but of his own son. Years later, many years later, when the happiness of his granddaughter is at stake, a dramatic incident and a letter from Abraham Lincoln reveal that he was not a traitor.

At the beginning of the play Milt Shanks is a man about forty-five years old. At the end he is a septuagenarian. This chance to play the same man at such widely different ages offers of course a *tour de force* opportunity for the actor lucky enough to get the part—but I do not know what particular thing I did in *Ibbetson*, whose character I had found in Herbert Tree's Colonel Newcome, that influenced Gus Thomas to believe I could play the bucolic patriot Milt Shanks. One of the deciding factors was that Williams and Thomas had nobody else.

They had tried indeed to find another actor, and the fact that they did not is one more example of the efficiency with which the agents of the Gentleman Upstairs look after me. Gus Thomas went all the way to Los Angeles to offer the part to Richard Bennett, who was in a Morosco play, and showed him a copy of *The Copperhead*. Dick, I suppose, had an engagement with a charmer that evening or was in a hurry to get over to the Alexandria bar or something of that nature, because it was obvious to Gus that he did not study the play carefully.

Bennett looked at the last act, at the great scene in which Milt puts on the Old Army uniform. This is the tremendous scene in the show. It is a curtain-lowering scene, the final scene, the one that makes the play.

"Oh, I don't know, I'm not sure, Mr. Thomas," Bennett said. "Dave Warfield had a curtain like that, you know. Wonderful play and all that, perfectly wonderful, you know, but I'm not sure. You'll excuse me now? Thanks so much."

Thus Richard Bennett turned down *The Copperhead.* Gus left Los Angeles heartsick, returned to New York, missed the train for New Rochelle, and offered me Milt Shanks.

As far as Mr. Shanks was concerned it certainly did no harm that I had been a lifelong admirer of both General U. S. Grant and of Colonel John Singleton Mosby, the brilliant Confederate cavalry raider who caused Grant more trouble than any other one man in a gray uniform. Mosby, as few persons realize today, lived until 1916 and wrote two books, *Stuart's Cavalry Campaigns,* and *Stuart's Cavalry in the Gettysburg Campaign.* It was part of the good fortune that has always dogged me that I had read these and all else I could lay hands on about Mosby, and that I had through my great regard for Grant studied all that I could about him and about his period. I thought his autobiography, which he prepared for publication by Mark Twain as he lay dying of cancer of the throat, was a magnificent effort. He wrote it to pay off his debts and to leave his children a little something. And so the hero worship I felt for these two men, the Confederate and the Yankee, led me on to find out something about what men were like and what the times were like during and shortly after the Civil War.

Since nobody else knows anything about Colonel Mosby, I am an authority on him. Perhaps you did not know that Grant and Mosby once met.

It was after the war. Mosby was bankrupt and desperate, a renowned captain without money and without opportunity. The South was on its knees trying to recover from the Occupation and from the carpetbaggers.

"Why don't you go to see the President?" Pauline, Colonel Mosby's wife, suggested.

"Ridiculous!" the Colonel snorted. "He would gladly see me shot."

"I don't think so," said Pauline. "He was a soldier."

Pauline must have been a remarkable woman. She made an appointment for Mosby to call on Grant at the White House and when the date had been set Mosby was in no position to decline it. He stood in the hall sweating out a long wait before he was ushered into the President's office. It was a big office and a long walk to the President's desk. Grant sat hunched over, chewing a cigar, looking down. Mosby squared his shoulders and stepped forward.

Grant looked up.

"Halt!" he commanded. "Come forward with your hands in the air."

Mosby told about this later. He said he knew damn well at that moment that he should never have been fool enough to present himself unarmed to General U. S. Grant. But he marched forward toward the President, his hands in the air.

Grant looked him over carefully before he spoke.

"Sit down, Colonel Mosby," he said politely. "You know, until this moment I was under the impression that you had horns, hoofs, and a tail."

The two had a talk and President Grant commissioned Colonel Mosby a United States consul on the spot. I think his post was Hong Kong.

At any rate, if there are any unreconstructed Confederates in the house I hope this anecdote makes them feel better toward U. S. Grant. He had warmth and humor after all. But as I was saying, it was reading stories like this and delving into the lore of the times that gave me a feeling for the people, North and South, during the Civil War, and made it possible to dramatize some of that feeling on a stage.

Most of my information was garnered in secondhand book stores.

To my mind there is nothing so beautiful or so provocative as a secondhand book store. In the instance at hand, it was secondhand book stores which built up my stage characterization and this, to be sure, comes around to echo the words about acting I set down some time ago. To me it is astonishing and miraculous to think that any one of us can poke among the stalls for something to read overnight—and that this something may be the sum of a lifetime of sweat, tears, and genius that some poor, struggling, blessed fellow expended trying to teach us the truth.

So, if you are going to play a part and that part, let's say, is a delicatessen shop owner, you are just as good in it as the total of all the delicatessen shop owners you know and have studied. If you are playing a boat builder, go to a boat builder and find out what he does. But since there were neither Confederate nor Yankee spies in New York for me to study in 1918, I went to the secondhand book stores and found them there.

I played as aforesaid two parts, Milt as a middle-aged man and Milt as an old man. Doris Rankin also acted in *The Copperhead.* She played Ma, my wife, in the early acts and Madeline King, my granddaughter, in the last act. If this seems like a confused family relationship, Doris actually being my wife, there was a precedent for it. In *Ibbetson* I had just enacted my brother's uncle and my nephew-brother had beaten me to death with a poker.

The Copperhead was Doris Rankin's debut on the New York stage. It came about simply enough one night at some restaurant when we were casting the show.

"Say, why not let Doris play that?" someone said. And we let her and she did it beautifully and that was all there was to it. She had been in and around the theater so much, all her life, that it did not surprise any of us that she could walk on and perform on Broadway. Only just now does it occur to me that she did an astonishing thing.

Jack had continued with *Peter Ibbetson* when I went into *The Copperhead.* On our opening night he was up in Hartford in his own show. Now, although as I have indicated before, none of the Barrymore-Drews then or now has ever been trapped into uttering a vis-à-vis compliment to another clansman, we did have and do still have tribal instincts. Years after *The Copperhead,* Jack called me—not to my face, God forbid with walls of fire—the best of the Drew-Barrymore tribe. I could wish sometimes that he had been a critic. He saw *The Copperhead* through an expedient that was typical of him. He bought out his own house in Hartford for one night, closed the show, and came down to New York to see me act. Ethel was there too. Well, the whole family always congregates to see the consecration of the bishop.

Ethel sat out front and suffered. So far as I was then concerned, nobody suffered enough. But it was worth it. I had a Galli-Curci triumph with fifteen curtain calls. I counted them carefully.

We had with us two young fellows, fifteen and sixteen years old, respectively, whom I had selected for parts and in whom I take pride, Chester Morris and Raymond Hackett. They were both excellent, although Chester gave me one extraordinary evening when he came down with a juvenile ailment, tonsillitis. In fact he had his tonsils out but arrived at the theater that evening late and had no time to reach my dressing room and inform me that he was going to work mute that evening.

He came on stage and opened his mouth at me and made gestures.

"Hah?" I said, waiting for my cue.

Chester mouthed and gestured.

"You mean to say that . . ." and I said his line for him.

Chester nodded his head affirmatively.

"And I suppose you also want to tell me that . . ."

We played it out that way for the rest of the evening.

The reviews were what we call "mixed," but I managed to come off all right for the most part. Here are some samples:

> If all the curtains in Mr. Thomas's new play were as strong as the final one, "The Copperhead" might be warranted to run till Johnny comes marching home. An audience that had listened all evening with respectful attention, but with interest slowly ebbing,

> burst into tumultuous applause which was deserved both by the dramatic moment itself and by the deep fervor and inward power with which Lionel Barrymore carried it. But in retrospect upon the play as a whole, the verdict is that of an ancient Yankee whose wife besought him to make the ball unduly high. "Woman," he said, "do ye think I'll drink through a rod of the brook to get a little rum?"
>
> The play is the dramatic (not very dramatic) rewagging of a tale by Frederick Landis.
>
> —*The New York Times,* February 19, 1918.

And John Corbin's comment in the *Times* on the 24th:

> ....From Lionel Barrymore, especially [speaking of the payoff of the play in the last act] all sense of remoteness fell away and one lived in the heart of the man, together with the majestic spirit of Lincoln. An audience that had sat for almost three hours in the doldrums rose in a mighty wave of exaltation and gave author and actor such an ovation as has seldom been witnessed in our rather cynical and trade-soiled theaters.

I insert these amiable comments without apology. The ones that break my back will come later. Barrymores and critics were never on hand-holding terms. I have, on principle, avoided knowing many of the fraternity because it sometimes turns out that when you get to know one you like him anyway.

While we are at liberty for a moment between plays, I believe this is as opportune a moment as any to tell a story about critics. Most of Jack's altercations in the theater were with audiences. He stopped his shows many a time to berate them for coughing and for laughing at the wrong time. In this instance, he proposed to stop the show and attack critics from the stage, a caper which was too drastic even for me to condone.

Heywood Broun told the story in the February 2, 1938, issue of *The New Republic:*

> .... But what I have in mind is *l'affaire* Barrymore. Scarcely a man is now alive who remembers the day and year. But one John Barrymore walked on the boards and used his entire head and not merely the lovely profile with which he now edges into pictures like a beautiful paper knife. He appeared in a play written by a friend and relative [probably Michael Strange's *Clair de Lune*]. It was a bad play and that opinion was set forth universally. The wrath of Barrymore, for some reason or another, centered upon two particular critics. One was Alexander Woollcott and the other your timid contributor.
>
> After reading the notices, Mr. Barrymore announced that on the second night of the play he purposed to make a curtain speech in which he would name and flay the miscreants. The other Barrymores advised delay, but Jack, quite justifiably, pointed out that the curtain speech must come soon, since the vehicle in which he appeared was but a reed in the wind.
>
> There was confusion and there were conferences. Ethel advised her brother that he had made his original mistake in reading the notices. The Barrymores, she pointed out, were an old theatrical family and aware both by tradition and experience that dramatic critics were less than the dust. Why stoop to single out one or two of the creatures?

Spencer Berger Collection

Lionel Barrymore directing the film debut of the Metropolitan Opera star, Lawrence Tibbett, in *The Rogue Song*, 1930

Spencer Berger Collection

Lionel Barrymore and Norma Shearer in *A Free Soul.* Academy Award Performance, 1931

Jack remained adamant. His speech was written and rehearsed and he intended to deliver it. Ethel Barrymore, in a panic, rushed out of the dressing room and managed to locate Uncle John at the Racquet Club. In those days he was the only player who had ever passed its portals. John Drew left his dominoes and toddled down to give his nephew Jack the party line. He supported the contention of his niece Ethel. Speaking with the weight of years behind him, he testified that never in his long career upon the stage had he ever committed the indiscretion of reading a review. He admitted that he was aware of the existence of a scribbling crew and he had also heard that these fellows undertook to instruct their betters in the art of acting. Fortunately their names escaped him. He had a vague impression that there was a reviewer called Charles Lamb. The idea of a Barrymore attacking any one of these persons seemed to him like shooting grouse out of season.

John Barrymore would not be moved, and so Lionel was summoned. He talked with far more vigor than any other member of the clan. Not content with advising Jack, he commanded him to hold his peace and preserve the honor of the family. Yet when he was done the rebel actor still shook his head and said, "My mind is made up. I know what I propose doing is unusual. That is the very reason why you can't dissuade me. I am going to talk about that pair of vultures in such clear and vigorous language that the story will make the front page of every paper in the country."

"You are mistaken," said the orthodox Barrymore. "The item on the front page will read 'Lionel Barrymore strangles his brother Jack in the dressing room before the performance.' "

And so the speech was never delivered but appeared in curtailed and milder form as a letter to the *Times.*

It remains, of course, to set the record straight. The play was indeed *Clair de Lune* and it was by Michael Strange, who was Blanche Oelrichs, Jack's wife. And it was not a bad play, it was a good play. It was excellently motivated, and besides its gossamer quality it had plenty of raw meat in it. If it had been written by some unknown instead of Jack Barrymore's wife it would of course have been hailed by the critics as a smash hit. Victor Hugo might have liked this play, and *come to think of it,* I believe he did. It was easy to tell that incidents and characters had been borrowed from his *L'Homme Qui Rit.*

As a coda to this chapter, I might add that to be inimical to critics per se would be a very great stupidity, but taking them by and large, after many years of necessary consideration of them, you are forced to the conclusion that had they been able to be executants of the things they criticize they would not have been critics. The constructive critics like George Bernard Shaw, or Hanslick, or Philip Hale (and I could if pressed name some more but not many) are the great ones. They could themselves excel in the arts they criticized. Anybody who has read Hale's astonishing book—an appreciation is what it amounts to —on Vermeer can easily discern that Hale would have to be a supreme painter in his own right in order to appreciate Vermeer as he does and in order to tell his audience about the various excellences of Vermeer. If Hale had not been such a talented executant himself he would not have been able to do this.

Even so, the fact that he wrote a book about Vermeer is a mere sort of table decoration. It wasn't necessary. Vermeer wasn't aided by the book. But thank God for that kind of critic, for Shaw and for Hale. They know the subject matter the artist is working in.

In our own times we have Mr. Virgil Thomson who is an eminent composer and also a critic. As great as Mr. Thomson is as a composer, candor compels me to say that he is a better critic.

Of course the artist, so-called, whether he be the author of music, or of drama, or the painter of a great picture, or whether he be an actor playing a part, does require the approval of an audience. There is no getting around that any way at all. He needs his audience, some kind of onlooker, some kind of auditor, and this can be a tremendous thing to him. But the matter for the artist, or actor, to understand is that the entire block in which he happens to be dying is not as interested in his personal life as he is. The trick, the skill, is to arouse somehow fifteen or twenty per cent of their interest so that this percentage of onlookers will be interested in his eventual demise. You cannot hope for a one hundred or even for a fifty per cent interest in any performance. If you could obtain that much you would be a miracle worker; but twenty per cent is something to be proud of. The great people, such as Balzac or Wagner, were able to induce about that much intelligent interest from their audience. I don't know which are the lower class of animals, audiences or critics.

I have been all kinds of a chore boy in the theater for a certain number of years but it goes without saying that I was never a critic. Once on a bemused evening, late, when my old friend Charles Darnton was grieving in a tavern because he had to write a review pointing out the deficiencies of a good companion in a Shakespearean offering, I tried to be of assistance by scribbling a few helpful lines on the beer-stained back of a tattered menu. I wrote:

"The Old Bird of Avon undoubtedly had an off day at the Mermaid when he wrote this part. It is not up to his usual standard."

For one reason and another this was never printed.

17. The Jest

DURING THE RUN OF *The Copperhead,* I became convinced that my memory was slipping. I might have employed this suspicion as a good excuse to escape from the theater back to motion pictures, which were silent then, requiring no recall of any kind, and back to my painting and my music; but it was beyond me at the moment to commit this intelligent fraud. I saw fright-shapes in the night, awakened in spasms of cold sweat, questioned my sanity, and fled in dismay to an alienist. That is what psychiatrists were called in those days. It had not yet become fashionable and routine to have a frustration for a conversation piece or to play with your libido. Anyone who went to an alienist was not more than a leap ahead of the loony cage, so I went in fear to Dr. Pierce Bailey, a distinguished specialist, and explained my predicament.

He asked me intimate questions. He found no snakes in my childhood recollections and no yearnings to marry my mother. So he said:

"Now, did you ever blow up on stage, forget your lines?"

"No," I said.

"OK," said the doctor. "You have a phobia. Everybody has a little phobia of some sort. Keep it. Good thing. I wouldn't tell anyone about it if I were you, but you won't forget your lines."

This reassured me and I went back to work, and to

sleep, securely coddling my private phobia, and to this day I have not missed an important cue. *The Jest* came along next for Jack and me and we had such a whale of a good time in this production that forgetting lines would have been nigh as improbable as mislaying the address of a favorite bar.

The Jest was a tragicomedy in four acts by Sem Benelli, one of the best-known modern Italian dramatists, in an adaptation by Ned Sheldon. It involved a conflict between Giannetto Malespini, a young poet of Florence at the time of Lorenzo the Magnificent, and Neri Chiaramantesi, a brutal captain of mercenaries. Jack played Giannetto and I played Neri. For years the poet has endured being persecuted and spat on by Neri and his rough henchmen. The final insult comes when Neri & Co. etch certain grotesque designs on his tender skin with the points of their daggers and throw him into the Tiber when he faints. There is also a girl they both love. In the end, Giannetto gets his revenge. This was a play of passion and crescendos in the high old tradition, as Latin as a poniard between the teeth. It was a lusty romp. Neri was a thankful role to me. He was by virtue of Benelli and Sheldon a hell of a guy, and after my years of hemming and hawing and uncertainty I enthusiastically took over in a part that cast me as the boss bully of the town.

The Jest went on the year Dempsey licked Willard, an event of importance to Ethel, who follows baseball and prize fights with the professional interest of a bookie. After seeing me in this play she commented that I could have thrashed them both. They were fortunately not in the cast, but it is a fact that I managed to have a commanding presence in *The Jest*, first, because I was playing that kind of a fellow, and second, because I was at least two inches taller than anyone else on stage.

Jack's Giannetto was even more of a character part than mine, despite the fact that I was full of sweetbreads in the way of muscle. He was supposed to be an esthetic, almost effeminate boy who achieved an enormous thrill out of being in personal danger. Then, as his character develops before your eyes, you see a person who is not physically supreme triumph over and kick the daylights out of a brute. This was Jack's personal interpretation of the part and his contribution to the writing of the role. He made his Giannetto bring about the absolute demolition of the great roaring heel Neri—then quailed when he saw how completely he had destroyed him. Jack was tremendous in the part and enjoyed creating it. It was Ned Sheldon, though, who made *The Jest* into a play that could be successfully acted.

There was never a complete playscript. The original Benelli play had been bought by Jack, but Ned took this and rewrote it entirely, especially the part that had been played in Europe by Bernhardt and Duse—Jack's role. *The Jest* as we played it was put together on scraps of old correspondence, on the back of envelopes, on paper napkins, on menus; and a great deal of it was never written at all. We created much of the play as we rehearsed it, in the manner of old-time vaudevillians:

"Now you cross over left and say this-and-that, and I'll say thus-and-so, and you say this, and I'll say that. Then So-and-so makes his entrance, and we both turn and you say . . ." and so on. Sheldon was a precisionist, but he could work this way too.

In the last act, when Neri lies in the dungeon in chains,

having been driven insane by Giannetto's murderous jest, a number of girls come to visit him. These are his former mistresses who are still in love with him, never mind that he has ruined them all and discarded them in the Roman gutter. These ladies were not in the original Benelli play. They were invented over bar and restaurant tablecloths and they were to the life. Each represented some girl one of us had, let us say, *observed.*

I suppose in the American theater there was never at any time such an astounding combination of professional writer, schooled by "Prof" Baker's workshop in the tight demands of "the well-made play," and fanciful creative artist, as resided in Ned Sheldon. As an instance of his playful genius I cite you this: for Neri's mad scene he needed wild, poetic words for the insane monster to mutter in his cell, in his chains, in his extremity. He had Neri say:

"Why do flies walk upside down? Where does the wind begin? Why do the stars come out, and why does an apple fall?"

I will reveal where Sheldon got those lines. One evening when we were discussing this scene and the lines that Neri should say in his madness, Ned suddenly got up and consulted the telephone book. He thumbed through it for a while and copied something. Then he returned to our table and gave Jack and me the words. He had taken them from an advertisement for *The Book of Knowledge.* More than likely you remember: "What will you say when your child asks these questions: 'Why do flies walk upside down? Where does the wind begin?' " and so on. So far as I know, no one ever nabbed Sheldon in this sparkling plagiarism. The Neri lines have always been accepted as near-poetry.

Many years after *The Jest,* when I was in Hollywood, J. Gordon Edwards acquired the motion picture rights to Sem Benelli's play. We met in a bar. Mr. Edwards began to give me the works.

"I have the Benelli play," he said, gloating. "Now I shall hire real actors for the parts and make a picture. Ha, I have the *original* play."

"So?" I said, because I knew something.

"So I'm a kind and generous man, I buy old actors drinks," said Edwards. "What will you have, Barrymore?"

"Beer," I said. "Better take my telephone number."

"Why?"

"You might want it some time. Never know," I said.

My telephone rang at 4 A.M.

"Hello, Edwards," I said.

"How in hell did you know who it was?"

"I knew you'd call me," I said. "You've read the Benelli play?"

"Yes, goddamit, and it isn't the same play at all. What the hell goes on? What play did you do?"

"Ned Sheldon's, of course," I told him. "Well, this is what you do. You see Alice Kauser. She's the manager. You have to see her, now, because if you don't Ned will give the whole thing away for nothing. You see Alice and you can buy *The Jest* more or less the way we did it on stage."

Jack and I wanted to do *The Jest* as a picture ourselves but we knew something else. It couldn't be made because of censorship.

Ned Sheldon was in love with the theater, as an ardent man may be in love with a lovely woman. When you were with him you almost believed that you too liked the theater. He was one of the most wonderful—and I use the word "wonderful" knowing what it means—persons I ever knew, one of the most extraordinary. He was utterly unselfish. It was he who took hold of Jack and made him say that he wanted to do something real in the theater and then made him do it. When he wrote he really wrote. No scene could go in unless it fulfilled his requirements: was it an important thing that was happening to these people at that time? did it actually mean something? He detested and deleted excess words, shearing off dross with the skill and the patience of a dedicated diamond cutter. The Barrymores owe him much.

Part of the success of *The Jest,* I think, can be attributed to the Sicilian Players who were in town and who fascinated us. We saw them many times and drew from them. Also, we drew from every Italian table d'hôte we had ever entered—from all the Italians who so far as we were concerned ever lived and breathed. No accents were required, since we were all Italians, but our Latin flavor was as high as the cry of "Vendetta!" in *The Mummy and the Humming Bird* or the squall of a street urchin in Piazzi di Spagna.

Arthur Hopkins produced and directed *The Jest.* I have never known a more erudite gentleman anywhere at all. Mr. Hopkins was a short, round man, designed on the teardrop architectural lines of a Billikin, who knew everything, but who possessed the extraordinary trick of making you think that you knew it first. Nobody, friend or foe, could tell when Hopkins had actually started directing a play. His company, like a kaleidoscope, had no pattern whatsoever at the beginning but invariably fell into amazing designs, which Mr. Hopkins apparently had nothing to do with. He operated on the principle of Machiavelli's great line in *The Prince:* "If you must do good, do it by stealth." That is precisely the way Hopkins directed. Anything he had to tell an actor was told a day or so after the blunder or the scene in question with such marvelous, dexterous stealth that the actor—being per se an egotistical dog or he wouldn't be an actor—believed that he had thought it up himself. So at the end of every production Hopkins found himself like Chouchard, the proprietor of the *Magasins du Louvre*, the father of ninety-seven children all of whom he denied.

The average person's heartbeat goes at the rate of seventy-two licks a minute. Battling Nelson, the prize fighter, had a pulse so calm that it never went as fast as fifty-four until after the fifth round. Hopkins was like that. His pulse never ticked normally until about the second act of the first night.

If Hopkins was like Battling Nelson, I myself share a peculiar distinction with a distinguished boxer, one George "Elbows" McFadden. Mr. McFadden and I are alike in that, in moments of extreme nervousness, we become sleepy. Maybe this is a kind of escape mechanism. At any rate, in moments of tension or danger, Mr. McFadden and I are almost certain to snore.

On the night of one of his big fights at the old Madison Square Garden, "Elbows" enjoyed his light rubdown before the battle, yawned prodigiously, stretched out on his table, and went to sleep. His opponent, a mean young fighter, tried to pull a fast one on "Elbows" by storming into his dressing room and yelling, "Hey, you big bum, come on out and get your licking!"

Presumably he thought that might intimidate the great

McFadden, but how wrong he was. McFadden was so genuine with his "I beg your pardon?" that the other fellow became scared to death and dropped the fight right there in the dressing room.

On the opening night of *The Jest,* I arrived at the Plymouth Theater in a state of nerves I might have felt if I had been waiting for the embrace of the Iron Virgin. "This, now, is the time they find me out," I said to myself. "I've got away with a few things so far with luck and chicanery, but they will catch onto me this time for certain."

In this frame of mind, and I promise you most sincerely that there is no more wretched frame of mind than an actor's terror on opening night, I sneaked into my dressing room, threw my overcoat on the floor, lay on it, and went instantly to sleep.

Hopkins came in just before curtain time, examined me, and sent for restoratives. Naturally he thought I was dead drunk. I suppose his heart may have gone a little faster at that moment, as he imagined the debacle in store before an opening night audience with a blubbering actor in one of the leading roles, but when he nudged me over with his toe I arose, applied my make-up, and went on stage, sober enough to feel like a man confronting the firing squad. Jack, poor devil, was not blessed with sleep. He was in the hands of hell.

Our first night went all right, after I had waked up. We performed with gusto, and then repaired to a table in a corner to await the words of our masters, the critics. As we toyed with claret and nonsense Jack and I play-acted, each pretending that he was concerned only with what the papers would say about the other.

"I am, of course, old man, merely taking a brotherly interest in whether the Neros will up their learned thumbs for your interesting performance."

"Nay, old fellow, the only matter of importance is whether they give you proper credit."

We raced each other for the newsboy. The verdict was for acquittal. Mr. John Corbin of *The New York Times* was in particularly good digestion that morning. He said:

> "The Jest" of Sem Benelli has fallen across the sky of a declining season like a burst of sunset color. It is probably not a great play. Even in the version which Edward Sheldon has prepared for American consumption, its welter of love and jealousy, hatred and revenge, is redeemed by no gleam of sweetness. . . . In the bravo, Neri, the glow of lurid passion is all but unrelieved. In the third act, much time is given to developing the fascination which he exerts upon erotic women—an episode which, however it may have interested Italians, impresses our Northern public as a rather sorry bore.
>
> . . . . A decisive share of the result is doubtless due to the brothers Barrymore. Neri is, to be sure, a part in which any competent actor, granted a sufficiently vigorous voice and body, could score notably. But it is nonetheless true that Lionel Barrymore illumines it with a touch of genius. Malicious bully though the huge mercenary is, he is yet comprehensibly deliciously human. An audience that is inwardly terrified at him, almost stunned by his ferocity, can yet laugh at his burly exhibitions of rage and strength, and his no less vigorous and picturesque oaths, with no dramatic letdown. Indeed, the effect is rather to intensify illusion. In Giannetto, John Barrymore has

> a more difficult part—a nature physically terrorized that yet burns bright in intellect and will and is thus able to cope successfully with his raging adversary. Except for the white flame of beauty, half spiritual half decadent, with which the actor invests the part, there is no phase which is not inward and subtly complicated. It is only on a second hearing that its involutions become clear. To the future of such actors, it is impossible to set any limit. Some day we shall see them, perhaps, as Othello and Iago.

A few days later, still amiable, Mr. Corbin rewarded us with these lines:

> The performance, (if I may venture a dramatic aside,) now ends at 11:35. This means a gain of three-quarters of an hour over the first night. When it has had time to boil down some more, I hope to see it again and satisfy my mind on the mooted question whether the text (which is translated by Edward Sheldon) is in prose or blank verse! I already know that much of it is iambic pentameter, and of a very high quality. Also I am confident that Lionel Barrymore has set a new mark in his development as a character actor, and that John Barrymore has revealed a new and distinct phase of his varied and extraordinarily interesting talent.

Mr. Burns Mantle selected *The Jest* for one of his ten best plays of the year and put us in his book. The play ran from April 9, 1919, through June 14, withdrew for the summer, resumed in September and ran through February 28, 1920.

No matter what your opinion of critics in general is (mine is not precisely that of Boswell's for Johnson), you are compelled, if you practice certain trades like mine, to depend upon them for your dinner. In New York these princes of foxes run in packs and are so potent that they can drag down any grape and you along with it, to make *their dinner*. The success of your show depends almost entirely upon how they react, often upon the state of their dyspepsia, sometimes upon the cordiality with which the producer's press agent bows them into the theater at the pass gate.

Save for the exigencies of eating, it being necessary to read the signs and know whether we could continue to pay the grocer or not, I have paid no attention to the critics and have not been guided by their numerous observations about how I should and should not act. I never saved clippings and have been hard put occasionally to dig up some necessary dusty quotes to go along with this apologia. This chore was doubly difficult because I seemed invariably to exhibit a tendency to search out criticisms which gave me the best of the deal. Sometimes these were difficult to come by. I have to confess, though, that there are a few critics who are apparently civilized gentlemen in spite of their ulcers and frustrations. Mr. Corbin was certainly generous when he called me a genius, a novelty, God knows; and so of course I have embalmed his words, although the pleasant epithet does not disarm me. The late Burns Mantle was a nice man: how could you dislike a fellow, even a critic, who said that "I have the greatest circulation in New York and the fewest readers"? And how could you be anything but fond of a man who told this story about his hard-of-hearing wife: In his early years

Burns could not scrape up enough cash to buy her one of those electric hearing devices, but by dint and frugality he finally got the money together, ninety-nine dollars and seventy-five cents.

He took the machine home, Mrs. Mantle clapped the thing on her head, looked at him expectantly, and said:

"Now, Burns, say something worth ninety-nine dollars and seventy-five cents."

Next go-round the foxes gnawed at my vitals. Next week *Macbeth*.

18. *Debacle at Dunsinane*

WALTER PRICHARD EATON used to argue that courage in the theater is after all nothing more than the imagination to see potential effects which the dullards cannot envision. It seems to me that there may be a large distinction between courage and imagination, especially in the theater, but however that may be, Arthur Melancthon Hopkins surely brought both qualities to any stage he directed. Merely to name some of his plays cinches the point: Ibsen's *The Wild Duck* and *The Doll's House,* Eugene O'Neill's *The Hairy Ape,* Don Marquis' *The Old Soak,* Laurence Stallings' *What Price Glory?, Holiday,* and *The Petrified Forest* are among his productions. And Arthur's dealings with Barrymores certainly required courage and imagination of high degree.

The qualities of speed and suspense in *The Jest* were largely written into the play by Ned Sheldon. It disturbed the senses like a musty odor, and under Hopkins' gentle direction it was well acted. It had something more. Hopkins gave it a production which created a haunting, heavy kind of beauty which a great many persons felt but few could analyze.

You found this quality again and again in Hopkins' plays. If you are like me you were always surprised and then puzzled about how he got it there.

After the two-year run of *The Jest,* when I had left the

cast, made a picture or so and appeared in *The Letter of the Law,* Hopkins sent Robert Edmond Jones to England to make detailed studies of the Tower of London, to pick up rare costumes and old pieces of armor for an enterprise that was pure speculation. He was going to star Jack in *Richard III,* one of the plays that the John Barrymore Board of Strategy, composed of Ned Sheldon, Constance Collier, Alexander Woollcott, Jones, and Margaret Carrington, included in their plans for a great and unique classical repertoire. This was one of the most remarkable dreams in the history of the modern theater, not only for its scope and integrity but for a negative reason also: the dream had nothing to do with money. There were no legal papers, no contracts. Either Jack or Hopkins was at liberty to call "Hold, enough!" after any curtain. The idea was simply to try to do some fine things in the theater, if you will believe there was ever anything so unselfish as that on Broadway.

Hopkins had discovered in *Redemption* that Jack was not indolent. That is to say, professionally. He had rehearsed endlessly. Now he flung himself just as ardently into *Richard III,* but there the partners found a flaw in their instrument. This was Jack's voice. It was good enough for comedy and it was an effective reed for most drama, but for Shakespeare you require the diapason of an organ. I suppose you could make a comparison by saying that Shakespeare is to all other theater what grand opera is to musical comedy.

Margaret Carrington was a retired singer who knew, as few persons in the world knew, the techniques of pulling out the stops and getting the most and the best out of a performer. She insisted on relation of words to meaning and she demanded hard work. Through Uncle Jack, she became my brother's coach.

And Jack found his voice. He toiled for months. The tones of Gloucester were the rehearsal for the iambics of Hamlet. Meantime, Hopkins did his job for *Richard III*. Working with Jones, he produced the sets which are still regarded as classic; then he went about directing the play in his own fashion.

Hopkins did what seemed to be a curious thing when he assembled his cast. He refused to allow any books of the play on stage. The actors were handed typewritten parts with no written directions, merely the words they were to recite. Hopkins then commanded them to treat Shakespeare with no respect whatever, explaining that respect invariably brought about a funereal effect. He told them that as he saw it *Richard III* was a melodrama and ought to be played as such. He especially cautioned his players against reading the lines as if they were cold verses in a dead language.

Those of you who have winced or yawned as some high school instructor with a degree in physical education dissected Shakespeare syllable by syllable and dactyl by spondee, scattering the meaning and the beauty on the oily floor to be trampled under his fallen arches, will applaud Arthur Hopkins' approach. He did not tremble in awe before Shakespeare's words and he did not underscore them, either. He assembled a cast with no professional Shakespearean experience and introduced them to literature as if it meant something. Jack was in thorough agreement with all this.

Hopkins found Jack unsparing in preparation. "Of all the actors I have known," he once wrote, "he was the most conscientious and untiring in preparation. Nothing was too much trouble. He would go to the costumer, the bootmaker, the wigmaker, the armor maker, twenty times each, forty if necessary to get everything right. He was the first to know his part. He would rehearse each time as though it were a performance. He was never late, never made excuses. To him perfection was the aim, and its attainment could not be too much trouble. He loved creating a part, and once that excitement had passed, the part interested him no more. He was not the actor who wanted to recline on a long run."

Later, Arthur Hopkins presented Jack in *Hamlet,* the role with which I suppose everyone associated my brother in the theater. It was *Richard III,* however, that Hopkins really loved. In that, he always said, he had glimpsed the real greatness of Shakespeare.

Richard III filled the Plymouth and might have run forever. There were plans for productions of *Cyrano, Peer Gynt, Faust,* and *Richard II*. But *Richard III* was abruptly closed before it had scarcely begun. Jack suffered from a nervous and physical breakdown which kept him out of the theater for eighteen months.

"He was that rarest of phenomena," Hopkins said, "the actor who hated to act. He loved to create, but once that had been accomplished, he was like an artist who could not bear to look again upon a finished painting, or a writer who was nauseated by a glimpse of some past creation. This is a feeling that artists will readily understand. That he would have had an unparalleled career there was no doubt, and he knew it. He did not forsake undreamed-of realms. His renunciation was with full knowledge of what he was leaving. He was in no sense what the theater knows as a trouper, what his forebears had been, what his uncle John and sister Ethel were. The creative part of the theater he loved. Its repetition was unbearable."

Arthur now turned to *Macbeth*. He was convinced I could excel in the part, and loyally took oath only a few days before his death that I was a good Macbeth; but unanimous opinion, including my own, is against him.

I have to confess the truth. I did *Macbeth* in a fit of pique. I had been working for Whitman Bennett in Yonkers because I still preferred the relatively easier labor of the films, with time off for my experiments in music and painting. And Whitman Bennett did not pick up my option. It occurs to me now that I had no particular reason to imagine that he would pick it up. At the time I thought it was outrageous, and I was in this sulking mood when Arthur Hopkins reached me on the telephone.

After the usual amenities he said, "What about *Macbeth?* Remember, we discussed a *Macbeth* for you during *The Jest?*"

We had discussed it. I had discussed it seriously, but like *The Jest* I had not meant it seriously. I knew in my heart that I was not a Shakespearean actor. But now, having been fired by Bennett, with my ego bruised and the grocers yelping for cash, I would have undertaken anything that the astute Arthur Hopkins offered. If he had asked me to play all the parts in the Last Supper, I suppose I would have tried to do it. I would have been about as successful as I was in *Macbeth*, too.

I did not prepare myself for Shakespeare with anything like the ardent dedication that my young brother put into his novitiate. It stands to my discredit that I did not, but at this hoary date almost thirty years after the event I believe that no one will accuse me of fumbling around for excuses for a failure. God knows I have had successes far beyond my merits, all of which I have thoroughly enjoyed, and I do not mind telling you that I was no good in *Macbeth.*

My voice was considered all right. Jack had gone to Mrs. Carrington to get a rasp out of his throat. He went to her humbly acknowledging his fault, conquered that fault, and emerged stronger in every other department. Many a champion, I suggest, has become great because he was compelled to overcome a weakness; whereas the smug man remains merely adequate.

Presumably it seemed like a fair enough wager that if one Barrymore could do Shakespeare so could the other, but they had the wrong Barrymore for *Macbeth.* They should have tried Ethel. I did not go to Mrs. Carrington, and I did not learn anything, and I was a failure.

Hopkins, on his part, gave *Macbeth* the same careful imaginative production with which he blessed Jack in *Richard III.* We had the sets by Jones and we rehearsed it with the same techniques I have already described. But let it stand at this: I had all I could do merely to master my lines, to remember my words, let alone create or even imitate an interpretation of a vast, complex, traditional, and disputed character. I was not afraid of Shakespeare, that gentleman being safely dead, but there are some actors who can "read" him and some who cannot. I was one of the illiterates.

The important thing to fix in mind about *Macbeth* is of course whether you consider that the Thane operated under his own free will or not. Was Macbeth indeed a man of evil and overpowering ambition following his own course of action and murder toward the kingdom of Scotland? Was Lady Macbeth his inspiration or only his "unsex'd tool"? Did the witches inspire Macbeth and lead him on, or did they merely not tell him what he wanted to hear and bolster his terrible aims? The scholars are split on these points. William Hazlitt holds that Macbeth was "tempted to the commission of guilt by golden opportunities, by the instigations of his wife, and by prophetic warnings. Fate and metaphysical aid conspire against his virtue and his loyalties." Charles Lamb says that Shakespeare's witches "originate deeds of blood, and begin bad impulses in men."

Against this, Hiram Corson, the Cornell scholar, argues that the theory is inconsistent with all of Shakespearean drama, that Shakespeare never presented any character as the sheer victim of fate at the outset. They were all free agents at the start, and the weird sisters in *Macbeth* represent merely the powers of evil which are ever attracted to the kind of soul which elects to get attracted. Following the same argument, it then seems that Lady Macbeth was more of a gun moll than an inspiration for the murders.

It can also be pointed out that Banquo interviewed the sisters as well as Macbeth and that Banquo maintained his integrity. Everybody who saw them did not necessarily, therefore, become a murderer.

As for the lady, it can certainly be argued that she was not ambitious on her own hook but was merely a wifely accomplice in the wicked yearnings and machinations of her bad husband. In the third scene of the second act, when Macbeth returns after his visit to the King's chambers and describes what he saw—including what Lady

Macbeth had done—in the lines including "the murderers, steep'd in the colors of their trade, their daggers unmannerly breach'd with gore," the lady faints. She is not pretending. It is a real faint. Macbeth shows no remorse, but Lady Macbeth does, constantly. It is she who cries: "What, will these hands ne'er be clean?"

As a portrayer of Macbeth I was confused by these considerations, and I am still confused. I am not sure to this day which of the scholars prevails in the argument, even though I personally was plagued by the crones and they were not. I had to get out on that stage and act, witch-ridden.

> Ere the bat hath flown
> His cloister'd flight, ere to the black Hecate's summons
> The shard-borne beetle with his drowsy hums
> Hath rung night's yawning peal, there shall be done
> A deed of dreadful note.

The dreadful deed was done, so far as I was concerned, on the night of February 17, 1921, when the curtain of the Apollo Theater went up.

If our *Macbeth* had been performed by a company of Siddons and Irvings capable of giving the production all it deserved, I think we would have had a very great evening. Jones had given us a spacious, abstract, beautiful setting. Figures came out of darkness and were invested in darkness again. There was a quality of nightmarish distortion in some scenes, a feeling of wicked dreams, and no reality. The whole thing was akin to the poisonous brew of the cauldron, and there was a score by Russell Bennett to accentuate the descent into dark places of the mind. All of this scenery of pure mood, beautiful and effective as it was, flew in the face of tradition and perhaps did not win the approval it deserved. I felt, though, that although we failed as a play and I failed as an actor, we had—or Arthur Hopkins had—put together a tremendous new kind of dramatic orchestration. But nobody liked us.

I don't regret it. I am happy that I did *Macbeth*. I might have wondered all my years if I might not after all have been cut out for a Shakespearean actor, having failed to find my comfortable niche anywhere else. I might have been accused, and I might have accused myself, of being afraid to try. I found out under the most impressive auspices.

The critics—and I reluctantly put incense on them by quoting them in my book—were as unanimous as the time of day on jewelers' painted clocks. They damned me. I grieved, but after consulting my conscience I decided that they were only voicing my own sentiments. Both Heywood Broun and Alexander Woollcott, having after all been to night school, were kinder in their observations than I was.

Master Broun delivered himself of a line that became famous and is quoted to me to this day, to my embarrassment. For the benefit of any members of the audience who might not know, I have to explain first that there is in New York a famous ticket agency named McBride's. Broun said:

> Lay on MacDuff, Lay off McBride.

Mr. Woollcott pinned me down as follows:

> The most willing and most expectant audience of the current season assembled last evening at the

Apollo Theater for the première of "Macbeth," which, properly enough, they looked forward to as the natural successor of "Richard the Third," which had been given a year before with the same imprint and with much the same talents or the same inheritance.

Here was another Shakespearean tragedy produced by Arthur Hopkins, produced for its own sake and as a separate masterpiece, rather than any mere part and parcel of some stock-room repertoire. Here was another Barrymore to play the leading role. And here was the extraordinary and still experimental Robert E. Jones to robe and light and color it and give it background. It bade fair to be a first night of great memories. That audience dispersed quietly a little before midnight suffering chiefly from shock.

Shocked they were to find that it was within human power to rob that swift tragedy of so much of its excitement and of every atom of its baleful nightmare quality. Shocked that Lionel Barrymore, while often good and occasionally very good, should never once have brushed greatness in all the length and breadth of the play. Shocked, above all, that Mr. Jones, for all the three or four high moments of great beauty that he achieves, should have indulged in such impish antics of decoration as to become the star of "Macbeth," a "Macbeth" that will be talked of till the cows come home—as an oddity.

. . . . But after all, the loveliest sight that the revival afforded was just the sight of Ethel Barrymore sitting in the royal box, and the moment of highest enthusiasm in the evening was the moment when she entered it.

Woollcott again:

> Last Thursday night an eager audience at the Apollo was deeply and reasonably disappointed by a revival of "Macbeth," which had promised well because Arthur Hopkins was to produce it, Lionel Barrymore to play it, and Robert E. Jones to weave its appeal to the eye. From Mr. Barrymore's workmanlike but by no means distinguished performance as Macbeth, the attention was distracted by Mr. Jones, who, in his effort to clear all the old rubbishy "scenic effects" out of the great play's way, was himself forever tripping it up.

And Burns Mantle:

> The "Macbeth" debacle in which Lionel Barrymore figured, [and others] were the outstanding features of the February productions. Much had been expected of and more had been hoped for the Barrymore "Macbeth." The revival was made under the direction of Arthur Hopkins, and the scenery designed by Robert Edmond Jones, both of whom had done much for John Barrymore's revival of "Richard III" the year before, but the result was unhappily disappointing. The scenic setting was extremely modern, modern to the point, in fact, of being weirdly fantastic, and neither audiences nor critics would accept it, with the result that the revival was withdrawn after twenty-eight performances.

Ethel had left the Flower Hospital to attend my Macbeth. She hurriedly returned to it after the performance.

Jack was on hand and added at least a smile to the obsequies. He thought that E. J. Ballantine as Malcolm and Sidney Herbert as Banquo looked alike when they stood together. "Like a pair of sleeve buttons on a coat," Jack observed.

Arthur Hopkins to the day of his death insisted on recording a dissenting opinion about my Macbeth. He said in a letter to a friend of mine on December 29, 1949, a few months before his death, some words that are the kindest I am sure that will ever be spoken of me. I print this letter wagging my eyebrows with joy, but not a word of it is true:

> That he was the most gifted character actor of our time was revealed by his unforgettable portrayals in such widely divergent characters: the Organ Grinder in "The Mummy and the Humming Bird," Colonel Ibbetson, Milt Shanks in "The Copperhead," Neri in "The Jest," and above all—"Macbeth."
>
> He more completely lost all personal identity in his portrayal than any other artist, man or woman, that it has been my privilege to observe in the process of unfolding creative wings. Other great artists with whom I worked were not so successful in leaving themselves wholly off stage when the characters took the stage.
>
> This, of course, is the ultimate magic of acting, the complete legerdemain. No one knows how it is accomplished. It is a gift that cannot be transmitted to another. For me, at least, the miracle disappeared when Lionel left the stage only to be seen again in the too seldom flights of Laurette Taylor. We had experienced it earlier with Duse. . . .

Emily Hapgood once spoke to me of Jack's abandonment of his gifts as "Roman extravaganzas, casting golden plates into the river." How doubly

> extravagant is the picture of Jack and Lionel seated together at the river's edge. I would not attempt to say which was the more wasteful.

Isn't that something?

Arthur never forgave either Jack or me for deserting the stage for Hollywood, but in unblushingly quoting the foregoing letter, I hope I have spun the prayer wheel and fixed his blessing on myself after all.

19. Good-by to Broadway

FAILURE BY ANY kind of an artist who has the egotism to thrust himself before the people and dare the consequences is bleak enough, but when you are an actor and have been snubbed you feel like the only sick goldfish in the aquarium. By this time I had built up a certain amount of confidence, although I had not signed a truce with the stage, and had come to believe because of the previous successes that, after all and in spite of everything, I was a player. The *Macbeth* accident chastened me; I sulked in my tent and grumbled that I had known all the time that working on the stage was a miserable and obscene way to make a living.

Arthur Hopkins understood, among the many other things he always understood, that salvation for me as an actor required the immediate application of psyche-solacing unguents, soothing syrups, and possibly a resuscitator. He set about working his therapy immediately and seized on *La Griffe*, a play by Henri Bernstein adapted by Louis Wolheim and Edward Delaney as *The Claw;* and he put me to work in this at once, slamming figurative doors so that I would no longer wince to the echoes of moans and groans over *Macbeth,* and if possible escape even from the leaping nerves of my own conscience. It was good medicine. It was a grand play—a play for young men to see, consider and soberly renounce some of their prunes and pride; for old men it is a rehash of their mistakes which they already know too well. Arthur Hopkins stinted nothing in making this a successful production, and he made it one; I would have departed the theater four years sooner if this one had not worked out.

The name of Louis Wolheim as the adapter of a play may surprise some of you. He is recalled as the rough and tough character player, one of the stars of *What Price Glory?* and as a hairy illiterate in many motion pictures. But Wolheim was a scholar. He was a distinguished mathematician and he was proficient in all languages I can name. I met him years ago in Ithaca when I played a villain in *The Romance of Elaine* with Pearl White and Crane Wilbur.

I was in *Elaine* as usual because of a stroke of fortune. Arnold Daly had been playing the villain and acting on the stage at the same time in this twenty-installment cliff-hanger. He took me with him to the studio one day. Somebody looked me over and offered me Daly's job. I refused, naturally, until I had consulted Arnold, but he told me that he was leaving the cast, and so I grabbed at this chore gratefully. I was some kind of terrible fellow who came up in a submarine and deviled poor Elaine. It amounted to nothing; the important thing was that I met Wolheim, who was earning thirty dollars a week and was happy. By the time we did *The Jest,* Wolheim was an old friend and I got him a job with the company; he took part in a battle in the third act, and made me look so good by losing that I won much more applause than I deserved. The next time I heard of him he was the star of Eugene O'Neill's *The Hairy Ape.*

Wolheim would have got anywhere he wanted to go on his own, but I claim to have started him.

I did *Laugh, Clown, Laugh* for David Belasco, which was either a bit of thinly veneered theatrical artifice or a grisly play of compelling power. Apparently the onlookers could not entirely make up their minds. Some of them were stunned. Belasco was an engaging fellow if not an authentic great man. He was the essence of what is theatrical. I think he had little or nothing in common with life itself. Other producers, the good ones, drew from life; but Belasco drew only from what was dramatic. He didn't steal his material but he was completely theater, and he viewed everything utterly in terms of the theater.

The Piker came next for A. H. Woods. It was a good play but it was not for me. I played the broken-down bank messenger who commits a petty theft and gets into trouble over his head. This was a bleak role and I could do very little with it.

Taps, for the Shuberts, came next. I was a bluff old sergeant and wound up sniveling in the third act. Not so good.

My third venture of the season was *Man or Devil,* by Jerome K. Jerome, again for the Shuberts. This was not an ambitious drama. It had no brains, no great problems, no sex. It was an old-style piece, the kind of thing Joseph Jefferson might have done superbly. It had the quality of a fairy tale, with its sailors, sea captains, and Gretchens. It frolicked and rambled—and it was all in all a pretty good show.

Man or Devil opened at the Broadhurst Theater on the evening of May 21, 1925, and ran for twenty performances. I am glad that this was a reasonably happy produc-

Spencer Berger Collection

Lionel Barrymore, 1932

Spencer Berger Collection

The three Barrymores in *Rasputin and the Empress,* M-G-M, 1932
Top: at ease on the sound stage. *Bottom:* in costume

tion, if far from a great one. *Man or Devil* was my last play.

And so the early Twenties saw the end of my work on the New York stage and the beginning of twenty-five years in motion pictures. They also saw the conclusion of something else which will be of little interest to the reader save only if, having hung on this far, he has tried to stick confused clues together and determine what manner of person this Barrymore really is. I am trying to indicate throughout that I am an unusually nice fellow, but I perceive that some of the evidence is against me.

Not to excuse myself for anything but simply to set down what seems to me to be true, I suppose that my frustrations as a painter, my preoccupation with music, and my obsession with the idea that I wanted to escape from the theater contributed toward making me a difficult person to live with. These and all the other weaknesses and instabilities which may mark even persons of the highest good will—and none of us in our hearts ever doubts his own essential good will—made me abrupt, made me thankless, made me thoughtless, made me sour. I suppose that if Doris and I had had a small independent income and the leisure which goes with it, and could have pursued and patronized the many things we actually had in common, I suppose then that our marriage would have had a better chance. As it was, in part because I was a triptych personality emotionally involved but unsatisfied in three arts, I made our marriage impossible and allowed it to dissolve. Doris was to blame in no respect. The only fault that can be laid to her is that in comparison with anybody else she always came off the better.

Doris was granted an interlocutory decree of divorce from me on December 2, 1922, after the findings of special referee J. Gordon Flennery, of Poughkeepsie, had been submitted to Supreme Court Justice Joseph Morschauer. Such papers and testimony as there were in this sad case were made decently inaccessible except to parties interested in the suit. We concluded our depressing business as quickly as we could and with as much privacy as possible, with no recriminations. We did not regard divorce casually, or as a matter in which actors and actresses are specially privileged. I do not so regard it today. The legal dissolution of a marriage is a serious and a tragic thing, and most certainly a thing which does not permit of exploitation for the mere satisfaction of anybody's curiosity. I am compelled to report my divorce because I have chosen to write a book and this is part of the record. It happened. There it is. Any reader who thinks the worst of me for it is not only privileged so to think, but is correct.

Miss Irene Fenwick was born in Chicago and made her stage debut under her own name, Irene Frizzell, in the chorus of H. W. Savage's production of *Peggy from Paris* in 1904. A month later she was the leading lady of this show.

She became one of Broadway's most engaging stars in light comedy roles, playing for Charles F. Frohman at the Lyceum in 1910 in *The Brass Bottle,* and going on from there to a number of interesting plays: *The Speckled Band, The Importance of Being Earnest, The Zebra, The Million, Hawthorne of the U.S.A., Mary's Ankle,* and *Lord and Lady Algy* at the Broadhurst in 1921.

She was Antoinette with me in *The Claw* and Simonetta in *Laugh, Clown, Laugh.*

Master Woollcott in reviewing *The Claw* found that "Irene Fenwick acquits herself handsomely as the wife," a line which was written purely as dramatic criticism and not as the prophecy it turned out to be.

Irene was divorced from J. F. O'Brien in April, 1923, and shortly thereafter announced her engagement to me. I sailed for Havre on the French Liner *Paris* on June 6, on my way to Rome to work with Barbara La Marr, Jack Daugherty, Montagu Love, and Bert Lytell in Sam Goldwyn's *The Eternal City.* Irene and I met in Rome and were married on the afternoon of June 14 by Captain Ciamarra, a war hero, one of the forty men then alive who had been decorated with the Gold Medal of Italy. Senator Cremonesi, Royal Commissioner of the Municipality of Rome, was to have performed the ceremony but had to be excused at the last moment because of state duties.

Among our wedding guests were George Fitzmaurice, Florence Lawrence, Adrienne Morrison, Ouida Bergere, Alice Lawrence, Barbara La Marr, Montagu Love, Richard Bennett, and Bert Lytell. The film was interrupted just long enough for us to make a brief trip to Venice.

There, one evening as we emerged into a spangled night, we saw a crowd of gay people gathering across the canal and we asked a waiter about it.

"Some actress or other is going to entertain," he told us. So of course we went across the canal to applaud, and there, working in a night club, was Marie Dressler. She was playing the equivalent of the Italian subway circuit, Venice, Naples, Rome, and so on, and we had a vast and funny reunion.

That was amusing. What struck us in Venice seriously, a thing that we never forgot, as we would look across seascapes of lapping tides almost bloodstained color in the sunset, catching the rippling reflections of pink palaces, and watching the red sails of fishermen signaling their return—and the frescoes and façades of great architecture and the cobbles of pavements where the Doges walked—what struck us was the knowledge that *we were not alone.* Turner and Whistler and Frank Brangwyn had been there before and had told us of these things. And there indeed on the walls was Tintoretto, his paint so fresh that he might have laid it on yesterday. It made us think that Tintoretto could not, in fact, have been the great artist that he was had he not been born in Venice.

We went to a house where they told us Wagner had lived for a while, and they told us a story. Verdi, when he heard that Wagner was in town, grumbled to himself and said: "Well, it is not my music, this new music, but it is great, and I must go and drop a card on him." So Verdi alighted from a gondola at Wagner's doorstep and presented his card.

"Herr Wagner cannot see you," a servant said.

Verdi drew himself up.

"Look at the name," he commanded.

The servant looked.

"Si, Signor Verdi, I am sorry, but Herr Wagner cannot see you. He died half an hour ago."

All of Venice, and all of Rome, too, was full of mystery and beauty and full of dark jokes, and all imbued with a strange atavistic familiarity. I suppose it is so for any fairly sensitive person who goes there with respect to ponder on the wellsprings of our literature and civilization. We felt always a kind of awe in the dusk of Roman evenings when we saw and recognized ghosts of centuries of history perched on the crumbling walls of the Old City.

Now it appears that about half the so-called motion picture colony has gone to Rome to make pictures or to make love. But there is nothing new under the sun, especially the Roman sun. We were there twenty-seven years ago and we were not the first.

20. Two for the Money

BUT IN 1925 I had no more notion of making a serious and permanent alliance with motion pictures than I had of becoming a tattooed man in a county carnival. I preferred pictures, of course, having found them much more relaxing than the stage, but having failed to add any luster to the Shubert escutcheon in my last play and having received no offers of employment from any source, I was again on view in a familiar attitude—at loose ends. Now enters Fate. As I have been at some pains to set down, the minions of Manifest Destiny never heralded their approach to me with trumpets, as in *La Forza del Destino,* or even with nods and becks. The subcontractors of *Le Papa Bon Dieu* have invariably caught me unawares, but I have this to say for them, with profound thanks: they never missed a performance.

I was rounding the corner of Broadway at 45th Street one late afternoon on an errand which I hoped would provide me with a job. I had proposed to the United Booking Office that I organize a company and take an abbreviated version of *The Copperhead* on tour. My eyes were on the pavement because I was avoiding a look at the Wrigley chewing gum sign. Jack and I for years had a superstition that it was bad luck for us to gaze upon this spectacular but harmless proclamation. I don't know why we thought so. We just did, and we avoided it as if it were a plague or a temperance worker.

In this stance I bumped into Maury Small, not a large man, and sent him staggering.

"What ho," said Small.

"Very little ho," I said. "Sorry to have damn near killed you."

"Think nothing of it," said Small. "What are you up to?"

"I am thinking hopefully of inundating the country with culture and superior acting," I said. "I am about to take out on tour a short chop of that great play, *The Copperhead,* starring that sterling actor, Mr. Barrymore. It occurs to me that this might be just the thing to save the nation. Also, but purely incidentally, I might make a dollar or so out of the enterprise."

Maury fell in stride with me but said nothing for a while.

"Don't do it," he said.

"So?" I said.

"So, remember me? I'm your agent."

"So you are. How could I forget?"

"You usually forget anything having to do with money," said Small. "Now, let's see about this thing. I think I can do better for you."

"How?"

"Movies."

"Sounds prosperous. You have a carefully nurtured sucker on hand?"

"No sucker at all. B. P. Schulberg. Let me talk to him first. Why not talk to him now? Here's my office, let's call him up."

We went into Small's office and he got Schulberg on the telephone in California.

"Ben, you know I always look after you," he said, "and I think maybe, just perhaps, there's a chance I could get Lionel Barrymore for you."

I couldn't hear Schulberg but I could imagine his first words.

"How much?" he said.

"Well, Barrymore isn't here just now, but I believe I could get him for you for say ten thousand dollars for one picture."

"Five thousand," I whispered to Small. "Four thousand."

"That isn't much money for him, but he'd like a trip to California," Small went on.

"For God's sake don't kid around. Take three thousand," I rasped.

"You'll confirm it? Ten thousand it is. You'll wire me, Ben? Thanks."

Maury waved me on my way. "There you are," he said. "We won't of course do a thing until he confirms that by telegram. Meantime, I'll go fishing."

"How do I get there?" I wanted to know.

"Why, that's understood. Ben will make reservations and everything. He'll wire us."

The remarkable Small did precisely as he said. He got out of town and went fishing, while Irene and I fumed about whether that deal was actually going through or not. Late the next evening Small called up, casually enough, and informed us that we were on our way to Hollywood. The picture was *The Girl Who Wouldn't Work,* with Marguerite de la Motte.

I have been here ever since. That deal ended my stage career entirely. I have never been back to the stage and I have never regretted it.

By long distance operation, Small then arranged for me to make four more pictures immediately at the same rate. Since pictures were made in four weeks or less at that time and since the income tax was not yet a devouring dragon, I felt flush and competent to exercise the one sure, never-failing talent that all Barrymores and Drews are heir to—extravagance. Irene and I put up at the Town House, which was and is exclusive and expensive, and I ran through the money as fast as I laid hands on it. We were soon broke again.

Hal Roach came to my rescue.

"I will give you fifteen thousand dollars for a picture," he said, and I took him up before his words could form an echo.

He cast me in a two-reel comedy in which my chief function was to let comedians bop me on the head with a rubber hose. Easiest work I ever did. I was content. But Small almost perished of apoplexy. He hurried to California to scold me.

"Are you crazy? Are you mad?" he yelled at me. "Don't you know what Roach is doing? He is hiring all the old-time stars, like Theda Bara and others, and putting them in these comedies for people to laugh at. This will kill you in pictures. Even a Barrymore can't survive this."

"You don't know Barrymores," I said. "We survive anything that pays."

Did, too.

Small himself moved to California shortly thereafter and through his offices I began to get the kind of work he preferred for me. My association with Metro-Goldwyn-Mayer began with a picture for George Hill.

I went to the studio one day, hopeful that they would

cast me in something, and I was referred to Mr. Hill, one of the powers. His face seemed familiar. I went home and worried about it, and then it hit me—this was "Tripod Hill," who used to carry Billy Bitzer's camera for D. W. Griffith. So I hurried back to Metro-Goldwyn-Mayer.

"I know you," I said, "but of course you haven't had the misfortune of seeing me in anything."

"Oooh yes," said George. "I know you. Let's go to work."

I went to work and I have been at work for Metro-Goldwyn-Mayer now these twenty-six years.

Jack grew weary of *Hamlet,* as he grew weary of everything. He shuttered his play after one hundred and one performances, just one more than the record set by Edwin Booth. He re-opened in November, 1923, closed again, and went on tour, abruptly calling a halt in Cleveland, where his last performance of his greatest role was seen in this country. He refused to appear in anything until two years later when, inspired by I know not what, he decided to take the great dare, that of challenging the British with an American Hamlet.

Why Jack did these abrupt things, why he always grew bored with his plays after he had mastered them; what he was escaping from, what antic personal gods he was defying, and what the lifelong search was all about that impelled him to acts that were sometimes mad, sometimes irresponsible, sometimes brilliant, I can explain no better than anybody else. I am inclined as the shadows grow longer to the theory that he was in revolt against the whole insecure pattern of his life, and that the insecurity sprang from the collapse of his frame of reference when Mum

Mum died when he was fifteen. He was at loggerheads with the world and he was at loggerheads with himself, and he knew it. We were always curiously alike. And just as I had never considered my real métier to be acting, so do I feel that it was not Jack's either. He could do it; but essentially Jack was another kind of an artist. He was a painter. My chief reason for saying this, now that so much is old in retrospect, is not that he had a talent for painting and drawing—and he did have it—but that I recall his way of talking. Invariably when he told something he eventually summed it up in terms of line and color. His words had more color than music in them. He was acute and biting and poisonously funny, but all this, come to think of it now, was defensive. Of course, exactly what frustrations he was defending I cannot be sure and exactly what personal Grail he pursued I cannot tell. He was a man who was in flight and in pursuit at the same time; no great wonder that his path was erratic, like some comet tugged by both earth and sun.

I have the feeling that I can understand this because on my own level closer to the ground I am a man who has been all his life in about the same predicament; but the understanding is more emotional than intellectual. Setting down the words to explain Jack Barrymore is like seeking the mystery of Hamlet himself in the monosyllables of Basic English.

More than that, I have to confess that even if I had the stark secret of my brother's life in my hand, I might not be inspired to open my fist. I am one of those who suspect that Will Shakespeare's shade takes gusty amusement in the puzzles he set up in his sonnets, and in his unidentified dark lady—all perhaps unintentionally—and I think that my brother's spirit may also be amused by people who try to figure him out. Master Will and Jack, whom Shakespeare obviously had in mind when he wrote *Hamlet,* as somebody quipped, would be having a high old time together now if psychic things work out the way they should.

But that is a bit of trick reasoning and a sentimental conceit, and I wrote it to confuse the issue. What was the matter with my brother I honestly don't know.

He went to London in 1925 and had a great success. His *Hamlet* was called "A Haymaker at the Haymarket," and was hailed as "a thing of intellectual strength" by such critics as Horace Shipp. As in New York, he spoke the lines of his Dane judiciously, with measured attention to every word uttered, and did not attempt to drug the senses with "emotional slither," to use Ezra Pound's good phrase. The British found this Hamlet a prince and philosopher rather than a man merely distracted by circumstance; and that, I suspect, is the way Master Will wanted his prince played.

There was one monumental dissenting opinion. This was expressed in a letter from Bernard Shaw, who attended the opening night with Michael Strange (who was the then Mrs. John Barrymore). Mr. Shaw applauded my brother as a performer, but he objected very strenuously to the way in which he had lopped out portions of Shakespeare's work. Here is part of his letter to Jack:

> You saved, say, an hour and a half of Shakespear by the cutting, and filled it up with an interpolated drama of your own dumb show. This was a pretty daring thing to do. In modern shop plays, without characters or anything but the commonest dialogue, the actor has to supply everything but the mere story,

> getting in the psychology between the lines, and presenting in his own person the fascinating hero whom the author has been unable to create. He is not substituting something of his own for something of the author's; he is filling up a void and doing the author's work for him. And the author ought to be extremely obliged to him.
>
> But to try this method on Shakespear is to take on an appalling responsibility, and put up a staggering pretension. Shakespear, with all his shortcomings, was a very great playwright, and the actor who undertakes to improve his plays undertakes thereby to excel to an extraordinary degree in two professions, in both of which the highest success is rare. Shakespear himself, though by no means a modest man, did not pretend to be able to play Hamlet as well as write it; he was content to do a recitation in the dark as the ghost. But you have ventured not only to act Hamlet, but to discard about a third of Shakespear's script and substitute stuff of your own, and that, too, without the help of dialogue. Instead of giving what is called a reading of Hamlet, you say, in effect, "I am not going to read Hamlet at all: I am going to leave it out. But, see what I give you in exchange!"

This depressed Jack. It would have floored me. I might comment *sotto voce* that Mr. Shaw *seemed* to be forgetful in saying that Master Shakespeare did not pretend to play as well as to write, for Shakespeare was known as an actor all his life and was not accredited as a famous playwright until after his death. As an actor, Shakespeare might have looked with more favor than did Mr. Shaw, a writer, upon the necessity to condense a play a little. But Mr. Shaw, in my sincerely humble opinion, was one of the mountain peaks of the world and I think I had better keep quiet.

All the British, so far as that goes, have a right to be offended with us when we tamper with the tabernacles of our common literature, as we so often do. The last time I was in London they were still chuckling over the credit line in a Douglas Fairbanks picture. It was billed by an American producer as *The Taming of the Shrew*—"by William Shakespeare with additional dialogue by Sam Taylor."

Constance Collier was with Jack. She played the Queen in *Hamlet*, and played it wonderfully. She writes in her engaging autobiography, *Harlequinade*, now unfortunately out of print, that my brother soon became quarrelsome in London, and that he worked up a strange resentment to the play itself. He began to despise the sight of the stage and the lines he had to speak. He became physically ill, whether from mental turmoil and weariness or something else, I do not know. I do not suggest that he began to hate the play because of Mr. Shaw's comment, for the great writer and the actor became close friends and exchanged many letters. I think that Jack merely followed the pattern he had set before. Once having accomplished something, from a play to a woman, he found it tedious and wanted to start a new quest.

As a matter of fact, he regarded all audiences as monsters. He went on record with this in an interview with Ashton Stevens, in the Los Angeles *Examiner* of February 5, 1905:

> Audiences? No; the plural is impossible, whether it be in Butte or Broadway, it's an audience. The same

> great hulking monster with four thousand eyes and forty thousand teeth. What a wonderful monster it is, with a hide that might have been born from a battleship, with warts on it like hills. And that monster unit with one great mind makes or breaks men like me. At least it gives or denies them the amusement of Success.

Jack might have played *Hamlet* in London for another record run, I take it, and he might have toured all Europe with his play, but he soon lowered the curtain.

There were recriminations, of course. There is a commonly held belief that an actor belongs to his public, that because his public has fed him and applauded him, he owes that public his life from then on; and so Jack was described in some quarters as an ungrateful deserter. To my way of thinking, such a point of view is nonsense. I think that if there is any possessiveness in the relationship between actor and audience, it is the other way around: an actor may *possess an audience* for an evening, if he is lucky. But any player who begins to think he owes his public anything immediately ceases to be an artist and becomes a dead duck. Jack knew this.

At the end of the *Hamlet* engagement, he signed a contract with Warner Brothers to make three motion pictures.

21. Galatea Speaks Up

THE EARLY PICTURES that my brother and I made together added a facet or so to the folklore that we were larcenous fellows.

"You'd steal a scene from your grandmother," an actor once said to me. Then he suddenly remembered that my grandmother was Mrs. Drew.

"No, by God, I guess you wouldn't," he recanted.

It is more than likely that we ourselves created the kleptomaniac legend, being a tribe given to certain exaggerations in small talk; and today it is true, of course, that if the magic could be accomplished short of slitting my throat before the camera I should relish the miracle of lifting at least part of one scene from the enchantress, Miss Margaret O'Brien; but as between Ethel and Jack and me, we always knew better as professionals than to blow the duke with competitive mugging. We had besides an experienced respect for each other, and for my part I was certain that reprisals would be lethal.

Exhibit A in the Hollywood indictment of my brother and me as scene-stealers is the sequence in *Rasputin and the Empress* in which we fought. Jack is the Prince and I am the Mad Monk. In shooting the film, we created an unholy row for a week on the Metro lot as we rolled, tugged, hit, bit, gouged, and wrestled in what purported to be a bloody and dreadful encounter. Jack finally did me in with a poker. But before my demise the director took pains to show facial expressions as the Battle of the Barrymores groveled into its final throes. First Jack's angry face, then mine. Then Jack's. Then mine. He downs me. I pop up, eyes to camera. I down him. He pops up. Profile to camera. It is commonly alleged that the fight took so long because each of us was battling for the limelight.

This wasn't, of course, the case. We could not have arranged those things. We were doing as we were told, and if the editor put the film together a certain way, it was not our fault.

Once, however, I did deliberately connive to theft a scene from my redoubtable relative. Money was involved.

When we were making *Night Flight,* our fifth and last film together, Jack played the role of the superintendent of a South American airport. I was an old man who had to be sent for and bawled out by the boss. All the lines and all the action were Jack's.

Clarence Brown, who was directing, considered this a larceny-proof act for Jack and put up a wager.

"I will lay you ten dollars that this is one bit that Lionel cannot possibly steal from you," he said.

"Taken," said Jack. "He will snatch it if he has to hang from the chandelier."

As played, Jack completely dominated the scene. He was brilliant in his rhetoric and his action while I stood dumbly in front of his desk taking the dressing down without a word to say or a movement to make.

I turned slowly, a bleak and defeated figure, droop-shouldered, and stumbled for the door. The big scene was still Jack's and I was through. I couldn't think of any way to make the act mine with my back to the camera and one second to go before Clarence was due to call "Cut!"

But just then it occurred to me to reach around and rub my bottom.

Jack wagged his head and turned to Clarence.

"Now there, sir, is a brother to be proud of," he said. "Pay me the ten dollars instanter!"

In the early days before the perfection of sound, a completely casual air pervaded all studios. We worked informally at Metro, largely because we were not inhibited by sound, or "talkies," as they were called in that unenlightened age, and also because many of us were stage actors who had known each other for years. We occupied dressing rooms in an old frame building with a porch running around it, and there we would sit, tilting our chairs back, as drummers used to sprawl on hotel piazzas on summer nights, saying "Yas, yas, yas," and "Did you hear this one?" There was even a quartet with Lionel Belmore, Lew Cody, John Gilbert, and Lewis Stone. Will Rogers not only kept horses on the lot but a dozen goats which he would rope for us, two at once, in exhibitions.

Lon Chaney was there. He stayed indoors most of the time, fussing with his make-up and experimenting with a gas-burner which he turned to mysterious uses. Weber and Fields, Louis Mann, Sam Bernard, De Wolf Hopper, and Willie Collier were around; Alice Brady and Trixie Friganza were on hand too. But there were only six real stars: Mae Murray, John Gilbert, Lillian Gish, Lon Chaney, Ramon Navarro, and Antonio Moreno. Lewis Stone and I have outlasted all of them in pictures.

Bottles were tilted on the lot in a manner now unknown

at any studio—and at few bars—and a good time was had by everybody.

Stanislaus Boleslavski, who wrote *The Way of a Lancer*, was one of the favorite people of that era. He was a mountain of a man and a mountain of good humor. One noon hour in the commissary, Charles Dorian, an assistant director then, couldn't find Boleslavski and said in a loud voice: "Where is that Russian son-of-a-bitch?"

A quiet rumble answered from behind.

"Polish son-of-a-bitch," said Boleslavski.

I presume, since the arbiter of good taste in the White House has dignified the appellation, that its use will be permitted by a mere actor.

The perfection of sound film frightened Hollywood as nothing has alarmed the village since, even the shadow of J. Arthur Rank. Up to 1927 our Galatea had been a silent wench and it was quite possible and indeed quite usual for an actress to express any emotion at all, from passion to intellectual concentration, by exertion of her eyes and her bosom. If she were happily endowed in both departments she was likely to become a star. Now, of a sudden, a man named Lee De Forest played Prometheus and gave Galatea a larynx. It became not only possible for the screen to talk but awesomely necessary for the screen to find something to say and to learn how to say it.

The news that we were vocal was received with sheer terror by actors and actresses who had had no stage training, or who had thin, bad voices, or who had unconquerable accents. In the upper echelons, in the executive production offices, there was scarcely a man who had any stage tradition. And I think this is remarkable: they set about learning to manage this new thing over night and they did learn to manage it over night.

Irving Thalberg, who was production executive at Metro during the early days there and on into the advent of sound, is the chief example of the genius of these pioneers. Irving was a motion picture man utterly. He was also extremely young. I used to go into his office with the feeling that I was addressing a boy. In a moment, I would be the one who felt young and inexperienced. I would feel that he was not one but all the forty disciples. One day he knew nothing about the stage and about speech in the theater. The next day he knew all about it. Others, not as brilliant as Irving, but with astonishing speed, also mastered the new grammar.

One of the main problems was to find directors who were supposed to know something about controlling the new noise. There was a scramble for directors who had had stage experience—and here again enters Chance in my story.

"Why, relax from your bad dreams, gentlemen," I said to the bosses. "As an old and experienced hand to whom nobody has paid any attention these many years, let me explain. Sound won't make quite as much difference as you fearfully expect. Action will remain the chief ingredient of these cultural dramas of ours. The main difference will be that the titles will from now on be uttered—hopefully in something approximating English—instead of printed."

The upshot of that declamation was that they decided among themselves, "Well, this fellow ran with that theatrical crowd in New York. Maybe he knows a thing or two. We will make him a director."

My first picture was a one-reel short from a sketch by Maude Fulton which had been used at a Lambs' gambol. It was called *Confession* and starred Robert Ames. Mr. Ames, a client of Small's, was at the moment at liberty and obsessed with delusions of undernourishment, so he consented to submit to my direction when six hundred dollars was mentioned. I cannot report anything dramatic or unusual about this early short subject. We made it in an enchanted hurry and marveled when it talked back to us.

I assumed the mantle of De Mille and made a prayerful bow to D. W. Griffith, whose every possible technique I determined to steal. I made five more films. None of them had classic outlines, but actually, as I look back, I like to think that they were pretty good for their time. The pictures were *The Rogue Song,* one of the first talking pictures in color, with Lawrence Tibbett and Catherine Dale Owen; *Madame X,* with Ruth Chatterton, Lewis Stone, Elliott Nugent, Michael Lewis, and Ulrich Haupt; *Unholy Night,* with Ernest Torrence, Dorothy Sebastian, Roland Young, Boris Karloff, and Lionel Belmore; *His Glorious Night,* with John Gilbert and Catherine Dale Owen; and, for Columbia, *Ten Cents a Dance,* with Barbara Stanwyck.

The Rogue Song introduced Tibbett to motion pictures at the height of his splendid career. I drew this challenging assignment because—I presume—I was supposed to know something about music as well as about acting and about motion pictures. It was the devil of a picture to make, because in 1929 the "playback" had not been invented. The "playback" is the system of recording voices or orchestras on records in advance and at leisure, then playing back the music, which is perfect by this time, while the singers or actors go through the motions of performing. In our picture, we had to record sight and sound in one take, at the same time. Tibbett's big baritone would blast us off stage and we would have to start all over again.

As we made the picture it gave me cynical pleasure to keep in mind that the Los Angeles public now paid through the nose to hear in concerts the performer they had previously begrudged five dollars for singing at local funerals—and that is the fact. Chanting five-dollar dirges at the obsequies of Los Angeles notables is how Lawrence Tibbett got his start.

Many artifices are employed in recording sound today, but when I started conditions were rugged. I remember first of all sitting high on my camera boom (a long, towering crane from which you take long shots) overlooking a scene which comprised the entire length of Stage 16 and embraced three separate rooms and a long hallway. At the farthest end of the great stage Tibbett started singing a big, round A-flat, which note he kept up for the entire length of the studio, still singing this lusty A as he sat down and poured a tankard of beer. This, mind you, was done ad infinitum, all afternoon, and as if this were not enough, in the middle of August; and as if that were not enough, in the thickest woolen uniform the Western Costume Company could provide. After this great scene, my mind's eye always goes back to the one immediately following it, which audiences did not see: Larry Tibbett, having shed his uniform and being clothed only in himself and a pair of suspenders, drinking another tankard of beer that this time was not a prop.

In *Madame X*, I was plagued by recording almost as much as in *The Rogue Song*. The sound engineers were absolute and tyrannical gods. They were the only people in the world who understood anything about amperes and decibels; if they said a certain thing could not be done, there was nobody on the directorial or actorial side who could even pronounce the proper words to give them an argument. Their sound equipment was mysteriously hidden away in vast boxes on the stages from which they emerged to lay down ukases. In order to capture the precious words of our actors, we had to hide microphones in geranium pots, behind screens, under tables. It was impossible to command a player to speak while he moved from here to there, as he would naturally. He had to telegraph his messages by stopping every time he recited, remembering to pause in front of the proper flower pot.

In *Madame X*, it seemed necessary to have Ruth Chatterton move from a seated position, walk across the room, meet some one in a tight-two scene, and continue her conversation while a native boy who was strumming a guitar continued to make his music over and above the conversation.

The sound people looked at me as if I had suggested recording the love life of the microbes.

"Impossible, Mr. Barrymore," they said and walked away.

"Now look, gentlemen," I said, following them, "consider me totally ignorant. I've got a tin ear but I also have an idea. If it doesn't work, it's all my fault, but let me try something."

My property man was a fisherman. He trolled the seas with great bamboo poles and brought in enormous finny specimens to prove his prowess. Some of those fish, I reckoned, were heavier than the weighty microphones (as large as old-fashioned telephones) then in use.

"Get me one of those damned fish poles and tie the microphone on one end. Then prop it out of camera range over Miss Chatterton's head. When she walks, move the pole along with her, keeping the mike right over her.

"Damocles' sword, my dear, but be a brave girl. It won't fall on you."

The sound engineers have not to this day admitted that my scheme worked. They will pull out their preposterous slide rules and tables of logarithms and *prove* that such an antic could not be possible. As a matter of fact, they even stoop so low as to get out statistics and show that somebody invented the sound boom a year before. Cecil B. De Mille is one of the claimants, and more than likely he did invent one. Eddie Mannix also invented a sound boom. All I can say is that in 1929 I recorded Miss Ruth Chatterton's voice with a fishing pole.

I discovered as a director that the Frohman and the Arthur Hopkins approaches were the best. I bespoke my actors quietly. I nurtured their tender egos. If a player performed poorly, I would say:

"Now, that was perfect, old man. No one could have done it better. But just for instance, suppose we try it *this* way."

While I was on stage working with actors I felt at home and as reasonably happy as I can feel any time when I am forced to engage in toil. I was blessed, as you can tell from my casts, with uncommon talented people. They could read their lines and they could act. But there is much more to directing than sitting on the set and yelling: "Players ready? Camera ready? Let's go! Camera! Action!"

A director labors for months ahead of his pictures, casting, approving costumes, approving scenery, and conferring with his producer (who is in effect his managing editor). He works early in the morning, before anybody else starts, getting his scenes ready for the day's shooting. He stays late at night examining his rushes, deciding which scenes he will have to retake. He spends hours after completion of his picture editing, splicing, cutting—and squalling for retakes. This sort of thing was totally unsuited to a man like me, whose admiration for *mañana* is only exceeded by his yearning for more *mañana.* At Columbia, for instance, where I directed *Ten Cents a Dance,* somebody transposed the reels, the picture was run off slaunchwise, and rumors flew about Hollywood that Barrymore had lost his wits and made a picture backwards at a loss of a million dollars. Eventually, the film was hung together properly. Pretty good picture, too, but the experience discouraged me. I sulked in my tent again and hummed funeral marches.

At this point Maury Small went to Thalberg and argued that they had better pull me back into the fold as an actor again before I lost all self-respect and assurance. By this time, young men who could really direct had come along and I was no longer a necessary Cincinnatus. They let me return to my plough. I did so with hosannahs and I bit like a carp at the bait when they offered me the part of the criminal lawyer in *A Free Soul,* a courtroom drama based on the life of Los Angeles' great mouthpiece, Earl Rogers, father of Adela Rogers St. John. The most remarkable boon of good fortune dropped into my lap with this picture in the form of one difficult scene.

This scene—and it would have been a ripe plum for any competent actor—is the one in which the attorney addresses the jury in heights of eloquence and passion, then falls dead. It was a wonderful, clever, theatrical, extended scene, almost an entire reel long, and it frightened me as much as the first night of *Macbeth*.

The day we were to take it I arrived at the studio in a torpor. I perceived little of anything, spoke to nobody. All I craved with every fiber of my being was to drop into some corner and be forgotten and go to sleep. But in the movies, you start acting at nine A.M., and whether your scene involves love or despair, you start acting and digesting breakfast at the same time.

I knew my words. I had no trouble there. I knew my character. I had studied him. I think I sincerely believed what I was saying to that jury of extras. I began quietly, then I let them have it with everything I possessed.

As I went into my collapse, feeling actually that I *was* falling dead, there were "Bravos" from the actors and extras. I appreciated this because that sort of thing is rare and is the actor's highest accolade. But Clarence Brown, who was directing, swore softly and quickly hushed the cheers, which had come too soon. When he finally called "Cut!" I picked myself up from the floor and approached him apologetically.

"It was swell, Lionel," Clarence said.

"Maybe, maybe," I said, "but I am sorry to tell you, I don't think I could possibly do it again."

Ordinarily, you go through a scene like that eight to ten times for the various close-ups, long shots, middle shots, and so on.

"You don't have to," said Clarence.

"Don't have to!" I exclaimed. "What do you mean? You're not throwing it out, are you?"

"Lord no. I had eight cameras on you. We got it all at once, from every angle. I was sure you couldn't do a thing like that more than once."

It was this scene, more than anything else, which won me the Motion Picture Academy of Arts and Sciences award—the "Oscar"—in 1931.

The late George Arliss, who had won his own gold statuette the year before, presented my Oscar to me at the annual awards dinner.

". . . . For great artistry, for a magnificent performance," he said as he addressed the audience and me in the same accents with which he played Disraeli and Alexander Hamilton. As he talked he stroked Oscar's poll reflectively. He became absorbed in the feel of it. "Here it is, Lionel," he finally said, "but from the shape of his head, y'know, I have the conviction that he isn't a very good actor!"

I mumbled my thanks. I am eloquent only in the back rooms, where it often comes out that I am learned and rhetorical. I have never been able to make a speech in front of an audience. At any rate, the only decent thing I could have done was to present my Oscar to Clarence Brown.

At this stage of the proceedings it would be nice and impressive to catalogue a large group of grateful and doting young players, now stars, who owe their start in the drama to the kindness of the Great Barrymore. I do not go so far as Jack, nor as a matter of fact did he mean it literally when he said, "Damn the understudy! My job is to keep him off that stage!" But most persons who obtain in any of the arts, however modestly they nod the credit to someone else, actually get there on their own hook. If you are going to be a sword swallower, I gravely urge you to keep in mind that it is your own gullet down which the blade must descend; nobody can do it for you. However, there was one young fellow in whom I took an interest some years ago because I thought he looked like Jack Dempsey.

He first appeared in a company of *The Copperhead* when we played Los Angeles in April, 1927, my only apostasy from the screen. I thought he had all kinds of makings at the time, although the only distinguished thing he did in that play was to drop his hat in a prop well—then reach in casually and pick it up.

Not to be mysterious about it, the boy was Clark Gable. On one of the occasions when I was making shift to direct at Metro, I remembered him, called him up, and said:

"This is for you. Got something. You get out here and I'll make a test and we'll put you in pictures."

One of the reasons that Clark seemed to resemble Dempsey at that time was that he was lean and hungry. He made haste to the studio.

The picture I had in mind was called *Never the Twain Shall Meet.* I did not direct it, for this and that reason, but it gave me a chance to run off a test of Clark.

I had him wear nothing but some orchids and a lei or something, and a blossom behind his ear. I made three or four scenes and had Gable stick out his chest in all of them.

"Brother, the guy's wonderful," I said to myself.

To Clark, I said: "OK, boy, I'm sure you're in."

I had my tests developed and called Irving Thalberg in to look at them. I expected to be crowned with laurels, but Irving looked at the test in utter silence, nodded his head in an indefinite negative, and walked out.

I was ashamed to call Clark and tell him that he and I had made a total failure, that Thalberg had turned him down. Then I began to study my part for *A Free Soul* and became so immersed in it that I forgot the matter.

A month later I reported to the studio ready to start. There was already some activity on the stage assigned for our first scene. I eased my way forward to see who was at work. A man was giving a girl one of the longest kisses of screen record. The man was Gable. The woman in his arms was Norma Shearer, Mrs. Irving Thalberg.

When the scene was over, Gable came over to me grinning wider than a Hallowe'en pumpkin.

"Sure, I'm in this too, what do you know? Forgot to get in touch with you. Day after you made that test for me, Irving called me up and put me under contract."

He established himself there and then for his work in *A Free Soul.* I happily went on from that picture, which had brought me such good fortune, to *Mata Hari,* with Miss Greta Garbo.

22. *Don't Sell Movies Short*

I HAD WORKED with the lady once before. Fred Niblo, the producer, had called me into his office one day and announced that I had been cast in support of the luminous and enigmatic Swedish beauty in *The Temptress.* I was delighted but bemused. The prospect of appearing in front of a camera with Miss Garbo, who was reputed to say "good morning" to nobody, was not precisely terrifying, but none the less I had certain qualms and curiosities about how one was supposed to get on with her. And so, following the precept I had learned on the stage, I sought advice from a man she was reputed to admire, who was supposed to know how to get on with great ladies—my brother.

Jack was perfectly silent after I had made my request.

I pursued him. "Surely you have at least some nonsense to mutter? Has the feline bit off your usually overarticulate clapper?"

Jack was silent a long time.

"You know, Mike," he finally said, "even Brillat Savarin occasionally ate other people's salad dressing."

I was answered.

As even a dolt's eye might perceive, Greta Garbo had the true nimbus of greatness; but she was difficult to understand. She was not knowable through the usual amenities. For want of a better approach to this ineffable lady, let me circle around for a moment and try it this way: if you had your morning coffee with Giuseppe Verdi you might possibly find him uninteresting or even downright eccentric. The lightning bolts he tossed like hot rivets when he wrote music would not appear. To know and enjoy the full shock and delight of the man, you would have to get yourself into a position to receive and experience the impact of his work.

This is a way of saying that the commonplaces about Miss Garbo have no significance; but unfortunately for her and unfortunately for us, the many things she was given to do in motion pictures, fine as some of them were, were really not worthy of her gifts, neither the popcorn peddling exhibitors nor John Q. Moviegoer being as yet ready to digest motion pictures of the level of William Shakespeare. There is more than an adequate literature for many other artists in other fields, say Horowitz and Heifetz; but as for Miss Garbo, I am reluctantly forced to conclude that in her day and time with us she was compelled to do her best with boogie-woogie.

I worked with her in *The Temptress,* in *Camille,* in *Mata Hari,* and in *Grand Hotel* without getting to know her. I would have attempted some sort of homey acquaintance save for the fact, regrettable for me, that it took me at least two days to emerge from the spell she always cast by her great acting; and when I might have pursued my amiable designs, I (having even then attained a certain ripening age) had forgotten my good intentions in this direction.

But after several years it was borne in on me that her apparent aloofness stemmed only from extreme shyness. It was as simple as that. The gods, in meting out their gifts, had neglected to endow her with the small chitchat of a head waiter.

Indeed, her unpretentiousness was so extreme that it amounted almost to a malady. She appeared and disappeared as silently as a wraith. She ignored the grace notes of "good morning" and "good night," but I am convinced that on such apparently cold-mannered occasions she was either preoccupied and consumed by the "hard gemlike flame" of her truly great art—or she was merely bashful. When you were fortunate enough to know her a little, she was very, very nice, and likable, and kind. She has real simplicity, the true simplicity of the genius—only she is so diffident that her psychology is comparable to the terror of a gun-shy bird dog.

She was not backward with her own workers when the time came to perform, but she would ice over and retire whenever kibitzers or other curiosity mongers elbowed their way onto her set.

I remember a saying of Peter Dunne's: "This general, now, could get madder than hell if there was anything to get mad about." Garbo could be funny—if there was anything to be funny about. She was—and is—a very great actress. I speak of her in the past only because she has now disappeared from our scene. Perhaps one day some genius equal to her genius will create the roles that she deserves, and she will return.

Next to Miss Garbo the most awesome actress I have encountered in Hollywood is Margaret O'Brien. After my first picture with her I remarked that if she had been unfortunate enough to be born in Salem, they would have burned her as a witch. This saying has been widely quoted, and somewhat out of context; I meant it as the most en-

Spencer Berger Collection

Lionel Barrymore as Scrooge in Dickens' *Christmas Carol*

Spencer Berger Collection

BOATYARD IN VENICE by Lionel Barrymore. Selected by the Society of American Etchers as one of the "Hundred Prints of the Year".

vious kind of compliment. And since this involves a little girl, suppose I tell a story:

Many years ago my grandmother gave me a jeweled pin of sapphires and pearls. It had been given to her by her father to wear for good luck on her first important performance.

Years later she offered me the pin with the wish that it might bring me the same happiness that it had brought her.

Being a rank sentimentalist in spite of a crusty exterior, I hoped that perhaps one day I should find an actress, young and fresh and beautiful, to whom I might appropriately present this pin. For many years I discovered no girl who quite came up to the requirements implicit in Grandmother Drew's brooch.

One day when I was working in *Dr. Gillespie's Criminal Case* the director brought over a mite in pigtails. She was wearing a long hospital nightgown and I was told that she was to play the little sick girl in the story. She was shy and polite and small, only five years old.

I thought—out loud, after she had made her curtsy and departed: "How bloody awful. She'll be bringing lollipops to the set and getting them tangled in everybody's hair."

She did indeed, but since she invariably brought me one I managed to condone this unusual type of refreshment and almost acquired the vice myself.

I soon realized that Margaret could perform like no youngster I or anybody else had ever seen. When she takes over, you might as well imagine yourself a design on the wallpaper. You could stand on your head and no audience would notice you. Impressed by this virtuosity, I set about wooing the lady and was somewhat more successful than I was with Miss Garbo. We often had lunch together and I was pleased to think that I had made a good impression upon such a fine actress.

I had already begun to consider that perhaps here was the girl for Mum Mum's pin. I was certain sometime later when she did *Meet Me in St. Louis,* and no one was happier than I when she won a special Academy Award for it. Right after that we were together in *Three Wise Fools,* in which Maggie dealt out a lesson in acting to Lewis Stone, Edward Arnold, and me. At the end of the picture we had a party on stage.

When the ice cream cake was cut, everybody crowded around and it appeared to me that it would all be gone before I could lay hands on a slice. Margaret got first cut. But did she rush off into a corner and gobble it? She did not. She brought it to me.

"Mr. Barrymore," she said, "this is the first piece and it is for you because I love you."

I gave her Mum Mum's pin there and then. She deserved it, with all the sentimental implications I attach to it.

As time went by and I recovered successively from the impacts of Miss Garbo and the redoubtable Miss O'Brien, I looked about me and discovered that there are many other performers in motion pictures who could have walked a stage with Sir Henry Irving, or with anybody. It would be an impertinence for me to take an eclectic stance, so I forbear from trying to name all these ladies and gentlemen. But I continue to be struck by the effectiveness of Spencer Tracy. I had come to Hollywood accustomed to the broad gestures and emphatics of the stage. This performer seemed to be doing nothing at all.

He acted with such subdued diffidence that it was always a surprise to me to observe, later, that he had made more impression than all the people who spoke louder and showed more emotion. Finally I recalled a story.

Years ago at the beginning of his career, Spencer had a minuscular part in one of my sister's plays. On opening night he wavered in the wings, prey to the horrors that beset victims on the way to the chair or high school orators on the way to the lectern. He was, I am reliably informed, a fit candidate for shock treatment when Ethel took pity on his predicament, approached him, laid a kind hand on his shoulder, and said:

"Relax."

He took her advice and he has been relaxing ever since.

Tracy is a master of the art of throwing lines away. The best lines of any author are barely audible, so casual is Spencer. The only other actor who comes anywhere near him in this department is Lew Ayres: I should ask no better entertainment than to watch a scene between these two men. I hasten to add, however, lest anyone surmise from these observations that an author receives scant courtesy from the Messrs. Tracy and Ayres, that the opposite is true. In their hands, any writer gains stature he didn't know he possessed.

There was another younger player who puzzled me, but not for long. I saw her first in *A Bill of Divorcement,* with Jack, and it had been reported that the pair did not get along well. But there was something about her, something reminiscent, and something great. I finally got it, but I went first to Jack and said:

"Who is she like?"

He gave me an immediate answer.

I asked Ethel:

"Who is she like?"

And Ethel answered.

The Barrymore opinion was unanimous. Katharine Hepburn is not only like Maude Adams, she *is* Maude Adams. This observation, of course, may mean little to the several generations that are younger than I am, but it may be of interest, by way of a certain happy recognition, to oldsters who remember *Peter Pan* and *What Every Woman Knows*, and the most piquant talent that ever graced the American stage.

The foregoing notes on a handful of interesting persons are merely an approach to a brief preachment I hope the reader will allow me to make. The players on whom I have scattered my doubtful blessing, probably ruining their careers from now on, are merely representative of the first-rate talents and the first-rate good will to accomplish that has long resided in Hollywood. You could fill these pages with the names and addresses of superior men and women in the arts and crafts of the theater and of the music halls who are only waiting for adult audiences for whom to produce adult art.

We might mention my own sister, if you happen to like her. Or a director like George Cukor, or a producer like Robert Rossen, or the delightful Walt Disney, as Exhibits A in the argument that the motion picture industry has on hand now, if under wraps, the genius to tell grown-up stories to grown-up people. Of course, however, the enormous sums of money that have to be spent to produce any kind of motion picture, from claptrap to *All the*

King's Men, precludes any attempt to make anything except what audiences of millions will support.

For my part I have often laid about me with ill-timed and ill-aimed rhetoric in criticisms of Hollywood. Hollywood is a place that requires frequent damning to keep it alive and bouncing. *But don't let anyone sell motion pictures short.*

Let me hand you an opium pipe.

Suppose Wagner were alive today. Let us imagine, since we are indulging in the utmost fancy, that Wagner lived in Glendale. Wagner, like Shakespeare if he were here, would most certainly take the great motion picture industry into his godlike hands and wrest great music and great poetry out of it. Imagine the Ring cycle on film! Imagine what Cedric Gibbons, with Wagner at his elbow, would do with the callipygian Rhine maidens!

Instead of producing the best he could for the small and wretched opera houses of his time, with the conventional limitations of scenery which inhibited him, imagine what might have happened had Wagner been able through motion pictures, which admit no horizon, to express *all* the glory that was in his head!

If such a miraculous thing, if such genius-work by some new Olympus-sent Wagner, using all the beauty and color and scope the screen now makes available, seems incredible, consider: why has the Metropolitan Opera broadcast on Saturday afternoons already got thirty million listeners? Be-bop and trombones are, of course, in pitiless ascendancy at the moment; nevertheless, countless millions listen to Toscanini. There is hope, brethren. The doors are already unlocked, the view is fair, and the sky is the limit, not only to aviation, but to motion pictures.

Pray do not sell us short, then, even when ennui or nausea is the only possible response to some of the unappetizing antics performed in Hollywood by overzealous flagpole sitters. In this salubrious climate of Southern California, almost precisely that in which civilization was cradled in aged Greece, in some gathering twilight in some not overpoliced park near one of the big cities, are perhaps marching two people who will meet under a tolerant moon and happily and in spite of all inhibitions beget the music drama of tomorrow.

23. A Bow to Louis B.

MY WIFE and I lived quietly on Roxbury Drive, Beverly Hills. Jack lived unquietly on Tower Road. By the early Nineteen-thirties, both of the Barrymore brothers had accomplished what for years had seemed incredible. We had escaped from the stage, we had found a place in motion pictures, we had acquired the leisure which we both craved for our various private enterprises, and we were earning money. Curiously enough, our so-called characters and our ways of life being so different on the surface, we had followed essentially the same pattern. This applied to money also. Neither of us could keep it.

In the spending department, Jack outdistanced me by far. In 1931, his income came to $460,000, which he disposed of immediately and in style, on a yacht, on his cacophonous and amazing private zoo, on travel, and on various highhearted escapades too familiar to this generation for gaudy repetition here. Possibly Jack forged ahead of me merely because he had more to forge ahead with. The sad fact is that, with money coming into my hands in quantities which should have insured me at least a third-row leather chair at some junior Union League Club, I managed without any effort at all to spend almost every cent of it. How I accomplished this I am bewildered to explain, just as I am still bewildered by anything that smacks of a decimal point. Neither Irene nor I had a taste for vast parties. I never owned a yacht or a horse. I acquired few valuable paintings. I stored up no treasure. We lived unostentatiously, and for the last several years of her life Irene was ill.

The best I can say is that this talent for throwing away money is not a unique or even a novel thing. In recent years there have appeared in Washington a number of gentlemen close to the White House who seem to possess comparable capacities for tossing dollars at birds. But Mr. Truman, if he is really sincere in his bi-partisan policies, should invite me into his Cabinet. The Barrymores were expert on the unbalanced budget long before the Fair Deal.

My chronic financial embarrassments were none of them extreme nor did they actually involve important sums. They were, however, harassments which threw me into moods of nightmare and frustration. It was the same kind of terror which used to strike me at Seton Hall when I was confronted with examinations involving addition and subtraction and other such mysteries which are the province of professional engineers only. And so, trembling and cursing myself, I would go out to the studio and plead with the fiscal executives for a handout.

They were always kind. They would advance my allowance or fend off the butcher or show me—sometimes—that I had money in the bank I didn't know I had. Now, of course, they solemnly allege that my exhibitions on these occasions by far surpassed in histrionics anything I ever performed on stage, screen, or radio. They allege that I influenced them with phony tears. With all respect to the generous gentlemen who so often helped and guided me, I have to deny this. The tears were never phony.

Of course, when my importunings became too frequent or my solvency seemed to be seriously threatened, they would refer me to Louis B. Mayer.

Now the mind's eye picture of a great studio chief is that of a cold and shrewd executive who dangles careers on strings, plays with actors like puppets, and discards them when they begin to unravel around the edges. In my earliest days at Metro I confess I had, perhaps, some such notion of Mr. Mayer. The first time I discovered that he had quietly done me a favor I shrugged it off as possibly an accident. The second time I blinked and thought it over. But when this sort of thing had happened about seventy-five times in a row, it finally came home to me that Louis B. Mayer's generosity was indeed on purpose.

And so, when it often happened that I had exhausted the patience of the paymasters, I would hurry up to Mr. Mayer's office.

"Lionel's on his way," they would telephone upstairs. "Tell the boss to get ready."

He was always ready. He counseled me without scolding, got me out of this predicament and that, succored me from the Federal dicks when my income taxes threatened to mount to jailworthy heights, and reached for a checkbook and salvation when necessary. Perhaps one explanation of this remarkable man is his own start in life.

His formal education, like mine, was casual. I believe he mastered the eighth grade before quitting school. His background was about as far from the theater as you can get, the seaport of St. John's, New Brunswick (also the home town of Walter Pidgeon). As a boy he worked for the seaport captains of both steam and sail and before he was twenty wound up as head of a salvage company of his own. From that he went into motion picture theater operation—luckily for me, he was theater-struck—and from that to production. I presume he learned the good will and the understanding which is so enormously his during boyhood, during those early days with the tough and honest sailors of New Brunswick. I would not presume to say. I am merely grateful for whatever happened and for what he did for me.

Under Louis B. Mayer's astute guidance I worked in a number of pictures. I am startled by my own dossier—it includes something more than seventy films at Metro, not counting all the Kildares or the loan-outs. There was *Dinner at Eight,* with Jean Harlow, Marie Dressler, Wallace Beery, and Jack; *Night Flight,* with Gable, Jack Barrymore, Helen Hayes, Robert Montgomery, and Myrna Loy; *Her Sweetheart,* with Marie Dressler; *Treasure Island,* with Wallace Beery and Jackie Cooper; *David Copperfield,* with Freddie Bartholomew and W. C. Fields; *Ah, Wilderness,* with Beery; *The Gorgeous Hussy,* with Joan Crawford; *Captains Courageous,* with Tracy and Rooney; *Saratoga,* with Jean Harlow and Gable; *A Yank at Oxford,* with Maureen O'Sullivan, Vivien Leigh, and Bob Taylor; *Test Pilot,* with Tracy and Gable; *Tennessee Johnson,* with Van Heflin; *Valley of Decision,* with Greer Garson; *Malaya,* with Tracy and Jimmie Stewart; and *Duel in the Sun,* with everybody.

Of course, I was not always so fortunate as to play with the likes of Miss Garbo or Mr. Tracy or Miss O'Brien or Mr. Ayres. Sometimes I was cast opposite talented dogs. My first experience in this line of work came with a picture called *The Thirteenth Hour.*

The dog was a collie, one of the precursors of the great female impersonator Lassie, and he liked me. He liked me, I suppose, because I liked him, and I liked him because I like all dogs. But I was the villain of this piece and the collie was supposed to attack me. He was supposed to leap through a window, discover me at my devilish work, and kill me.

He leaped all right. He would come through the window with a well-trained snarl, then jump on me affectionately and ask for a romp. In the end, they had to mistreat and deceive that dog in order to have him make-believe that I was a bad man. They underfed him for two days, then put a sirloin steak in my wig. He almost tore me to pieces. He was a better actor, come to think of it, than most of the performers today, but Uncle Jack would have frowned.

A problem of another nature involving dogs arose in the picture called *The Voice of Bugle Ann.* For this one, Tom Bash, a Missouri sheriff, brought out his famous Walker dogs and it was suggested that I take home the bitch who was to play Bugle Ann in order to get acquainted with her.

I had at that time a chauffeur named Harry Hinkley who fed Bugle Ann. The upshot of this was that Bugle Ann fell in love with Harry and ignored me. That was all right, for what we had become chiefly interested in was her voice, which was essential to the picture. We waited for her to cut loose but she uttered not a note.

One night I came home late and anxiously inquired of Harry: "Has she bugled yet?"

"Yes, *sir,* she shore has," said Harry, "once under the piano and twice on the rug."

That should take care of the animal department for the time being.

As I was saying when I interrupted myself to make a small bow to Louis B. Mayer and to tell the dog stories, Irene and I were no contribution to the night-side life of Hollywood. Irene never formally retired from the stage, but having left it three thousand miles behind, and having proved to everybody's pleasure that she was a fine actress, and being unwell for many years, she was content to manage a charming home and to watch, with amused eyes, my various attempts at this-and-that. I learned to play the oboe passably, and I began to make a few etchings.

Like anything else that an amateur does, etching is an absorbing and a rewarding pastime if you have the knack of it and if you do not confuse yourself with Mr. Whistler. I began to enjoy this tedious art intensely and produced all told, I suppose, about a hundred plates. I was handsomely complimented by a membership in the Brooklyn Society of Etchers, and the Milch Art Gallery in New York astonished me by actually selling a few prints. So, at long last, I have been paid money for drawing. I do an occasional etching now but I should hate to have to make my living at this in competition with real artists.

I should hate also to be caught playing the oboe by any member of the New York Philharmonic, but I do play it when I am alone and a toot of odd music seems appropriate. I live in the country.

With such pursuits as these and in our small circle we found life pleasant. We became close friends with Mrs. Mary Ellen Wheeler and her three daughters, Murdie, Violet, and Florance. These ladies, who had nothing to do with stage or screen, had a house in Pacific Palisades, and were so kind to us and taught us so much about how to live that we often imposed upon them to the extent of visits that lasted as long as two months at a time. Mrs. Wheeler, who is many years younger than I am, considered me an irresponsible fellow and began to call me "Son." Naturally, I retaliated by calling her "Mother."

As Irene's illness grew worse, the Wheelers were more frequently at our home on Roxbury Drive. Their presence and friendship is one of the blessings that have been showered on me, one of the arrangements made from above, for they were with me in the garden on the afternoon of Christmas Eve, 1936, when Irene suddenly died.

I was supposed to go on the radio in *A Christmas Carol* the next day. With hardly a moment to read through the lines in advance, Jack took my place and gave that memorable performance which perhaps you recall. I went home with the Wheelers. I never went back to Roxbury Drive.

24. Brass and Woodwind Section

MY HOME stood empty. It stood as Irene had left it. I did not want to live in it again and I could not accept the idea of anyone else's living in it.

I said, "Do you know what I think about the political situation today? I think it is going to eventuate into a fight between whisky and vodka. I am not going to take a chance on renting my house to anyone who might have a leaning toward vodka."

I was more prophet than I knew. I also said:

"Or to someone who might have a leaning toward Romberg or Lehar. Oh, great composers, give them their due, but I am still on the side of Bach, Brahms, Beethoven, and even Bruckner. And not merely because their names begin with B."

I gave these reasons for not wanting anyone to live in my house. They had a certain validity; but the truth is as I have said.

Still, as the housing shortage increased I began to be ashamed, and I looked around for the right kind of guest. I said a silent *Requiescat in pace* to certain good memories and decided to find a tenant. And I was hit immediately with an idea.

A young friend of mine was preparing to fly to Europe to marry his beautiful fiancée. I said to him:

"Now, old man, if by any chance, if it just happens,

that you accidentally meet Richard Strauss over there, you tell him that he is the only man on earth to whom I would gladly give my home. Tell him to leave Europe and come and live quietly in the blessed sunshine of California."

Can you imagine my surprise and my delight when only two weeks later I received a letter from Strauss? He thanked me for my generosity and said that he would arrive in a couple of months.

I was overjoyed. I wired back at once: "I will be more than happy to see you here as soon as possible." And in a letter I offered him not only my home but its staff of help and any other support necessary to make him happy and comfortable in this new country. As I have said before somewhere in this account, I never took myself seriously as a musician for obvious reasons, but I took music seriously and great musicians seriously. I felt then somewhat like a Greek peasant of Athenian days who has supplicated Apollo and been rewarded with a promise of a personal visit.

Strauss wrote that he was very happy. He made his reservations on the *Queen Mary* and, as a mere formality, he asked me to make a necessary affidavit with the American consul in Switzerland to make it possible for him to obtain his immigration visa. That is where the tragedy began.

I hastened to seek advice on how to make out this affidavit—but my lawyer refused to have anything to do with it.

"Don't you know that Richard Strauss is a Nazi?" he said. "My God, Barrymore, don't you know that it would not only ruin you but would be an injury to him to bring him to this country where people remember seeing him photographed with Goering and Goebbels?"

I was shocked and bewildered. I think, at that time, that I would have argued that great artists are superior to politics. And as a matter of fact I was completely unaware of the rumors that compromised Richard Strauss with guilt by association. I had read none of the stories about his alleged Nazi activities and I had seen none of the pictures said to have been taken of him with Hitler's officials. Out in Chatsworth, where I now lived, no one had suggested that Strauss was a Nazi.

I went from place to place and from man to man in almost frantic haste trying to solve a problem I could not understand. I felt queer and resentful that such a problem should even exist.

I consulted attorneys, officials, and consuls, anybody who would listen to me. In every instance the reaction was the same.

"But, sirs," I would say, "we play all his compositions in this country. We have not interdicted *Till Eulenspiegel*, or *Salome*, or *Don Juan*. Are his works welcome but not the creator of them?"

Everyone was adamant and explicit. It became clear that, though Strauss were the most innocent man in the world, it would be not only disagreeable but positively dangerous to him to fetch him to California. Sadly and in grave embarrassment I had to write to Strauss and tell him that our wonderful plans could not be accomplished.

He answered me with kindness in one of the most touching letters I have ever received, or have ever seen. He told me that he of course was not a Nazi. I will quote only a few lines, for this was a tragic thing. He said:

I regret so deeply that your noble purpose of inviting me to America could not be fulfilled. Don't let anyone take away your faith in me. I will wait with patience and we will hope that the world will become more honest and that the noble arts will be cleansed of politics.

With kindest regards from me and from my very sad wife who was looking forward so much to our new home,

Very gratefully yours,
RICHARD STRAUSS.

Richard Strauss died not long ago without enjoying the California sunshine. It strikes me bitterly and ironically now to think that he might have been alive if he had come to 802 Roxbury Drive, Beverly Hills, to live in the house I did not need.

Not long ago I asked a lady to do an errand for me. She was going downtown and I inquired if she might not stop at a certain music store and buy for me a number of lullabies and short pieces by Johannes Brahms.

"No particular compositions, Mr. Barrymore?" she said.

"No, just get me some songs," I said. "Get me about forty of them."

The lady knew, of course, that I amuse myself and astonish others by putting notes together to see how they may come out. She asked me without expression:

"Mr. Barrymore, did Johannes Brahms ever steal anything from you?"

"No, ma'am," I said, "but if you will bring me those songs I suspect that he is going to commit a wholesale theft this afternoon."

In my own so-called "works" I have, like Mahler, borrowed from everybody except the studio gateman, and I shall undoubtedly get around to him later if he can sound an A. Not in defense of my own pilfering but as a matter of fact and record I decline to believe that any composer sprang full-tuned from the brow of Jove; the exceptions might be Wagner and Debussy, who indeed did flash upon us uniquely like planets from another world; but if real asteroids should crash into your own backyard you might call in all the knowledge and science in the world to define their chemical and atomic content without ever piercing, actually, the secret of their flaming grandeur. I think that is how it is with the truly great. The rest of us, including the near-great, are derivative and imitative.

Nothing is new. You may remember that H. G. Wells once asked his illustrators to clothe the characters in one of his fantasies in costumes that were like none that had ever existed—and the poor technicians were utterly stumped. In the end, they copied the costumes from some vase that was eighty thousand years old, or thereabouts. Just so, if your modern composer wants something "new" he goes back to Scarlatti and Corelli and Couperin and borrows their style and dresses it up. And then it comes out as the last word. But for the most part, every melody you hear is "Tristan-like" or taken straight from Debussy. It is a marvelous thing; where would we be for music without these men?

So far as I am concerned, whenever I begin to think that I have evolved some philosophy in these matters, I am always jerked back to the conclusion that I do not actually know a thing. I may know something Tuesday but I don't know it today. In the true tradition of criticism, this will by no means prevent me from firing off broadsides. My aim may not be steady. Let the prudent and the learned be prepared to stand back.

I began to write a little music when I was about thirty years old and I have continued to compose various small things for these forty-two years. A number of persons will be surprised, of course, to be assured that I can not only read notes but can put them together and even orchestrate them, but this is the simple fact; and it is not as difficult as it may seem to the uninitiated. It is like the explorer who was away back in the Belgian Congo where he had to employ native runners to trot twenty miles for supplies.

One day he wrote on a piece of wood that he wanted some tobacco. The native sped off, obtained and delivered the tobacco, then disappeared for several days. The explorer discovered that he had showed the "talking wood" to his tribe, which regarded it as a miracle and a marvel, and had buried it with respectful ceremonies. The tribe had been awed by something that was actually exceedingly simple. If you are not a musician, then, do not bump your head before some tenth-rate "artist" merely because he knows a technique that seems mysterious to you. So does the side-show performer know stunts that are esoteric to the average person. Orchestration is usually something to leave wrapped up in pleasant ignorance; if people understood it better, perhaps they wouldn't enjoy it so much when they hear it.

One of my friends, a respected friend for many years, was Mrs. Edward MacDowell. I had always had a tremendous feeling for her husband's piano compositions, and at her suggestion I orchestrated four of the sea pieces. This took me about a year; I did it when I was working in pictures, staying up late or getting up early, setting down the orchestration a little at a time as I could.

Mrs. MacDowell astounded me by suggesting that I send the work to Fabien Sevitzky, conductor of the Indianapolis Symphony Orchestra. I should never have mustered the courage to do an impertinent thing like that if she had not assured me that it would be all right, that I had done well enough not to be too presumptuous. Sevitzky, thank God, was pleased, played the pieces, and kindly wrote to me every year asking what else I might have done that might be worth consideration. I finally met Sevitzky, pumped him for his advice, and did write from time to time a number of things which he and his fine orchestra have considerately played—to my *enormous* satisfaction.

I doubt if there is a greater, more exhaustingly emotional experience possible than hearing your own music brilliantly performed, performed big, by a great orchestra, with those twenty violins picking up the fugues that were imaginary to you, and a renowned conductor welding the whole thing into something far better and more impressive than you had dreamed.

Paul Dresser wrote what turned out to be Indiana's state song, "On the Banks of the Wabash." Sevitzky decided that I should orchestrate it, and I did, most happily. This was played at one of the state festivals. It was kindly received, even by persons who knew about music, but I appreciated most of all a warm letter of thanks from the Chamber of Commerce.

That same year I finished *In Memoriam,* a tribute to Jack, and Eugene Ormandy was good enough to perform this one.

Partita, a more ambitious composition, was performed

in New York by the Philharmonic under Artur Rodzinski.

Ethel heard it, and later she said to me:

"Lionel, have you *seen* that program?"

"No, I just listened to the radio," I said.

"I think you should look hard at this," she said, handing me the printed folder.

There was a symphony by Beethoven. There was an overture by Brahms. And there was *Partita,* by Barrymore. I hid my head.

Listening to *Partita* with Rodzinski and the great New York Philharmonic was, I have to confess with no modesty and no shame, an enormous experience. I felt as certain religious folk have been said to feel at their devotions, as if they had to snatch at something of reality fast lest their souls evaporate in sheer bliss. An orchestra of one hundred pieces, the best musicians in the world, performing me! I took care to be alone that Sunday when they played *Partita* because I did not want anybody to see me weep.

It goes without saying—save that I enjoy saying it—that I am grateful to Fabien Sevitzky and to Eugene Ormandy and others who have helped me. My efforts in music, diffident and modest as they are, have brought me great pleasure, as such efforts will bring pleasure to anybody, no matter how small his talent, who pursues them enough to master the fundamentals and reach the stage where he can begin to have fun. If you like music, do something about it. Sing in your local choral club, join the church choir—learn to play the oboe!—or try out for first tenor in a barbershop quartet. If like me you have the temper for it, write your own music by committing honest thefts from real composers.

But don't, of course, get yourself confused with Wagner.

I wrote some music for "The Mayor of the Town," which I used to do on the air, and this had a pleasant ring which I always liked, though I could never quite decide where I stole it. I set to music a poem by Heinrich Heine at the request of Madame Schumann-Heink shortly before her death, but since this was done especially for her and for no one else, I destroyed it. I did a Piano Concerto in 1946 which Sevitzky has performed, and I have at various times set down a number of things which no one has performed and which I am sure no one ever will perform. In 1949 I enjoyed hearing my *Opera Buffa,* the kind of thing that might have been written by any fairly bright young student of Mozart, performed by the Burbank Symphony under Leo Damiani. Since this was near home, I took pains to be on hand to take a bow if any such opportunity arose. Damiani thoughtfully pointed me out, so I got the bow.

Sometime ago I was smitten with an ambition to do a symphony based on "Mairzy Doates," but for one reason and another did not, and just as well.

From time to time, in the pursuit of Euterpe and money, I have made recordings involving music. One Saturday night in 1948 in the Hollywood Bowl I had the great pleasure of hearing Miklos Rozsa and the Hollywood Bowl Orchestra, with Roger Wagner and the Los Angeles Chorale and Kathryn Grayson and Mario Lanza as the soloists, do a composition of mine called *Hallowe'en.* I spoke the words. This and other narrations with music, such as *A Christmas Carol* and *Rip Van Winkle,* have been caught on wax. If you are full of curiosity and reckless with your money you can buy them in stores, and I hope you do. I get a small percentage.

Sometimes, in the preparation of things like this, I run into an argument. There was a gentleman, who shall be nameless, having a definite say-so about these records, who, when asked if he thought any emoluments would accrue from these works of mine, declared: "Yas, yas, yas, maybe a little, but this Barrymore really costs us money. He likes this music stuff, these big orchestras. Outside of that, he may be good sometimes as a narrator."

I said: "Now get this. It is only great modesty which makes me demand large orchestras. Beethoven and Brahms did indeed write quartets and quintets, but, good sir, these great men were surpassing geniuses. Beethoven sometimes used only four fiddles. For my part, I really hate to enter the lists against the gods with only seven fiddles behind me.

"However, since I am an actor and therefore an egotist, if you say so we will proceed with the recordings with an accompaniment by a Hammond organ."

Be that as it may, Hollywood is still a wonderful place in more ways than one. The war, which so stunned us with horror while it was going on and has in these sad and frightening days left us some horrors even worse, and with despairs we never dreamed of, did at least one thing for America. It sent many of the finest musicians to our shores, a great many of them to Hollywood where they could make a living. It is almost as if you might today pull into a Sunset Boulevard drive-in and sit down between Beethoven and Brahms, and never of course know it.

I almost killed Rachmaninoff on Sunset Boulevard.

Preoccupied with some fancy of my own I almost ran him down. As the car swerved I recognized him. I nearly went to pieces. My emotion was uncontrollable, and I had to pull over and thank God, who has helped me out so many times in so many ways, for sparing me this accident.

As I looked around, Rachmaninoff raised his fist and cursed me in choicest Russian blasphemy. I bowed and was proud to be addressed by him in any tongue.

I never met Rachmaninoff, but as you see I have a lively memory of that great man. I am proud of having had a word from him, like the fellow who said:

"Mr. Whistler, I passed your studio today."

"Thank you," said Whistler.

I am fortunate in knowing Dr. Eugene Zador, one of the greatest of the great. He came from Europe with the others, and through some quirk of Fate, more than once kind to me, I managed to meet him and we became friends. He looks at my effusions on music paper and like some medieval alchemist of old who transmutes mud into gold, he can often perform precisely the same kind of service for me.

Today it is increasingly borne in on me that the lighter forms of music, such as bugle solos and the glissando bleats of boy and girl baritones on the networks, are the own true loves of the listening public, not merely in the hinterlands but in the allegedly cultured metropolitan centers as well. Perhaps, though, we should not complain about this but should take wry kind of pleasure in observing that even our hillbilly tunes derive from old English folk music. It is amusing to know, for instance, that it was really Beethoven who brought Kathleen home; he did it briefly in the E Flat "Emperor" Concerto. It is also interesting to note the quivering excitement of the large-breasted ladies of Pasadena when Toscanini and his NBC Symphony come to town. Toscanini is great and unique, of course; but no one in Pasadena seems to be aware that one of the finest conductors in Europe, Dr. Richard Lert, lives and works in that community virtually unknown and certainly neglected.

But I remind myself that I have already talked too much about the art of painting and that I am making the same mistake by holding forth fulsomely about music. Forgive me. Any intelligent pessimist with half a brain cell in operation these fateful days is bound to feel like a victim in a tumbril on the way to the guillotine. It is later than we think, we have a few things on our minds, and there is not time to be concise as the shadows gather over the crowd.

If at this point anyone begins to think he detects a bitter note in these lubricities—well, perhaps he is right. But I can only repeat that you must not take me seriously as a composer or as a critic in anything pertaining to great music. I have my fun.

25. *Brave Exit*

HAVING HAD ADVENTURES in the temples of several arts but still not feeling that I belonged to the priestcraft in any of them, I was in the proper mood to try something new when the radio people came to me in the early thirties to convince me that my presence would lend distinction to the wireless. They had a minimum of difficulty persuading me that I was most probably a great radio actor, and they put out broadsides to the public announcing acquisition of this new gem. I was the more eager to try because the first show they gave me involved music.

This was an arrangement of Romberg tunes in which I played the part of narrator, telling the operatic stories to a little girl, Cora Sue Collins; she, I suppose, is by now telling the same tales to her own children. I enjoyed doing this and I enjoyed the other opportunities to work on the air that came my way, but I wonder what those gentlemen think now who advertised so widely that the renowned Barrymore would bring so much to radio. Obviously, I brought nothing. I merely acquired a new string to my bow, learned a new technique, and myself greatly profited from the experience. Truthfully, I am always amazed by the general excellence of the air and by the skill and craft of the professionals on it. The American public is besplattered with luxury by their radio programs: they have only to flip a little switch and turn a button to command in their living rooms the presence of the world's best entertainers, musicians, and dramatists. The choice is astonishingly wide. And if you don't like what you get you turn to something else or silence them all.

At the moment, of course, there is a controversy about whether television will hurt radio or not. Of course it won't hurt it. It will improve it vastly, just as the addition of sound improved motion pictures. It will be exactly the same thing with television. It's merely radio with pictures added.

"The Mayor of the Town" show with which I was identified for a good many years was actually a wartime show, else, as a matter of fact, I should never have been allowed to do it.

I had been hankering for a production of my own and had cut some records of Arthur Train's "Cappy Ricks" stories, "Cappy" being a crusty but intelligent old gentleman appropriate for me to play, I thought; but that enterprise was forestalled by World War Two. At this moment, the advertising agency of Ruthrauff & Ryan came up with a patriotic notion. Our ships and the ships of our allies were being sunk on the high seas by submarines and it was increasingly necessary to encourage the nation to save scrap iron. It is a curiosity now, of course, but they first thought of "The Mayor of the Town" program as a war propaganda program, framed in entertainment. They approached Metro about permitting me to play in it.

Permission was instantly granted, naturally, and I went to war as the Mayor. I invite anyone to suggest that my labors failed to shorten the conflict by a split moment, but as has so often happened in my story, the whole undertaking worked out splendidly for me. I stayed on as a radio actor, to my profit.

An adaptation of Dickens' *Christmas Carol* came later, in 1942, and has, apparently, become a fixture which people expect and accept because after all somebody ought to read the *Carol* to the children at Christmastime. An odd thing about this is that we have produced it differently from year to year, with various players and with various cuts and additions to the original, but no one has seemed to notice.

Jack too was on radio. I could wish that it might have been different, that he might have been permitted to take his curtain call in the black tights of the Dane, or even as Lear. I could wish that as he went down, destroying himself, the accompaniment might have been an echo of *Götterdämmerung* instead of the sneers of the envious and the witch-whispers of gossipmongers. Of course, I do not wish these things at all. What actually happened was that my brother did a brave and honest thing.

I have no heart to reiterate all of his story. It is well known. Jack and Dolores Costello had enjoyed an idyll and had been divorced. Then came the Elaine Barrie escapade, another marriage and another divorce, which undoubtedly sold a number of newspapers. Then the inability to remember his lines in pictures and the necessity of reading them from blackboards (and Jack's wonderful remark: "At that, I am one of the few actors out here who *can* read and act at the same time"). And with all this, bankruptcy and great debt, and illness.

He could have quit. He could have said, "Depart, jackals, I am ill and tired and I have no more money and

I cannot pay you a farthing." He could have done that without dishonor. He chose to pay up. Against all the errors that can be properly charged against Jack Barrymore, this can be entered in his record: he was consumed with a passion to remit what he owed.

It was for this reason that he dragged himself between hemorrhages and fainting spells to play a travesty of himself on the Rudy Vallee show. It was called disgraceful. There were sincere persons, old friends among them, who turned away under the understandable conviction that he had sold out the last sacred cup on the altar, his self-respect, his art, as he appeared ridiculously on the air week after week in slapstick shows in which he held himself up to mockery.

He did it simply to get tax money. It was all he could do. He used a tarnished and broken tool in his extremity, in this willful, tongue-in-cheek impersonation of an old tragedian, but he used it like a master. He was utterly conscious of what he was doing and why it was necessary to do it. Nor was Rudy Vallee either callous or selfish in employing Jack. He understood perfectly. He respected my brother and stood by him as he played out the last act of his tragedy in his own way.

If you will not think it immodest of me to say so, I will set it down for the record that far from shame it was a gallant thing that Jack did on that burlesque show in his final days. It was also, I have to say with professional pride for a brother who was a very great actor, an enormous example of his spirit and art that with the shadow already on him, he was able to do it at all.

No one could help him. It was tried, God knows. There were friends who did all they or any humans could. Gene

Fowler, for instance, who later wrote magnificently about Jack in *Good Night, Sweet Prince,* and found himself at the end of 468 pages still, like the rest of us, unable to utter the final and complete explanation of Jack Barrymore.

During the buffooneries with Rudy Vallee that Spring of 1942, my brother often went on the air in great physical anguish. He collapsed several times in early May, but was bolstered up and enabled to continue by the quick and gentle ministrations of Dr. Hugo M. Kirsten. He did several shows with the doctor at his side, and those performances by a haggard actor, barely able to stand but always able to read his lines, were as funny as any Jack Barrymore ever did.

Jack's last show with Rudy was on the evening of May 14, when he read a line that was unhappily prophetic.

"I'm retiring," he said to Vallee.

"Not really?" said Vallee. "You mean you're leaving acting flat?"

"Why not? That's how it's left me," said Jack.

Some one argued during rehearsal that these words were in bad taste.

"Bosh, old man," said Jack. "Leave them in. It's only a gag."

On the night of May 19, at a rehearsal for the show scheduled to go on the following Thursday, Jack was unable to continue. He staggered and Rudy Vallee came forward to support him.

"I guess this is one time I miss my cue," my brother said. He was in severe shock and pain and there were tears streaming down his face. Dr. Kirsten was called at once and Jack was taken to the Hollywood Presbyterian Hospital. He suffered from the chronic kidney ailment which had pained him so long, and also from hypostatic pneumonia.

"The show must go on" is a hackneyed phrase, but it means something to old actors. I took Jack's place on the Rudy Vallee show on the evening of Thursday, May 21, and though my voice and heart were heavy, I did the best I could, as Jack had done for me that Christmas after my wife died.

I was unable to walk due to an accident, but I had my wheel chair rolled into Jack's room and stayed with him. He was unconscious most of the time, but occasionally he would recover and his mind would be clear and sharp. He spoke now and then to Gene Fowler, who knew that Charon was waiting at the dock for his old friend; but Gene managed somehow, despite his grief, to come up with badinage and affectionate bullying to ease my brother's last moments. I shall always be in Fowler's debt, not only for what he did for Jack but for his staunch support of me during those hopeless days and nights.

During his comas, my brother dreamt of our grandmother, Mrs. John Drew.

Again and again he mumbled her name:

"Mum Mum."

Several days after entering the hospital, Jack rallied enough to speak seriously about something to Dr. Kirsten. I could not hear what was said, but I was not surprised when I learned that he had asked for a priest.

The Rev. John O'Donnell, pastor of the Roman Catholic Church of the Immaculate Heart, came to Jack immediately. He was an old friend. We had known him in Culver City years ago when he was a pastor of a church near the studio. And Father O'Donnell came not once, but often, sometimes twice a day.

I would not know, of course, what was said between my dying brother and the good father, but I do know that they prayed and talked together and that Jack was taken back into the Church. He received the Sacrament of Extreme Unction at the hands of Father O'Donnell, and so met his Maker in the grace of the Church to which his mother had brought him as a little boy. I have been at pains to put all this in because I understand that the general impression is that my brother did not die in the Church.

With me as I kept my last watch were Alan Mowbray, the actor, and John Dekker, the artist, both old friends of Jack's and mine, and, of course, Gene Fowler.

Suddenly, late in the afternoon of May 28, my brother raised himself on an elbow and asked for Gene, who was sitting in the hall.

"Lean over me," he said. Gene complied.

I did not hear what they said, but there seemed to be some special joke between them.

A few minutes later he looked at me and tried to tell me something.

I did not understand.

"What did you say, Jake?" I asked.

"You heard me, Mike," he said clearly and fell asleep. And those were his last words. Jack died the next evening, May 29.

But the show went on. It went on that night in Boston, where Ethel was playing in Emlyn Williams' *The Corn Is Green.* She would have been at her brother's bedside, but ten days earlier he had asked me to wire her.

"Tell Ethel to go on, not to come," he commanded. She understood and obeyed.

When Ethel walked on in the first scene, the audience stopped the show for many minutes with an ovation while she stood with bowed head and waited. Then she finished the play without a tremble in her voice. I like to think, of course, that she was supported in this performance by an actor whom neither she nor the audience could see.

Months later I asked Fowler a question.

"I realize it is none of my business, and perhaps it is something that I would not be supposed to know. But would it be all right if you told me what Jack said that afternoon?"

"Of course it would be all right," said Gene. "I was going to tell you, but not for a while because it was a joke. He said:

" 'Is it true that you are the illegitimate son of Buffalo Bill?' "

"And what did you reply?"

"Why, I said that I had always understood that I was the natural son of Colonel Cody. I added that we mustn't let anyone else know about it. This seemed to please him and he closed his eyes with a smile."

An autopsy revealed that Jack had cirrhosis of the liver. He suffered in addition from chronic gastritis, from ulcers with hemorrhages, from hardening of the arteries, and from pneumonia. I authorized the autopsy and I have since been thankful many times that I had the sense, in spite of shock and sorrow, to have it done. It is better to know than to wonder.

But no medical or literary scalpel revealed, or could reveal, I regret to say, the sources of the revolt, the uncertainties, and the always-questioning consciousness of unfulfillment which impelled Jack Barrymore to his death.

The greatly gifted are not the fortunate persons of this world. Today we are forced to read all these astute papers in the magazines about the values of "adjustment." We must all, it seems, "adjust" ourselves to the world and to everybody else. How fortunate, I say, for the sheep who can munch in unison and adjust. How painful for the artists, the statesmen, the pioneers, the musicians, and the actors who fail to keep time—but what a gift for us that they do fail.

26. *Tomorrow and Tomorrow*

THE ACCIDENT which had me trapped in a wheel chair at the time of Jack's death occurred one afternoon late in 1936. I was in my so-called studio industriously and happily adding lines to some unimportant drawing on a heavy metal drafting board, the kind you are familiar with in the art departments of newspaper offices. I leaned on this thing, upset it, tripped and fell.

I felt the stab of a hard and wrenching pain in my left hip. I fumbled and scrambled but I could not get up. When help reached me and I had been carried to the hospital it was discovered that I had broken my hip.

Aside from the pain, which I bore with bellows and no fortitude, I felt betrayed and outraged. My Fates, who up to this time had run errands on my behalf with a good deal of imagination, had nodded and had allowed me to suffer from a mere commonplace accident. I was reminded of a remark of Jack's: "Die? I should say not, old fellow. No Barrymore would allow such a conventional thing to happen to him." Ethel has gone on stage on numerous occasions with a temperature far above par, and Mum Mum, as you will remember, was confidently scheming a new play the day before she passed on. But here was I, who had never suffered anything save wounds of the spirit, hoisted and trussed like a chicken, helpless but not inarticulate.

I yelled for Louis B. Mayer. I was under the impression that he would take charge, dismiss the entire thing as a piece of nonsense, and get me out of that hospital.

Whatever Mr. Mayer was doing—and whatever he was doing was important—he dropped it and came to me. He found me clamoring to escape my harness and (I wish Adolphe Menjou had not used the line first) suffering from the greatest pains known to medical science.

I was not only uncomfortable and dismayed, I was suffering from the not unreasonable assumption that I was through as an actor, washed up, kaput.

I revealed all this to Mr. Mayer in outrage and tears. He tried to soothe me.

"It will be all right, Lionel, it will be all right. We will think of something," he said.

And later on he did think of something, brilliantly. But on that day he left me in spite of his reassurances in a state of hopeless bewilderment. I lay in that hospital bed like a creature on the Venetian rack, tugged by ropes and pulleys, tortured in body and sour of mind. And the possibility of my demise as an actor was not all in my imagination.

This went on for months and I was not a good patient. I admire men who can meet misfortune with a stern British lip or a "Heigh Ho!" but I am not one of this breed. In adversity I dree my weird with full diapason, keen like a crone at a hanging, and call pitifully upon the gods to drop all nonessential affairs and give me their full attention.

Days were black and nights were blacker. Both my backside and my conscience bothered me. I seem to recall, although this does not now seem probable, that I repented my sins, especially those of omission, and resolved to amount to something. But I was mainly frightened and convinced that if I could not walk I would, like an old broken-legged horse, never be of any use to myself or to anybody.

The report was out, and I knew it, and there were persons in high places at Metro-Goldwyn-Mayer who were willing to confirm it, that I was indeed through.

Naturally I did not hear a certain conversation that Mr. Mayer had a few days later with one of the financial wizards in the New York office, but I was told about it later.

"Tell everybody," he said, "that if Lionel is out I am through too."

There are times when even to comment on an act of friendship and loyalty is to make a lugubrious ass of yourself. This is one of those times. Mr. Mayer did what he did and there is, of course, no way to express my gratitude.

It came about after I was limpingly on my feet again that, following Mr. Mayer's instructions, Metro-Goldwyn-Mayer writers had found it not so troublesome after all to invent scenes for me in which I did not have to walk, run, and leap. I could sit behind desks. I could act in beds. I could stand. And gradually, I was able to move around. Gradually also I realized that it had been years anyway since I had attempted a grand jeté before the camera. The sun came out and it appeared that save for an aching bottom and a well-exercised temper, I was not so badly off after all. Gradually, I learned to walk a little.

Then came the picture *Saratoga* with Clark Gable. I came on the set one day in gay spirits, tripped over a sound cable, fell heavily, and snapped my hip again.

I had it all to do over. They had to park me in the hospital again with those racking ropes and pulleys. Again it was a matter of months. This time I did not come out on my feet.

Now comes a part of my story that I would explain in detail if I could. The reason I cannot explain it is that no one at Metro, least of all Louis B. Mayer, will stand and take a bow and say "I thought up the *Kildare* series." Nothing greater, of course, could possibly have been contrived for me than the character of the grumpy but likable old physician in the wheel chair. His locale is in the hospital. He moves all over it in that chair, wheeling from operating room to ward, riding the elevators—and riding his young protégé, played originally by Lew Ayres. I liked the part so much that I subscribed to *The Lancet* and other medical journals, and have as a result become a second-class quack and a first class hypochondriac. We made at least a dozen *Kildares,* during which time Dr. Ayres and I accomplished cures which would put the medical profession centuries ahead of itself if they would only pay attention to our diagnoses. But seriously, the *Kildares* were carefully produced and I pride myself and Metro that the good doctors have at least smiled tolerantly on our impersonations.

As I was saying, it has never been revealed to me how the *Kildare* series came about. If they were not invented specifically for me by human kindness, then they were indubitably inspired from a Very High Place. If in this discursive testament you have been pained to find little of a good moral tone, perhaps you can find something thoughtful in that.

At any rate, the successful mechanics of the *Kildares* revealed that it is possible for a man in a wheel chair to do considerable acting, particularly if he needs the money. I have made at least forty pictures since the second accident.

Since that mishap did not actually interrupt anything, except temporarily, I might have thought it not worth commenting on at such length except for one important matter. Along with another peculiar legend that devils me, this is one that I want to correct.

I do not have arthritis.

I emphasize this because of the many letters I get—by the thousand—from arthritics. Some of them are pitiful, some of them are gallant. They are from sufferers who assume that, because of a certain prominence that has befallen me, I have been able to command special cures and techniques for the treatment of this malady.

There are times when I could wish that this was so. There are indeed new and wonderful panaceas for arthritis, and there are remarkable instances of recovery. Perhaps if I too had arthritis I might benefit by one of these new methods. It would actually be a comfort (but I say this sympathetically and in no worse-off-than-thou spirit) to *know* exactly why I ail and why it is difficult for me to get around. I am handicapped only by a twice-broken hip which has, as a matter of fact, knitted well but which still makes walking a burden. I shall most certainly be up and about again. It is ridiculous that I have already reposed for so long on my rear.

Of course, in several departments being a nonwalker has its pleasant advantages. I do not have to get up and go fetch things for people. I do not have to go to them. They come to me. I can, if I want to, employ a despised crutch to get where I want, but I loathe these devices and avoid them. I am by way of being an expert chair jockey and can wheel my contraption almost anywhere there is a smooth surface. I can drive a car anywhere and I do.

And so, at an age when a few conversational debilities are to be expected anyway, I am not badly off at all. One of these vernal days when the sun shines and the sap runs fast I shall start prancing about again. Meantime, I do not envy Mr. Crosby and Mr. Astaire and others their golf. I despise golf. And perhaps these gentlemen envy me my chair.

The other legend that I have to dispose of is the embarrassing gossip which made me out a bitter and vindictive personal enemy of Franklin Roosevelt's. It is an unfortunate thing for actors that when they exercise their rights of opinion and free speech merely as citizens of the Republic, they often manage to bestir more ill-will and more misunderstanding than anybody else. I suppose this is because the actor is always thrusting his chin out as a target for criticism anyway, and also because almost everybody in Hollywood actually lives in a kind of crystal aquarium, subject always to the gaze and disdain of the curious.

Of course I did oppose the re-election of President Roosevelt's party on one of the occasions in which he ran, and I appeared briefly on the platform at a Los Angeles rally to growl a few words against the Democrats. Now, as any reader who has persisted thus far knows, I detest overstatements of any kind, but at this political whingding it is possible that I purpled up my prose a bit. I merely did it out of sincere conviction, however, and whatever hyperbole I engaged in was immediately replied to in gaudier tones by Mr. Harold Ickes, no mean mixer of word colors himself.

Be all that as it may, the fact is that I always had and still do have nothing but the highest form of personal admiration for Franklin Roosevelt. I did not have, unluckily for me, the privilege of knowing him, but he was the kind of man I would have liked. He had things that I liked. He collected ship models. He had a fine house. He had humor. He had nerve. And—if you will agree that it is the best compliment I can pay—I always considered him a superb actor. There is no question of it: if I could have known the President I should have adored him.

Due to the exigencies of his great office and the necessary secretariat which surrounds the Presidency, I am certain that President Roosevelt never received a letter that my dog wrote to his dog. I am certain that it was not received because I am convinced that had Mr. Roosevelt been handed this note he would have collaborated with Fala on a reply.

It had seemed to me as the war wore on and had begun to swing our way, that, awful as it was, we might concern ourselves with smaller things occasionally, such as the predicament of the faithful dogs left at home by soldiers. Many were forlorn and neglected, fine, intelligent, beautiful dogs; and they were either starving or being cruelly snatched by the wagons and hurried off to die in the pounds. It was, to be sure, a small and sentimental notion, but it seemed to make sense to me one evening by my fireside as I pulled the ears of my Johnnie, a Scottie like Fala. I seized on this excuse, thin as it was, as perhaps a way in which an old actor could establish contact with the President. With Johnnie's co-operation, we prepared a let ter and addressed it to Fala, care the White House. We said:

> Dear Fala:
>
> I have been thinking about the sad plight of the thousands of dogs left at home by soldiers now away fighting for our country. Some of these dogs are having a terrible time, being very lonesome for the boys that belong to them, and many of them are hungry and starving. Now, this man that belongs to me is in some respects a very nice man, but I have looked into the matter and discover that he has no influence.
>
> This man that belongs to you, though, has got a lot of pull. I thought perhaps you might take up with him this matter of the poor dogs who have sent their men away and are now in trouble.
>
> It might be that you would come out this way sometime. If you do, please look me up. I have a long line of trees and posts. Yesterday I bit the postman. He is a Republican.
>
> Respectfully yours,
>
> JOHNNIE.

Unless I miss entirely the humor of the man, Mr. Roosevelt would have replied to that if he had ever seen it.

After the President's death, it was proposed at Metro-Goldwyn-Mayer that I appear as F.D.R. in *The Beginning of the End.* I made a test and it was considered all right. I did not get the part, however, because when Mrs. Roosevelt heard about the casting she said firmly that she would withhold permission if the terrible Barrymore played her husband. This, of course, is all over the dam now, so I think I will not be misunderstood if I say that although I was naturally disappointed by her rejection of me, I had then and I have now nothing but admiration for Eleanor Roosevelt for her attitude.

I did not say, or even think, the things about her husband which I was supposed to have said, but these alleged sayings were reported to her and she had every reason to believe them. Therefore, good for her! How lucky a man was Franklin Roosevelt to have such a wife.

I wrote another letter during the war, even more improperly, to Winston Churchill and received a reply.

I had met Mr. Churchill many years ago in London. Why I was there I cannot at the moment recall, but Ethel was on hand, and at Willis's Rooms one evening, particularly memorable for me because I kept my eyes all night on the two most beautiful women I ever saw in my life, Lady Muriel Wilson and Lady Beckett, I was presented to Churchill. For him, it was precisely as if he had been introduced to the gas man, the shoe clerk, or any of the people you come in contact with but have no particular reason for seeing again. And as a matter of fact, I myself did not realize until years later whom I had met.

I had a Scott hat. Very good hat, the one thing in the world that I possessed at the time, and when I left Willis's Rooms I picked up another man's hat, also a very nice hat, and left mine. I wore this thefted bonnet for about ten years, impressed but not awed because it was Winston Churchill's; and then, realizing I had an important souvenir, I put it away. As things like that go, I was never able to find it again. If an unlikely occasion should arise, I would inquire of Mr. Churchill if he wore *my* hat and what happened to it.

I wrote to him one evening during the "blood, sweat,

and tears" times and I did this, I assure you, only because I had tilted a bottle too far and because the friends at my house had also looked into their cups too long.

I scrawled, as I recall it, some such sincere but idiotic note as this:

> Dear Mr. Churchill:
>
> You do not know me but you do know my sister. I am a brother of Ethel Barrymore and I have a request to make. It is this: when the time comes, as it surely will, and you get ready to spring the trap on that S.O.B. Hitler, may I ask for two front-row reserved seats?
>
> Respectfully,
>
> LIONEL BARRYMORE.

Several days later I remembered this impertinence. A search around the house failed to disclose the letter. We created a household whirlwind looking for it. Finally, with great misgivings, I got hold of the preposterous friends who had put me up to this.

"You destroyed that fool letter of course?" I said.

"Destroyed it hell," they said, "we mailed it to him."

I hoped, of course, that the Churchill secretariat would be as efficient as the Roosevelt staff and would not put my nonsense in Mr. Churchill's busy dispatch case. But they did. Indeed they did. The reply came in Mr. Churchill's own handwriting:

> 10, Downing Street
>
> (CREST) Whitehall
>
> 13 October 1940
>
> Dear Barrymore:
>
> It was kind of you to write me such a charming letter and I am touched by what you say. We feel

confident of success over here but it cheers us to know that we can count on the sympathy and good will of people like yourself on the other side of the Atlantic.

Yours sin'ly
WINSTON CHURCHILL.

Mr. Lionel Barrymore

My domestic arrangements today are as pleasant as any man's. I live in Chatsworth, a place about the size that would be sneered at as a farm back East but is solemnly called a "ranch" in Southern California.

At first, it was my ambition to raise chickens. When marauding weasels got them, I decided that there was no profit in producing rodent food and purchased a cow. The cow constantly became unhappy and set up such a roar of bellowing and moaning in her quarters that we couldn't stand it. It was then explained to me that she required male companionship. This was provided successfully, the hollering ceased, and our cow was soon with calf. Her progeny, however, turned out to be a bull, so in disgust we got rid of both.

Johnnie, the Scottie who wrote to Fala, was a constant and intelligent companion for many years until his death. He led a happy life, devoted to the extermination of gophers. A jackrabbit took up homesteading in the garden and became tame. And numerous cats arrived. At the moment, the census reveals that there are approximately forty.

I drive to the studio, a distance of about twenty miles, and since it is needful to arrive early because of make-up and wardrobe requirements, I am usually on the road through the San Fernando Valley by six o'clock in the morning. Unlike most actors in this as well as in everything else, I enjoy getting up early and always have enjoyed it. Aside from that, the early morning is the best of all possible times to look at the world and find it good, to see it sharp and clean and clear in a good light, to drink up with your eyes its color and beauty. I am grateful for what little experience I have had in so-called art, for at least I have learned how to see.

On long drives, which are occasions for any man to let his thoughts run as tall and long as they can, I discover that I am capable of gratitude, that I am thankful for a staggering series of surely *directed* happenstances and kindnesses which have carried me through absolutely in spite of my own perversities and stubbornness. It has, though, not been a good thing to be a triple-decked person, lightly touched in three arts, for even today—and it does not seem to me like a late hour at all—I am hopeful that somehow I may find my correct métier. I have not obtained, have not succeeded, or achieved, in any of the three branches into which I have thrust myself. Persons with one talent, or no talent, are perhaps luckier than some of us who are dealt three-of-a-kind but can't make up our minds whether to stand pat or draw for a full house. Mostly, I have bluffed.

Of course, in the end, in imitation of all intelligent men today, I wind up a pessimist. The current state of the world would frighten anyone possessed of at least the brains of a Congressman. I mean, of course, the threat of self-destruction which looms over us now, but I mean also something else: when I am asked by young interviewers how, during my numerous years, the country has changed most, for better or for worse, I know the answer instantly. It is a discouraging answer.

What has affected our lives most, it seems to me, is not the astonishing march of science. Certainly we have not marched anywhere spiritually. But we have marched backwards, laying up stumbling blocks as we retreat, in a determined effort to defeat free enterprise. It is no longer possible for a young fellow to hope for any reward from his brains or from his talents.

I do not want this interpreted to my disadvantage, please, as a partisan political view. It just happens to be so in my opinion that these curious economic theories which we have borne since approximately 1913 are the forerunners of disaster. If you will consult your history books, the ones you studied in the eighth grade, you will discover that the harbingers of the destruction of all the great civilizations before us were strangulating taxes.

So far as this applies to actors—I hasten to get back into my own bailiwick—these appalling income levies mean that anyone who wants to be a star these days does it purely for love of theater, or for love of his art. No fortunes can now be laid up by reciting on the stage or by posing for pictures.

If, since I have the years if not the privilege of speaking as one of the elder sages, I may sum up what is worth while, I should put it simply.

These are the important things: Youth, and health, and someone to love you.

As for this record, there are some lines in *Macbeth* which say it all.

> Tomorrow, and tomorrow, and tomorrow,
> Creeps in this petty pace from day to day
> To the last syllable of recorded time;
> And all our yesterdays have lighted fools
> The way to dusty death. Out, out, brief candle!
> Life's but a walking shadow, a poor player
> That struts and frets his hour upon the stage
> And then is heard no more. It is a tale
> Told by an idiot, full of sound and fury,
> Signifying nothing.

Appendix

THE RIVALS—Play in three acts by Richard Sheridan. Mr. and Mrs. Sidney Drew presenting Mrs. John Drew in Sheridan's Comedy, 1893. Cast included:

Mrs. John Drew, Mr. Sidney Drew, Mrs. Sidney Drew, George Osbourne, Chas. E. Verner, Clarence E. Holt, Albert Harris, Pierre Traiteler, Edwin Wallace, Lional [*sic*] Barrymore, Helen Mason Osbourne.

THE ROAD TO RUIN—Holcroft's comedy, in four acts. Produced under the direction of Sidney Drew at the Star Theater, New York, January 15, 1894. Cast included:

Mrs. John Drew, Mr. Sidney Drew, Mrs. Sidney Drew [Gladys Rankin], George Osbourne, Clarence E. Holt, Edwin F. Mayo, Al. Harris, Charles Erin Verner, Edwin Wallace, Carl St. Aubyne, H. D. Gibbs, Fred. McClelland, Helen Mason Osbourne, Kate Horan, and Mrs. Drew's grandson Lionel Barrymore footing the list of male artists as Footman.

THE BACHELOR'S BABY—Military comedy in three acts by Coyne Fletcher. Produced by Mr. and Mrs. Sidney Drew at the Park Theater, Boston, October 21, 1895. Directed by McKee Rankin. Cast included:

Mr. McKee Rankin, Mr. J. B. Booth, Mr. Sidney Drew, Mr. Sidney Booth, Mr. Thomas Tuther, Mr. Lionel Barrymore [as Sgt. Jones], Mr. Charles Crosby, Miss Annie Lee Rodgers, Miss Lillian Lawrence, Miss Nita Sykes, Miss Julia Ring, Miss Annie Mortimer, and Mrs. Sidney Drew.

MARY PENNINGTON, SPINSTER—Comedy in four acts by W. R. Walkes. Produced by Miss Georgia Cayvan & Co. at Palmer's Theater, New York, October 12, 1896. Directed by Charles Burnham. Cast included:

Mr. George Woodward, Mr. Frank Atherley, Mr. Orrin Johnson, Mr. Albert Brown, Mr. Lionel Barrymore [as Watson], Miss Georgia Cayvan, Miss Anne Sutherland, Miss Mary Jerrold, Miss Kate Ten Eyck, Miss Winifred McCaull, and Miss Louise Palmer.

Also at the Star Theater, Buffalo, January 12, 1897.

SQUIRE KATE—Pastoral drama in four acts by Robert Buchanan. Produced by Miss Georgia Cayvan & Co. at Palmer's Theater, New York, October 26, 1896. Directed by Charles Burnham. Cast included:

Mr. George Woodward, Mr. Frank Atherley, Mr. Orrin Johnson, Mr. William Herbert, Mr. Albert Brown, Mr. Lionel Barrymore [as Lord Silversnake], Mr. Thomas Bridgeland, Mr. Charles Thropp, Miss Georgia Cayvan, Miss Florence Condron, Miss Annie Sutherland, Miss Winifred McCaull, Miss Mary Jerrold, Miss Kate Ten Eyck, Miss Louise Palmer, Mr. Joseph Henry, and Mr. Henry Howe.

Produced under the stage direction of Mr. Napier Lothian, Jr.

Also at the Amphion Theater, New York, January 25, 1897.

CUMBERLAND '61—Romantic drama in four acts and five tableaux by Mr. Franklin Fyles. Produced by Augustus Pitou at the 14th Street Theater, New York, October 18, 1897. Cast included:

C. G. Craig, W. J. Ferguson, Frank Losee, Edgar L. Davenport, Lionel Barrymore [as Adolfus Drayton Lenox, a cadet], John E. Kellerd, S. K. Chester, Richard Malchien, Alvin Drehle, Richard Webster, Florence Rockwell, Amelia Summerville, Viola Black, and Millie Sackett.

Produced by Augustus Pitou at the Bijou Theater, New York, February 14, 1898. Same cast, except that Marie Shotwell took the place of Florence Rockwell, and Louise Galloway that of Viola Black. Also at the Boston Museum, Boston, January 17-22, 1898.

Mr. McKee Rankin presenting Miss Nance O'Neil in the McKee Rankin Company season of summer repertory at Minneapolis, Minnesota, beginning June 19, 1898. Repertoire included *Oliver Twist, Camille, New East Lynne, Leah the Forsaken,* and *Magda.* Lionel Barrymore is on record as playing the part of Richard Hare in *East Lynne* and Max in *Magda;* but no programs of this engagement are available.

UNCLE DICK—New play, in four parts, founded on the German, by Martha Morton. Produced by Mr. Sol Smith Russell at the Star Theater, Buffalo, October 6-8, 1898. Cast included:

Sol Smith Russell, Alfred Hudson, William Farnum, William Bernard, Lionel Barrymore [as Lawrence Sherman], Jacques Martin, Florence Rockwell, Ethel Winthrop, Fanny Addison Pitt, Lila Convere, and Alice Thill.

Also at the Stone Theater, Binghamton, New York, September 27, 1898, and at the Tremont Theater, Boston, October 23, 1898, for a week's engagement.

HONORABLE JOHN RIGSBY—Comedy in three acts by Charles Klein. Produced by Sol Smith Russell at the New National Theater, Washington, November 28, 1898. Cast included:

Mr. Sol Smith Russell, William Farnum, Alfred Hudson, James Lackaye, William Sampson, Jacques Martin, William Cullington, Lionel Barrymore [as Harold Marson], Florence Rockwell, Lila Convere, Alice Thill, and Fanny Addison Pitt.

Also at Powers' Theater, Chicago, for two weeks beginning January 23, 1899; same cast.

ARIZONA—Play in four acts by Augustus Thomas. Produced by Kirke La Shelle and Fred R. Hamlin at the Chicago Grand Opera House, Chicago, February 11, 1900. Return engagement at the end of a grand tour in the East and elsewhere. Cast included:

Mr. Theodore Roberts, Mr. Edwin Holt, Mr. Stephen B. French, Miss Mattie Earle, Miss Grace Henderson, Miss Adora Andrews, Mr. Vincent Serrano, Miss Eleanor Robson, Miss Jane Taylor, Mr. George O'Donnell, Mr. George Nash, Mr.

Edgar Selwyn, Mr. Malcom Gunn, Mr. Lionel Barrymore [as Sergeant Kellar], Mr. Sidney Ainsworth, and Mr. Almeric Grigsby.

SAG HARBOR (76 performances)—Play in four acts by James A. Herne. Produced at the Republic Theater, New York, September 27, 1900. Cast included:

James A. Herne, Frank Monroe, Forrest Robinson, Lionel Barrymore, William T. Hodge, C. Dibdin Pitt, John D. Garrick, T. H. Burke, Robert Gillig, Mrs. Sol Smith, Marion Abbott, Julia A. Herne, Chrystal Herne, Mollie Revel, Harriet McDonald, and Margaret Dibden Pitt.

Settings by Frank E. Gates, E. A. Morange, and Ernest Albert.

BRIXTON BURGLARY (48 performances)—Farce in three acts by Frederick W. Sidney. Produced by Sam S. Shubert at the Herald Square Theater, New York, May 20, 1901. Cast included:

Joseph Holland, Sam Edwards, Lionel Barrymore, W. J. Ferguson, Grace Filkins, Elita Proctor Otis, Channez Olney, Jessie Busley, James Kearney, and Richard Baker.

THE SECOND IN COMMAND (128 performances)—Comedy in four acts by Robert Marshall. Produced by Charles Frohman at the Empire Theater, New York, September 2, 1901. Cast included:

Guy Standing, John Drew, Oswald Yorke, Lionel Barrymore, Reginald Carrington, Robert Schable, George Harcourt, Percy Smith, Robert Mackay, Lewis Baker, H. Hassard Short, George Forbes, Ida Conquest, Ida Vernon, and Caroline Keeler.

THE MUMMY AND THE HUMMING BIRD (85 performances)—Play in four acts by Isaac Henderson. Produced by Charles Frohman at the Empire Theater, New York, September 4, 1902. Cast included:

John Drew, Guy Standing, Lewis Baker, Lionel Barrymore, Reginald Carrington, Robert Schable, David Henderson,

Thomas Gibson, Margaret Dale, Marie Derickson, and Constance Bell.

This play, with the above cast intact, returned to the Empire Theater, April 20, 1903, for two weeks.

THE BEST OF FRIENDS (65 performances)—Drama in four acts by Cecil Raleigh. Produced by Charles Frohman at the Academy of Music, New York, October 19, 1903. Cast included:

Frank Burbeck, Joseph Wheelock, Jr., Ray Rockman, Rose Lemoire, Eugene Santley, Lionel Barrymore [as Kid Garvey], Richard Bennett, Herbert Standing, Thomas McGrath, Louis Le Bay, Tully Marshall, Madeleine Rivers, Geoffrey Stein, Ralph Delmore, Prince Miller, Katherine Grey, Agnes Booth, Thomas Griffin, Willis Linderman, Albert Cowles, Stanley Jessup, John B. Cook, Douglas Stanfield, Josephine May Mack, Marion Childers, May Davenport Seymour, Edwin Hale, John C. Tremaine, O. B. Davis, Thomas Grant, Stewart Thomas, Davis Barnes, Thomas Daly, Harry Elton, Frank Murray, and Thomas Felton.

Staged by Joseph Humphreys.

THE OTHER GIRL (160 performances)—Comedy in three acts by Augustus Thomas. Produced by Charles Frohman at the Criterion Theater, New York, December 29, 1903. Cast included:

Frank Burbeck, Ralph Delmore, Frank Worthing, Drina De Wolfe, Elsie De Wolfe, Joseph Wheelock, Jr., Lou Middleton, R. R. Neill, Selina Fetter Royle, Maggie Fielding, Richard Bennett, Lionel Barrymore, Ida Greely Smith, and Joseph Whiting.

This play moved to the Empire Theater, New York, January 25, 1904, and then moved to the Lyceum Theater, New York, May 2, 1904.

PANTALOON (81 performances)—Play in one act by J. M. Barrie. Produced by Charles Frohman at the Criterion Theater, New York, December 25, 1905. Cast included:

John Barrymore, John F. Kennedy, Lionel Barrymore, Leona Powers, and Beatrice Agnew.

This play preceded ALICE SIT-BY-THE-FIRE, also by J. M. Barrie. Produced by Charles Frohman at the Criterion Theater, in New York, December 25, 1905. Cast included:

Ethel Barrymore, Beatrice Agnew, John Barrymore, Mary Nash, Bruce McRae, Cyril Smith, Florence Busby, Lillian Reed, May Davenport Seymour.

THE FIRES OF FATE—Modern morality play in four acts by Arthur Conan Doyle. Produced by Charles Frohman at the Illinois Theater, Chicago, December 6, 1909. Cast included:

Hamilton Revelle, Wm. Hawtrey, Edwin Brandt, Percy C. Waram, Thomas Mills, Hale Norcross, Ernest Perrin, Robert Reese, Lionel Barrymore [as Abdulla, a dragoman], Courtenay Foote, C. E. Harris, F. E. Hill, Charn Chandra Gen, Helen Freeman, Ina Hammer, and Grace Carlyle.

Lionel Barrymore withdrew from the cast at the end of the month, stricken with appendicitis.

THE JAIL BIRD—Vaudeville play by George Shiels. At Hammerstein's Victoria the week of January 31, 1910. Played by McKee Rankin, Doris Rankin, and Lionel Barrymore.

Withdrawn because of bad notices, and *The White Slaver* substituted.

THE WHITE SLAVER—Vaudeville play by Lionel Barrymore. With Lionel Barrymore as the Italian laborer, Doris Rankin as his daughter, and McKee Rankin as the slaver. At the Majestic, Chicago, February 22, 1910; at Hammerstein's, New York, March 18, 1910; Hartford, April 27, 1910; at the Orpheum, Los Angeles, November 10, 1910; at the Orpheum, Minneapolis, January 23, 1911; Indianapolis, February 7, 1911; at the Colonial, Chicago, March 3, 1911.

BOB ACRES—Scenes from Sheridan's THE RIVALS [The Challenge and The Duel]. Produced in vaudeville with Lionel

Barrymore as Sir Lucius O'Trigger, Sidney Drew as Bob Acres, Berasfort Lovett, and Frederick Bernard. In Brooklyn, September 11, 1911. At the Majestic in Chicago, September 27, 1911, with S. Rankin Drew taking the place of Berasfort Lovett as Captain Absolute. At the Grand in Pittsburgh, October 1, 1911.

THE STILL VOICE—Vaudeville play by George Cameron [Mrs. Sidney Drew]. Presented on the Keith circuit, at Cincinnati, March 26, 1912; at Chicago April 9, 1912; at Milwaukee April 16, 1912. Cast included:

Mr. and Mrs. Sidney Drew, Lionel Barrymore, Doris Rankin, and S. Rankin Drew.

PETER IBBETSON (71 performances)—Dramatization by John N. Raphael of George du Maurier's novel, in four acts. Produced by the Messrs. Shubert at the Republic Theater, New York, April 17, 1917. Cast included:

John Barrymore, Wallis Clarke, Leo Stark, Alexander Loftus, Lowden Adams, Laura Hope Crews, Barbara Allen, Nina Varesa, R. Bogislav, Lionel Barrymore, Montague Weston, Eric Hudson, Cecil Clovelly, Benjamin Kauser, Alice Wilson, Catherine Charlton, Martha Noel, Joseph Eagles, Vernon Kelso, Viva Burkitt, Madge Evans, and Constance Collier.

Staged by Clifford Brooke.

This play was revived by Lee Shubert at the Shubert Theater, New York, April 8, 1931. Wallis Clarke played his original role.

THE COPPERHEAD (120 performances)—Play in four acts by Augustus Thomas, from a story by Frederick Landis. Produced by John D. Williams at the Shubert Theater, New York, February 18, 1918. Cast included:

Raymond Hackett, Eugenie Woodward, Lionel Barrymore, Gladys Burgette, William Norton, Chester Morris, Thomas Carrigan, Albert Phillips, Evelyn Archer, Ethelbert Hales, Harry Hadfield, Doris Rankin, Grace Reals, and Hayden Stevenson.

THE JEST (77 performances)—Drama in four acts, adapted from the Italian of Sem Benelli's "La Cena delle Beffe." Produced by Arthur Hopkins at the Plymouth Theater, New York, April 9, 1919. Cast included:

John Barrymore, Lionel Barrymore, Paul Irving, H. Charles Smith, Maude Hanaford, Jacob Kingsberry, Alexander F. Frank, Gilda Varesi, Arthur Forrest, E. J. Ballantine, George Casselberry, Maude Durand, Rankin Davenport, Cecil Clovelly, Martha McGraw, Thomas Williams, Walter P. Richmond, and Margaret Fareleigh.

Staged by Arthur Hopkins.

THE LETTER OF THE LAW (89 performances)—Drama in four acts, adapted from "La Robe Rouge" by Eugene Brieux. Produced by John D. Williams at the Criterion Theater, New York, February 23, 1920. Cast included:

Zeffie Tilbury, Leona Hogarth, Russ Whytal, Josephine Wehn, Goldwin Patton, Maud Hosford, Clarence Derwent, Charles N. Greene, Lionel Barrymore, Charles Coghlan, James P. Hagen, Wallace Jackson, Frank Kingdon, Jacob Kingsberry, Herbert Vance, L. R. Wolheim, Charles White, Doris Rankin, Ada Boshell, and Lionel Hogarth.

MACBETH (28 performances)—Revival of the Shakespearean tragedy in three parts. Produced by Arthur Hopkins at the Apollo Theater, New York, February 17, 1921. Cast included:

J. Sayre Crawley, E. J. Ballantine, Burford Hampden, Lionel Barrymore, Sidney Herbert, Raymond Bloomer, Alfred Shirley, Lionel Hogarth, Herbert Jaap, Bernard Savage, Haviland Chappell, Mary Hughes, John Washburn, Guy Cunningham, Helen Chandler, Henry Vincent, Harry Winston, Albert Shrubb, Frank Sylvester, Stuart Black, Lawrence Cecil, Julia Arthur, Helen Robbins, Marguerita Sargent, Eleanor Hutchison, Nina Lindsey, and Doris Fellows.

Staged by Arthur Hopkins.

THE CLAW (115 performances)—Tragedy in four acts by Henri Bernstein, English version by Edward Delaney Dunn and Louis Wolheim. Produced by Arthur Hopkins at the Broadhurst Theater, New York, October 17, 1921. Cast included:

Charles Kennedy, E. J. Ballantine, Irene Fenwick, Marie Bruce, Lionel Barrymore, Giorgio Majeroni, Doris Rankin, Joseph Granby, Ian Wolfe, Harold Winston, and S. B. Tobias.

Staged by Arthur Hopkins.

LAUGH, CLOWN, LAUGH! (133 performances)—Drama in three acts by David Belasco and Tom Cushing, from the Italian of Faurto Martini's "Ridi Pagliaccio." Produced by David Belasco at the Belasco Theater, New York, November 28, 1923. Cast included:

Lionel Barrymore, Ian Keith, Henry Herbert, Guy Nichols, Vaughn De Leath, Thomas Reynolds, Sidney Toler, Irene Fenwick, Myra Florian, Susanna Rossi, Leah Le Roux, Nick Long, Jose Yovin, Rose Morison, Giorgio Majeroni, Kathleen Kerrigan, Lucille Kahn, Agnes McCarthy, Jenny Dickerson, Micheline Keating, Alice Horine, Charles Firmback, Jr., and Harry Craven.

Staged by David Belasco.

THE PIKER (44 performances)—Drama by Leon Gordon, based on a story by Oliver Eastwood. Produced by A. H. Woods at the Eltinge Theater, New York, January 15, 1925. Cast included:

Lionel Barrymore, Alan Brooks, Robert Cummings, Harry E. McKee, James C. Malaidy, Irene Fenwick, Frank Conroy, Adrienne Morrison, W. A. Norton, and Charles Slattery.

Staged by Priestly Morrison.

TAPS (32 performances)—Play in three acts by Franz Adam Beyerlein. Produced by the Messrs. Shubert at the Broadhurst Theater, New York, April 14, 1925. Cast included:

Lionel Barrymore, Edwin Maxwell, McKay Morris, Ullrich Haupt, Egon Brecher, Milton Stiefel, Frederick Macklyn, Thurlow Bergen, Herbert Standing, Robert Thorne, Lauman Davis, George Gilday, Sydney Smith, and Irene Fenwick.

Staged by Lawrence Marston.

MAN OR DEVIL (20 performances)—Play in three acts by Jerome K. Jerome. Produced by the Messrs. Shubert at the Broadhurst Theater, New York, May 21, 1925. Cast included:

Ruth Findlay, Herbert Standing, Milton Stiefel, Lionel Barrymore, Milano Tilden, Isabelle Winlocke, Georgina Tilden, Marion Ballou, Thurlow Bergen, McKay Morris, and Egon Brecher.

Staged by Lawrence Marston.

Index